Insight and Solidarity

Philosophy, Social Theory, and the Rule of Law

General Editors
Andres Arato, Ferenc Fehér, William Forbath,
Agnes Heller, Arthur Jacobson, and Michel Rosenfeld

Insight and Solidarity

A Study in the Discourse Ethics of Jürgen Habermas

William Rehg

UNIVERSITY OF CALIFORNIA PRESS
Berkeley · Los Angeles · London

University of California Press
Berkeley and Los Angeles, California

University of California Press
London, England

Library of Congress Cataloging-in-Publication Data

Rehg, William.
    Insight and solidarity : a study in the discourse ethics of Jürgen Habermas / William
Rehg.
      p.   cm. — (Philosophy, social theory, and the rule of law)
    Includes bibliographical references and index.
    ISBN 0-520-08204-4 (alk. paper)
    1. Habermas, Jürgen—Ethics.   2. Ethics, Modern—20th century.
I. Title. II. Title: Discourse ethics of Jürgen Habermas. III. Series.
B3258.H324R445   1994
170′.92—dc20   93-23800
                                                        CIP

Printed in the United States of America

1 2 3 4 5 6 7 8 9

The paper used in this publication meets the minimum requirements of American
National Standard for Information Sciences—Permanence of Paper for Printed Library
Materials, ANSI Z39.48-1984 ⊚

For my parents

Contents

Abbreviations

The following lists a key for more frequently cited works of Jürgen Habermas.

CES   *Communication and the Evolution of Society.* Trans. Thomas McCarthy. Boston: Beacon, 1979.

"Critics"   "A Reply to My Critics." Trans. Thomas McCarthy. *Habermas: Critical Debates.* Ed. John B. Thompson and David Held. Cambridge: MIT Press, 1982. Pp. 219–283.

DE   "Discourse Ethics: Notes on a Program of Philosophical Justification." Jürgen Habermas, *Moral Consciousness and Communicative Action.* Trans. Christian Lenhardt and Shierry Weber Nicholsen. Cambridge: MIT Press, 1990. Pp. 43–115.

Discourse   *The Philosophical Discourse of Modernity: Twelve Lectures.* Trans. Frederick Lawrence. Cambridge: MIT Press, 1987.

EzD   "Erläuterungen zur Diskursethik." Jürgen Habermas, *Erläuterungen zur Diskursethik.* Frankfurt: Suhrkamp, 1991. Pp. 119–226.

FG   *Faktizität und Geltung: Beiträge zur Diskurstheorie des Rechts und des demokratischen Rechtsstaats.* Frankfurt: Suhrkamp, 1992.

JS   "Justice and Solidarity: On the Discussion Concerning Stage 6." *The Moral Domain: Essays in the Ongoing Discussion between Philosophy and the Social Sciences.* Ed. Thomas E. Wren. Trans. Shierry Weber Nicholsen. Cambridge: MIT Press, 1990. Pp. 224–251.

LC   *Legitimation Crisis.* Trans. Thomas McCarthy. Boston: Beacon, 1975.

LM   "Law and Morality." Trans. Kenneth Baynes. *The Tanner Lectures on Human Values*, Vol. 8. Ed. Sterling M. McMurrin. Salt Lake City: University of Utah Press, 1988. Pp. 217–279.

MC   "Moral Consciousness and Communicative Action." Habermas, *Moral Consciousness and Communicative Action.* Pp. 116–194.

ME   "Morality and Ethical Life." Habermas, *Moral Consciousness and Communicative Action.* Pp. 195–215.

NR   *Die nachholende Revolution.* Kleine Politische Schriften 7. Frankfurt: Suhrkamp, 1990.

PT   *Postmetaphysical Thinking: Philosophical Essays.* Trans. William Mark Hohengarten. Cambridge: MIT Press, 1992.

PV   "Vom pragmatischen, ethischen und moralischen Gebrauch der praktischen Vernunft." Habermas, *Erläuterungen zur Diskursethik.* Pp. 100–118.

"Reply"   "A Reply." *Communicative Action: Essays on Jürgen Habermas's "The Theory of Communicative Action."* Ed. Axel Honneth and Hans Joas. Trans. Jeremy Gains and Doris L. Jones. Cambridge: Polity Press, 1991. Pp. 214–264.

TCA   *The Theory of Communicative Action.* 2 vols. Trans. Thomas McCarthy. Boston: Beacon, 1984; 1987.

W   "Wahrheitstheorien." Jürgen Habermas, *Vorstudien und Ergänzungen zur Theorie des kommunikativen Handelns.* 2d ed. Frankfurt: Suhrkamp, 1986. Pp. 127–183.

Preface

Although Kant's moral theory has long been familiar to Anglo-American philosophers, in recent years a remarkable surge in interest has generated not only a number of close interpretations of Kantian moral theory but a bevy of broader "neo-Kantian" extensions of it as well. At the same time, an equally remarkable, likewise broadly neo-Kantian development in moral theory has been less accessible to Anglo-American audiences. The "discourse ethics" (or "communicative ethics") elaborated by German theorists such as Jürgen Habermas, Karl-Otto Apel, Albrecht Wellmer, and others has only gradually found its way into the English language, its debt to American pragmatism notwithstanding. And even in translation, an often impenetrable style, in addition to the particular presuppositions of German contexts of debate, tends to put off readers who have not made German philosophy their specialty. The fact that the various presentations of discourse ethics are scattered throughout a variety of books and articles, the fact that these presentations are often occasional in character and sketchy in details, makes an already difficult task of appropriation still more formidable. It is thus all the more remarkable that, despite such obstacles, interest in discourse ethics continues to grow on this side of the Atlantic.

That the above obstacles also pertain to Jürgen Habermas's contributions to moral theory may appear somewhat surprising. For, of contemporary German philosophers, Habermas is probably the best known to English-speaking audiences, and his works are almost certainly the most extensively translated. However, despite some significant early forays, Habermas only recently turned his full energies on moral theory. The central articles, published in Germany in 1983, first appeared in English in 1990 (in the book entitled *Moral Consciousness and Communicative Action*); the first book devoted solely to discourse ethics (*Justification and Application*) only became available in English in 1993. Moreover, important background studies for understanding Habermas's position remain untranslated or buried in a variety of places. Nor will the recently translated works disappoint anyone accustomed to the challenges of Habermas's at once dense and suggestively elusive idiom and style. All this helps explain why Anglo-American thinkers have only just begun to study Habermas's moral theory in its full scope and depth.

To be sure, since Thomas McCarthy's *The Critical Theory of Jürgen Habermas* provided a clear, comprehensive survey of Habermas's writings prior to *The Theory of Communicative Action*, a number of authors have brought us up to date on various aspects of his more recent work. Some of these have even dealt with discourse ethics, albeit always in broader contexts. But discourse ethics itself has not yet received a full, separate treatment. In fact, besides the various scholarly obstacles noted above, an additional circumstance has made such a study still more difficult. For discourse ethics has been caught up in a number of rapidly developing debates concerning critical theory, modern societal rationalization, social-political analysis, moral psychology, and other issues. A relatively developed discourse ethics has only gradually emerged from the various issues in these debates. The time is now ripe, I think, for a more detailed exploration of discourse ethics simply as a moral theory.

This book is intended to provide such an exploration for English-speaking scholars working in the areas of moral, social, political, and legal theory. Toward this end I examine Habermas's most important writings on the subject of moral theory in order to arrive at a clear, systematic statement of discourse ethics. Such an examination is also an exploration, however, in the sense that I go beyond a straightforward exposition of discourse ethics and attempt to develop it further. This is necessary, in my opinion, to make discourse ethics plausible in Anglo-American contexts of debate. More specifically, certain debates in moral-political theory—such as those sparked by "communitarian" and feminist challenges to the liberal tradition stemming from thinkers such as Locke, Kant, and Mill—confront discourse ethics with imposing conceptual hurdles; clearing these hurdles requires a further elaboration of Habermas's suggestive but sometimes incomplete analyses. In most cases this simply means extending and developing initiatives present in Habermas; in some cases a critical analysis is appropriate. But I doubt one could accomplish either of these tasks if one did not first grasp the central idea behind discourse ethics. Only from that standpoint can one both criticize and develop a philosophical project with the systematic intent of discourse ethics. In developing a systematic account, then, I first formulate or "reconstruct" the guiding idea to discourse ethics, the chief contribution or advance it makes in moral theory. I then test and further develop this central idea against the potentially most damaging criticisms.

Given the focused systematic character of my analysis, there are a number of things I will not do here. First, I do not develop the discourse ethics of thinkers other than Habermas; at most I can refer to such alternative views in passing or for the purposes of bringing out a systematic point in Habermas's approach. Second, I do not provide a historical account of Habermas's own path in developing discourse ethics, although at certain points it will be necessary to note certain shifts in his position in order to gain some insight into the systematic issues. Finally, I cannot even provide a full account of discourse ethics in all its systematic ramifications. These reach across the boundaries of moral theory into philosophical theories of language and agency, as well as into psychological theories of moral development and theories of modernity, which include historical, sociological, and institutional analyses—to name only the more obvious. Again, I can only touch on these ramifications, noting the various points where discourse ethics, as a theory of practical reasoning, opens on other issues. My hope is that, if this entails a loss in comprehensiveness, it allows a gain in systematic clarity and depth.

I should perhaps warn readers in less philosophically inclined disciplines that the present work is primarily concerned with elucidating the rational structure or intrinsic logic of moral reasoning. As a moral theory in the Kantian tradition, discourse ethics represents an attempt to elucidate the notion of impartiality connected with the moral point of view. This elucidation is accomplished primarily through a principle of universalization. Such principles typically attempt to reconstruct what we might call the idealized logic or norms governing impartial moral thinking. Although such a normative account must have a connection with how people actually think about moral problems, attaining sufficient clarity about the ideal requires us, at least provisionally, to minimize many of the complications (and shortfalls in achieving an idealized impartiality) that characterize actual reasoning. This is not to dismiss such complications as unimportant for moral theory; in my opinion, they pose difficult problems that discourse ethics must eventually deal with. Inasmuch as the purpose of this book is to get clear about discourse ethics itself, however, I can only confront the questions raised by such complications in the last chapter, where I can at most provide some indications for future research and analysis.

Regarding the problem of sexist language, I have sought to avoid overly awkward solutions. Where formulations such as "he and she" are not too cumbersome, I use them; otherwise, I simply alternate by chapter between feminine and masculine pronouns.

I am grateful to the editors of the journal *Inquiry* for their permission to use material from my article, "Discourse and the Moral Point of View: Deriving a Dialogical Principle of Universalization," which appeared in *Inquiry* 34 (1991): 27–48. I also wish to express my gratitude to a number of individuals and groups for help with this book. Perhaps more than any other single individual, I am indebted to Thomas McCarthy for his careful criticisms, insightful suggestions, and continual encouragement. I am particularly grateful to Jürgen Habermas for his willingness to read and comment on the manuscript. I would like to thank David Michael Levin, Samuel Todes, Lutz Wingert, and Klaus Günther for their very helpful feedback; Michel Rosenfeld and the other reader for the University of California Press for some quite useful suggestions; Jeremiah Alberg and John Kavanaugh for their suggestions and, more importantly, encouragement; and Thomas J. Farrell for a very careful reading that caught a number of infelicities. I also wish to thank the Fulbright Commission and the Northwestern University Law and Social Science Program for their financial support, which made possible a year of research at the University of Frankfurt. Finally, the book would not have been possible without the support and encouragement of Edward Kinerk and Robert Costello.

Introduction

This is what it is all about

↓

What constitutes the moral basis of social cooperation? In the late twentieth century this question has taken on immediate, indeed overpowering worldwide relevance: even as a growing plurality of national groups presses for sovereignty, networks of international exchange and interdependence continue to grow and thicken. Thus the conflicts that arise today, both within and between nations, pose an increasingly acute problem of cooperation. These conflicts involve not only economic, technological, and ecological issues but moral ones as well. At stake often enough are human rights, or questions of freedom, equality, fair treatment, and so on. Thus an adequate resolution to such conflicts must respect the legitimate claims of different individuals and groups without destroying the complex bonds that link these individuals and groups, all their differences notwithstanding.

The United States has traditionally understood its democratic form of government as a framework for dealing with problems of this sort at the national level, for it allows people of different ethnic and religious backgrounds to unite into a single nation. Here too the moral dimension is crucial. From its inception in the eighteenth century, the American polity has been conceived as a pluralism of (largely religious) communal traditions bound together democratically on the basis of a moral consensus, i.e., a consensus that could brook differences in religious and philosophical outlook while converging on a set of normative expectations guaranteeing the inviolable dignity of the individual person. At the same time,

1

the break with Old World tradition and authority has given individual
entrepreneurship a scope hardly equaled in other nations—a tendency
that finds political reinforcement in the strong tradition of individual
rights. This background poses an ongoing problem of social consensus,
which takes on increasingly sharper contours, both practically and theoretically, as the range of ethnic, religious, and philosophical variation in
the United States continues to grow. The current intense debates over
"multiculturalism" attest to the power of this problem.

The theoretical issues involved in the problem of social consensus
cover a broad range of topics touching on a number of disciplines. Central to these issues, however, is a concept of practical reason. That is, how
one approaches contemporary social conflicts, whether and to what extent one thinks a morally based consensus is possible, and what one recommends for reaching such consensus depend crucially on one's views
about practical reason and its relation to morality. A theory of practical
reasoning is therefore of systematic importance for reflection on such issues, and it is my aim in the present volume to present such a theory.
More specifically, I want to introduce Jürgen Habermas's discourse ethics
(or "communicative ethics") as a vehicle for systematic reflection on the
problems attending consensus in pluralistic societies. As a neo-Kantian
theory of practical reason that takes the form of a theory of argumentation, discourse ethics offers considerable promise for reflection on the
moral bases of cooperation in a society committed to individual initiative
and communal bonds. Although a number of theorists have contributed
to discourse ethics, Habermas's formulation recommends itself because
he has continually kept systematic issues in view, attempting to relate
discourse ethics to a number of other areas, such as legal theory, theory
of modernity, theories of social-psychological development, and so
forth.[1] Moreover, the central texts for Habermas's version of discourse
ethics are just now becoming available in English, so that one might expect attention to his work to grow.[2]

1. In fact, Habermas's discourse ethics owes much to Karl-Otto Apel, who in turn
draws on C. S. Peirce's consensus theory of truth; see Apel's *Towards a Transformation of
Philosophy*, trans. Glyn Adey and David Frisby (London: Routledge, 1980). Habermas
also draws on George Herbert Mead's proposal for a discourse ethics; see especially Mead's
"Fragments on Ethics" in *Mind, Self, and Society from the Standpoint of a Social Behaviorist*, ed. Charles W. Morris (Chicago: University of Chicago Press, 1934; Charles W.
Morris, 1962), pp. 379–389. A still further proposal is Thomas Scanlon's "Contractualism
and Utilitarianism," in *Utilitarianism and Beyond*, ed. Amartya Sen and Bernard Williams
(Cambridge: Cambridge University Press, 1982), pp. 103–128.

2. The two main texts are Jürgen Habermas, *Moral Consciousness and Communicative Action*, trans. Christian Lenhardt and Shierry Weber Nicholsen (Cambridge: MIT

In my opinion, the theoretical power of a discourse-ethical approach to the issues confronting contemporary moral theory can be measured against two recent challenges to neo-Kantian moral theory. In both cases, the critics develop objections Hegel and Schopenhauer leveled against Kant. To anticipate, the so-called "communitarians" question the neo-Kantians' attempt to define morality in terms of the primacy of justice and individual rights; in their view, this misses the role that shared conceptions of the good life play in grounding our moral intuitions.[3] For the purposes of a systematic theory of practical reason, I consider this criticism to call for a discourse-ethical account of how one justifies generally binding moral norms. Proponents of an "ethics of care" raise questions that call for an account of how one applies norms, i.e., how one reaches actual moral judgments in concrete situations. In their view, the neo-Kantian focus on universalizable norms cannot capture the moral features of particular interpersonal relationships in concrete situations. In what follows I will map the contours of these debates in turn; this will indicate the points a plausible discourse ethics must address. I will then briefly outline the argument of the book.

The Communitarian Critique of Liberalism. The burst of liberal moral-political theorizing beginning with John Rawls's *Theory of Justice* set off a bout of debates over morality and social order.[4] Rawls's effort to rework Kant's Categorical Imperative into a decision procedure that would lead every rational person—irrespective of his or her particular lifestyle, religion, and other interests—to accept a certain concept of justice as the most reasonable basis for social coordination met with skepticism along a number of lines. A number of these critics, primarily neo-Aristotelians and neo-Hegelians, have been loosely grouped under the term of art, "communitarianism." Fundamentally, the "liberal-communitarian" debate turns on the question of how, or even whether, the liberal commitment to individual autonomy and relations regulated by rights and duties can do justice to the more substantive bonds tradi-

---

Press, 1990) and his *Erläuterungen zur Diskursethik* (Frankfurt: Suhrkamp, 1991), now available in English under the title *Justification and Application: Remarks on Discourse Ethics*, trans. Ciaran P. Cronin (Cambridge: MIT Press, 1993).
  3. Habermas's discourse ethics has already had to deal with this debate in Germany; see the essays in *Moralität und Sittlichkeit: Das Problem Hegels und die Diskursethik*, ed. Wolfgang Kuhlmann (Frankfurt: Suhrkamp, 1986).
  4. John Rawls, *A Theory of Justice* (Cambridge: Belknap-Harvard University Press, 1971); other leading statements of the liberal view can be found in Ronald Dworkin's *Taking Rights Seriously* (Cambridge: Harvard University Press, 1977) and "Liberalism," in *A Matter of Principle* (Cambridge: Harvard University Press, 1985), pp. 181–204; and Bruce Ackerman's *Social Justice in the Liberal State* (New Haven: Yale University Press, 1980).

tionally ruling community life and stylized as conceptions of the common good, or of the telos of human life.[5] Here Sandel's criticism of Rawls in *Liberalism and the Limits of Justice* has become something of a minor classic, although MacIntyre's *After Virtue* also deserves mention as one of the more eye-catching communitarian salvos.[6]

The liberal-communitarian debate takes in a number of topics. Sandel's critique of Rawls, for example, focuses on the concept of moral agency. Another set of issues revolves around the theory of modernity, how one assesses the historical emergence and current status of Western social and political institutions. It is unlikely that one could address these topics, however, without to some degree presupposing a theory of practical reason. Moreover, one cannot understand Habermas's position on agency and modernity without having his theory of rationality in mind. Hence the focus of this book. But even with this restriction in focus, we find ourselves confronted with a potentially confusing array of subtopics. One could ask about the role played in practical reason by the concept of the good; in that case debates over the importance of the *common good*, or of the telos of human life, come to the fore,[7] perhaps postmetaphysically transformed into questions about the role *tradition* has for

5. A number of overviews of this debate are available. See, for example, Amy Gutman, "Communitarian Critics of Liberalism," *Philosophy and Public Affairs* 14 (1985): 308–322; Allen E. Buchanan, "Assessing the Communitarian Critique of Liberalism," *Ethics* 99 (1989): 852–882; Nancy L. Rosenblum, introduction, *Liberalism and the Moral Life*, ed. N. Rosenblum (Cambridge: Harvard University Press, 1989), pp. 1–17; and Henry S. Richardson, "The Problem of Liberalism and the Good," in *Liberalism and the Good*, ed. R. Bruce Douglass, Gerald M. Mara, and Henry S. Richardson (New York: Routledge, 1990), pp. 1–28; also Will Kymlicka, *Liberalism, Community and the State* (Oxford: Clarendon, 1989); more recently, see Stephen Gardbaum, "Law, Politics, and the Claims of Community," *Michigan Law Review* 90 (1992): 658–760.

6. Michael Sandel, *Liberalism and the Limits of Justice* (Cambridge: Cambridge University Press, 1982); Alasdair MacIntyre, *After Virtue* (Notre Dame: University of Notre Dame Press, 1981; 2d ed., 1984); see also MacIntyre's *Whose Justice? Which Rationality?* (Notre Dame: University of Notre Dame Press, 1988). Other prominent critiques somewhat more difficult to categorize are Michael Walzer, *Spheres of Justice: A Defense of Pluralism and Equality* (New York: Basic Books, 1983) and Bernard Williams, *Ethics and the Limits of Philosophy* (Cambridge: Harvard University Press, 1985).

7. Besides MacIntyre, Charles Taylor has been a prominent representative of this approach; see, for example, his *Sources of the Self: The Making of the Modern Identity* (Cambridge: Harvard University Press, 1989), chaps. 1–4; "Justice after Virtue," in *Kritische Methode und Zukunft der Anthropologie*, ed. Michael Benedikt and Rudolf Burger (Vienna: Wilhelm Braumüller University Press, 1985), pp. 23–48; a somewhat modified German translation of this is available under the title "Die Motive einer Verfahrensethik," in *Moralität und Sittlichkeit*, ed. Kuhlmann, pp. 101–135; and two articles in his *Philosophy and the Human Sciences*, vol. 2 of *Philosophical Papers* (Cambridge: Cambridge University Press, 1985): "The Diversity of Goods," pp. 230–247, and "The Nature and Scope of Distributive Justice," pp. 289–317.

moral thought.[8] The latter move encourages in turn a hermeneutical approach emphasizing the necessity of *phronesis* for concretely realizing the good in practice.[9]

In my opinion, one does best to organize these topics around the question of the relation between justice and the good, be it the community's good or that of particular individuals in concrete situations. This way of posing the question brings out its systematic significance for a theory of practical reason: one can think of the relation of justice to the common good as central to an account of the justification of moral norms, while the issues raised by particularity and situational concreteness call for an account of the application of norms, i.e., concrete moral judgment. Unless discourse ethics can give a plausible account of justification and application in relation to the good, it will fall victim to the difficulties that have plagued deontological moral theories since Kant. The remainder of this section will use the liberal-communitarian debate to display some key issues involved in the relation between justice and the common good. The next section will then turn to the ethics of care debates to elaborate on the problems attending concrete moral choice, where the general demands of justice often seem to conflict with the welfare of particular individuals.

If we phrase the issue in terms of social cooperation, then the relevant issue in the liberal-communitarian debate concerns the role that notions of the good have in adjudicating conflicts, or in keeping potential conflicts at bay. Liberal theorists typically argue that cooperative solutions to social conflicts (generally thematized in terms of the distribution of scarce resources) can be reached if the participants put aside, as privately held opinions, those more intractable disagreements over particular conceptions of the good life. For example, Rawls's principles of justice define the fair distribution of certain "primary goods," which incorporate no more than a "thin theory of the good" acceptable to anyone whose more comprehensive views about the good of human life allow for tolerance; Ackerman proposes a "neutral dialogue" ruled by "conversational restraint." In both cases argumentation tries to avoid unnecessary controversy, seeking out instead noncontroversial or "over-

---

8. In Anglo-American circles MacIntyre is a good representative of this line.

9. For examples of the hermeneutical approach, see especially Hans-Georg Gadamer, *Truth and Method*, 2d, rev. ed., trans. Joel Weinsheimer and Donald G. Marshall (New York: Crossroad, 1990); also Martha C. Nussbaum, *The Fragility of Goodness: Luck and Ethics in Greek Tragedy and Philosophy* (Cambridge: Cambridge University Press, 1986), chap. 10.

lapping" premises as a common point of departure for reaching further agreement.[10]

By abstracting justice questions from the plurality of conceptions of the good, liberals hope to give a cognitive sense to morality, identified now with the impersonal rules that regulate fair social cooperation. Precisely because assent to moral rules does not depend on thicker values and ideas of the good, social conflicts can be resolved by rational procedures for generating such assent. Hence a key issue in the liberal-communitarian debate concerns whether and to what extent practical reason can or ought to abstract in the way some liberals propose. Generally, liberals admit at least some goods into their rational procedures. For example, Rawls's list of "primary goods" includes the basic rights, liberties, and goods that enable the exercise of moral personality, which Rawls defines as the capacity for a sense of justice and the ability to choose and pursue one's particular conception of the good and life plan.[11] In any case, a presentation of discourse ethics must address this question: what exactly is meant by a "good" and how does it function in practical reasoning or, more narrowly, argumentation aimed at just conflict resolution?

This question admits of a number of approaches. Thus one might ask *how thick* a consensus on the good life is required before rational conflict resolution can get under way. MacIntyre, for example, considers the liberal consensus too thin, stopping just short of the threshold beyond which particular conceptions of the good life appear as subjective preferences that cannot be rationally mediated. Since justice issues touch on such preferences, however, rational conflict resolution is not possible on the basis of the liberal consensus. Other variants of this last question could be added. Thus one may ask *how teleological* the shared notion of the good has to be. The Rawlsian "thin theory of the good" seems hardly teleological at all: what individuals actually do with their primary goods, what ends they pursue, remains their private decision. Or one may address the so-called *incommensurability* of the different values, goods, and social ideals at stake in argumentation. However overblown the

10. See John Rawls, "The Idea of an Overlapping Consensus," *Oxford Journal of Legal Studies* 7 (1987): 1–25; also his "The Priority of Right and Ideas of the Good," *Philosophy and Public Affairs* 17 (1988): 251–276, esp. 255–261; Bruce A. Ackerman, "What Is Neutral about Neutrality?" *Ethics* 93 (1983): 372–390; his recent "Why Dialogue?" *Journal of Philosophy* 86 (1989): 5–22; and also his "Neutralities," in *Liberalism and the Good*, ed. Douglass et al., pp. 29–43.

11. See Rawls, *Theory*, pp. 90–95, 567–577; also his "Kantian Constructivism in Moral Theory," *Journal of Philosophy* 77 (1980): 515–572, esp. 525–528, 543.

communitarian charges along this line, it remains unclear exactly how one argues over conflicting social ideals, or "weighs" the conflicting justice principles that come with them, or fits them together in a *bricolage*.[12] Rawls's solution of a lexical ordering of various primary goods agreed to behind a veil of ignorance, for example, only postpones the issue if it depends on a prior consensus over a Kantian ideal of moral personality.

A second major issue is closely connected with the above. The liberal abstraction from particularistic goods—or the attempt to consider such goods only from the impartial standpoint of justice—also gives *priority to justice* (or the "right"). In fact, the consensual outcomes generated by rational procedures are fair precisely because these procedures give primacy to justice. The point here is that the procedure as such—at least within certain limits—is impartial or "neutral" vis-à-vis conceptions of the good: it does not favor (or damage) any individual's particular interests or good any more than that of any other individual. The communitarian challenge to this neutrality claim represents one of the more troublesome arguments for liberals. Communitarians argue that the liberal prioritization of justice, far from achieving neutrality, in fact privileges a particular conception of the good life. Taylor, for example, has argued that the Kantian notion of moral personality operates as the good for liberal thought in its Rawlsian vein. To some extent, Rawls concurs on this point: justice as fairness presupposes consensus on the good of a well-ordered democratic political society in which citizens can responsibly choose and revise their own life plans. If one accepts this use of the term "good," the question then becomes this: is the Kantian good of moral personality simply one particular—indeed European bourgeois—conception of the good life among others, or is it rather a "metavalue" which can be properly understood neither as a particular conception over which reasonable persons may disagree nor as something from which a concrete life plan can be deduced?[13]

Rawls, of course, denies that justice as fairness is "comprehensive" in the manner of particular conceptions of the good life.[14] As a metavalue,

12. On the incommensurability question, see Jeffrey Stout, *Ethics after Babel: The Languages of Morals and Their Discontents* (Boston: Beacon, 1988).

13. See Rawls, "Priority of Right," pp. 254, 259 n10, 269–271; Taylor, "Inwardness and the Culture of Modernity," in *Philosophical Interventions in the Unfinished Project of Enlightenment*, ed. Axel Honneth et al. (Cambridge: MIT Press, 1992), pp. 88–93; also his "Justice after Virtue," pp. 33–34; for the metavalue interpretation, Gerald Doppelt, "Is Rawls's Kantian Liberalism Coherent and Defensible?" *Ethics* 99 (1989): 821–831, is to be recommended.

14. See, for example, his "Priority of Right"; also "Justice as Fairness: Political not Metaphysical," *Philosophy and Public Affairs* 14 (1985): 223–251.

however, it would seem that the basic structure of society allowing the pursuit of individual ends must present something like a "liberal telos" or "modern project."[15] So long as this project can meaningfully be ranked as one project among several alternatives, employing a concept of justice based on that project would seemingly contradict the liberals' neutrality claim.

Besides addressing the role of the good in practical reasoning, then, a plausible account of discourse ethics should also explain in what sense justice takes priority over the good. Moreover, it will be important to ask whether or how discourse ethics itself represents a theory of the good. To anticipate, I shall argue that discourse ethics does presuppose the value of social cooperation based on mutual understanding, but that this value is not just one conception of the good alongside other equally viable alternatives. Rather, the affirmation of this value draws on a solidarity so basic to being human that to deny it runs counter to rationality itself.

The neutrality question can also be framed in terms of the notion of *tradition*. Here a relevant question is, To what degree must practical reasoning operate within a tradition and its linguistic framework? More radical communitarians such as MacIntyre take a rather hard line on this question: until participants have made the existential commitment to a common tradition, any conflict resolution is either accidental, manipulated and thus irrational, or impossible. If this hard line is on target—if the argumentation involved in conflict resolution eventually hits upon notions of the good life and social projects, which unavoidably refer to value-laden terms whose meanings are inextricably embedded in traditions and social ideals—then the problem arises of how one can rationally motivate those outside one's tradition to enter into it, in order to see one's arguments as persuasive. This would seem to locate rational motivation at that depth where experiences are opened up through a tradition and its language, hence within a particular community or form of life. If conflict resolution always had to take matters down to such a level, then a rational consensus would have to involve, in some sense, an exchange and comparison of experiences. This would hardly be promising for speedy decisions.

To address the relation between practical reason and tradition, I shall distinguish between two kinds of discourse, which Habermas calls moral and ethical, respectively. This allows us to preserve the benefits of liberal

15. As Sandel, *Liberalism*, pp. 175–177 argues; see also Taylor, "Justice after Virtue," p. 46; "Distributive Justice," pp. 316–317; and his *Sources* for an extensive and nuanced argument along these lines.

conceptions of justice (in moral discourses) without denying the importance of tradition for some forms of practical reasoning (especially for
ethical discourse). In fact, we shall see that even moral discourse depends
in important ways on the ability of agents to appreciate, at some level,
one another's different traditions; moreover, moral discourse must draw
upon a tradition of moral values.

Application and the Ethics of Care. In the same year that Sandel's *Liberalism and the Limits of Justice* appeared, Carol Gilligan published *In
a Different Voice*, a critique of Lawrence Kohlberg's attempt to construe
individual moral development primarily in terms of justice, i.e., as the
development of the capacity for taking an impartial "moral point of
view."[16] The feminist ethics of care developed by Gilligan and others contends, among other things, that liberal notions of impartiality and universalizability denigrate the thicker, more particularistic attachments existing between individuals. Not unlike the communitarians, proponents
of the ethics of care also question the liberal prioritization of justice and
abstract right.[17] In terms of our argumentation-theoretic approach to social cooperation, the ethics of care asks whether it suffices to conceive
practical argumentation solely in terms of impartialist or neutrality-
securing principles. Insofar as real conflict situations are always concrete,
involving a specific set of individuals with particular needs and relationships, must not their cooperation take precisely these particularities into
account, rather than setting them aside for the sake of a universalistic
neutrality? This issue involves a number of challenges to mainstream
moral theory. Here I will only mention the issues that are more significant
for the present study.

16. See Carol Gilligan, *In a Different Voice: Psychological Theory and Women's Development* (Cambridge: Harvard University Press, 1982); an earlier critique of Kohlberg
along similar lines is found in Norma Haan, "Two Moralities in Action Contexts: Relationships to Thought, Ego Regulation and Development," *Journal of Personality and Social
Psychology* 36 (1978): 286–305. For Kohlberg's position see, for example, his "From *Is*
to *Ought*: How to Commit the Naturalistic Fallacy and Get Away with It in the Study of
Moral Development," in *Philosophy of Moral Development: Moral Stages and the Idea of
Justice*, vol. 1 of *Essays on Moral Development* (San Francisco: Harper & Row, 1981),
pp. 101–189.

17. For a systematic philosophical account of the ethics of care, see Nel Noddings, *Caring: A Feminine Approach to Ethics and Moral Education* (Berkeley: University of California Press, 1984). The ethics of care is located in broader feminist concerns by Jean Grimshaw, *Philosophy and Feminist Thinking* (Minneapolis: University of Minnesota Press,
1986); also important is Lawrence Blum, *Friendship, Altruism and Morality* (London:
Routledge, 1980); to get a sense of the debated issues, see *Women and Moral Theory*, ed.
Eva Feder Kittay and Diana T. Meyers (Savage, Md.: Rowman & Littlefield, 1987); more
recently, *Explorations in Feminist Ethics: Theory and Practice*, ed. Eve Browning Cole and
Susan Coultrap-McQuin (Bloomington: Indiana University Press, 1992).

A key point of departure for the ethics of care, at least historically, is the problem of the appropriate *application* of general norms. This problem appears most sharply in moral dilemmas, i.e., cases in which an agent confronts conflicting moral duties.[18] Gilligan's critique of Kohlberg focused precisely on his assumption that a straightforward ranking of duties in terms of a formal principle of justice represents the most morally appropriate (or "adequate") resolution of such conflicts. The fact that many women eschew such abstract solutions demonstrates not their moral immaturity but rather their sensitive recognition of situational complexity. The ethics of care thus draws on the intuition that an ability to gather further information in concrete situations is a mark of moral maturity. Of course, how one then processes such information in order to arrive at a moral judgment represents a further question, the point of contention in debates generated by the ethics of care. I take up these further issues below. First I want to draw attention to the general problem of application or particular moral judgment. Given our focus on social cooperation, we might pose the problem something like this: The cooperative regulation of potential conflict situations involves a tension between the general rules geared to *typical* situations and the particular judgments required to maintain cooperation in the face of the complications that can arise in *concrete* situations.

Even aside from the need to address criticisms of neo-Kantian moral theory, the notion of application deserves treatment in any systematic theory of practical reason. I thus consider it important to provide a discourse-ethical account of application and concrete moral judgment, and my response to the ethics of care will consist first and foremost in such an account, undertaken from an argumentation-theoretic point of view. However, the topic of application involves a number of complex issues. Although I will not be able to deal with each of these in the same detail, my analysis of application is undertaken with the following issues in mind.

Perhaps the issue most immediately connected with application is that of *moral perception*, i.e., the agent's capacity to perceive elements of a situation as morally relevant. According to the ethics of care, such perception involves more than subsuming a situation under general rules. In fact, even the straightforward application of general rules must pre-

---

18. Philosophers not typically associated with the ethics of care have also grappled with this; e.g., R. M. Hare, *Moral Thinking: Its Levels, Method, and Point* (Oxford: Clarendon, 1981); Henry S. Richardson, "Specifying Norms as a Way to Resolve Concrete Ethical Problems," *Philosophy and Public Affairs* 19 (1990): 279–310.

suppose that the agent can perceive the morally relevant features of the situation.[19] To redress Kant's neglect of this point, one must insist that morality involves a sensitive apprehension of situational particulars, especially those pertaining to the "weal and woe" of other persons.[20] An ability to take account of and respond to the other's concrete predicament and needs constitutes a properly *moral* task; according to an ethics of care, it is morally counterintuitive to ignore individual differences in favor of an "impersonal right."[21] My account of discourse ethics will thus indicate how one can take such factors into account when applying norms.

This attention to the concrete and nonuniversalizable immediately raises several further significant challenges to justice-centered moral theory. One of these concerns the scope of *the moral domain*. Not unlike certain communitarian proposals, the ethics of care would broaden the definition of what counts as "moral" or what enjoys "moral worth." One might allow for the importance of impartiality and universalizability while insisting that morality as a whole involves more than this, in fact includes spheres of action in which morally right decisions are properly *not* universalizable. One finds a prime example of such a sphere in the relationships that one enjoys with particular individuals—such as family members, friends, and so on—who seem to deserve a certain *partiality* of treatment.[22] At the very least, there would be something odd, if not repulsive, about testing every act of friendship for its universalizability: friendship could hardly exist on such terms. Nonetheless, the kinds of considerations that do properly pertain to friendship are, at some level, moral considerations, in our everyday use of the term "moral." Of

19. See Blum, *Friendship*, pp. 137–139; for a sympathetic attempt to develop Kantian moral theory on this point, see Barbara Herman, "The Practice of Moral Judgment," *Journal of Philosophy* 82 (1985): 414–436; more recently, Lawrence Blum has argued for a more complex analysis of "situational perception" in his "Moral Perception and Particularity," *Ethics* 101 (1991): 701–725.

20. Blum, *Friendship*, pp. 129–139; also his "Gilligan and Kohlberg: Implications for Moral Theory," *Ethics* 98 (1988): 472–491; here pp. 484–487.

21. See Lawrence A. Blum, "Iris Murdoch and the Domain of the Moral," *Philosophical Studies* 50 (1986): 343–367; also Iris Marion Young, "Impartiality and the Civic Public: Some Implications of Feminist Critiques of Moral and Political Theory," in *Feminism as Critique: On the Politics of Gender*, ed. Seyla Benhabib and Drucilla Cornell (Minneapolis: University of Minnesota Press, 1987), pp. 57–76; and her *Justice and the Politics of Difference* (Princeton: Princeton University Press, 1990), esp. pp. 96–121.

22. But note that such partiality need not attach only to special relationships. Blum's concept of altruistic action is not limited to these, but applies whenever one responds directly to another's need without basing this response on a sense of duty or on a claim that anyone in a similar situation would also have to respond in such a way; see Blum, *Friendship*, pp. 84–92.

course, it may be possible to justify impartially such relationships as a whole, as equally permissible for all. But this would hardly catch hold of the intrinsic moral worth of such relationships, how they constitute a set of values affecting one within a specific domain, values to which one ordinarily responds *without* first resorting to universalizability tests, even on the whole.[23]

To a large extent, the domain problem results from the liberal prioritization of justice, and so I treat the problem most directly in the context of the liberal-communitarian debate. There one can see that neo-Kantians need not deny that morality, taken in a broad sense, covers more than the domain of universalizable principles. Thus it is not surprising that neo-Kantians have also attempted to incorporate aspects of care into a principled morality.[24] This becomes especially interesting, however, in the face of attempts by some proponents of an ethics of care to radicalize the domain distinction, a move that raises the prospect of irreducibly different *moral perspectives* or orientations. Gilligan, for example, has argued that the justice perspective and the care perspective constitute two different ways of organizing one's moral thinking. As such, they cannot be mediated under a single metaperspective; rather, one can only switch back and forth from one perspective to the other, in a manner similar to the perception of Gestalt figures.[25] In response to Gilligan, the discourse-ethical concept of application shows how one can do justice to both perspectives within a single framework. In particular, I shall be concerned to show how moral judgment can involve a very con-

23. See Blum, *Friendship*, esp. pp. 58–83; for a broad challenge to the ubiquity of (narrowly construed) moralities, see Susan Wolf, "Moral Saints," *Journal of Philosophy* 79 (1982): 419–439.

24. See the selection of recent essays in Thomas E. Wren, in cooperation with Wolfgang Edelstein and Gertrud Nunner-Winkler, eds., *The Moral Domain: Essays in the Ongoing Discussion between Philosophy and the Social Sciences* (Cambridge: MIT Press, 1990). It is interesting in this regard to trace developments in Kohlberg's position: compare Lawrence Kohlberg, "A Reply to Owen Flanagan and Some Comments on the Puka-Goodpaster Exchange," *Ethics* 92 (1982): 513–528; Clark Power, Ann Higgins, and Lawrence Kohlberg, "The Habit of the Common Life: Building Character through Democratic Community Schools," in *Moral Development and Character Education: A Dialogue*, ed. Larry P. Nucci (Berkeley: McCutchan, 1989), pp. 125–143; and Lawrence Kohlberg, Dwight R. Boyd, and Charles Levine, "The Return of Stage 6: Its Principle and Moral Point of View," in *Moral Domain*, ed. Wren, pp. 151–181.

25. See, for example, Carol Gilligan, "Moral Orientation and Moral Development," in *Women and Moral Theory*, ed. Kittay and Meyers, pp. 19–33; also her "Remapping the Moral Domain: New Images of the Self in Relationship," in *Reconstructing Individualism: Autonomy, Individuality and the Self in Western Thought*, ed. Thomas C. Heller et al. (Stanford: Stanford University Press, 1986), pp. 237–252. For a criticism of this move, see Gertrud Nunner-Winkler, "Moral Relativism and Strict Universalism," in *Moral Domain*, ed. Wren, pp. 109–126.

crete care for particular individuals, though it can never boil down to friendship.

Once one broadens the moral domain beyond that of impersonal rules and impartial judgment, questions of *moral emotions* or feelings naturally acquire greater prominence. At one level we find the question of motivation: by challenging the Kantian view that moral action is motivated by respect for universal law, the ethics of care makes room in the moral domain for actions motivated by emotions such as compassion, sympathy, care—what one might call the "altruistic emotions."[26] More pertinent for our focus on argumentation, however, is the role of emotions in moral perception and reasoning. If special relationships generally involve close bonds of affection, and if the emotions or feelings arising from such bonds have a decisive impact on the decisions one takes, then moral reasoning—at least in the realm of care—should be closely tied to moral feelings of care, compassion, and so forth. If nothing else, feelings of care and love for another should make one more perceptive of the other's needs, and thus more likely to respond to the other, and respond appropriately.[27] To be sure, the manner in which the violation of moral norms (and especially norms of justice) evokes an emotional response has long been noticed.[28] But what implications might such observations have for the role of emotions in a theory of practical argument?

An answer to this partly depends on how one analyzes emotions, i.e., whether one attributes a "rational structure" to emotions.[29] Certainly a question of this scope deserves a separate study of its own. Here I simply want to indicate three levels at which emotions and feelings might play a role in argumentation. First, inasmuch as moral argumentation turns on the various needs at stake in a problem of social cooperation, moral emotions will play an important part in revealing the dimensions of the problem, i.e., the needs at stake. Emotions—particularly the negative ones—partly define the moral issues. Second, attempts to incorporate empathy into the moral point of view suggest that "feeling" (in some

26. Blum, *Friendship*, pp. 1–42.

27. Blum makes this argument in *Friendship*, pp. 129–139.

28. Habermas draws on just this link in DE, pp. 45–50; EzD, p. 143. See P. F. Strawson, "Freedom and Resentment," in *Freedom and Resentment and Other Essays* (London: Methuen, 1974), pp. 1–25.

29. For an overview of this debate, see William C. Spohn, "Passions and Principles," *Theological Studies* 52 (1991): 69–87; also the collection, *Explaining Emotions*, ed. Amélie Oksenberg Rorty (Berkeley: University of California Press, 1980). One of the most cognitivist views of emotions is that of Robert C. Solomon, who considers them "systems of judgment." For a summary of his position, see his "On Emotions as Judgments," *American Philosophical Quarterly* 25 (1988): 183–191.

sense) could actually improve one's understanding for the other's position, and thus allow for a fairer moral judgment.[30] To be sure, definitions of "empathy" vary, and a purely cognitive concept of empathy would not support this claim.[31] Nonetheless, even if one defined empathy as a cognitive grasp of the other's predicament, one might draw on some of the arguments sketched above and propose that feelings of care and concern could guide and enhance such empathetic understanding. In either case, the attempt to grasp the other's position and arguments in a process of moral argumentation might be considerably aided by certain emotions. Third, one might argue that emotions can actually amount to something like arguments or counterarguments. For there are cases where one withholds consent from a reasoned conclusion one feels is wrong without being able, at the time, to articulate why the conclusion is wrong. Such cases lie at the limits of rational articulation, where the moral person must trust her character and experience. In these cases one might say that the emotions "test and tutor reason."[32]

An adequate treatment of these issues ultimately exceeds the scope of this book. Nonetheless, a plausible account of discourse ethics must at least set out the systematic basis for developing the above connections between reason and feeling. Hence, I will attempt to indicate, first, how moral norms are internally related to moral emotions and, more broadly, the interpretation of needs. Second, I shall develop a concept of moral discourse for which empathy is essential. Third, I shall attempt to make room at the level of application for more particularistic dimensions of argumentation; this will at least suggest that emotions (as well as shared histories, narratives, and concrete bodily gestures) could enter into a rational consensus.

Outline of the Argument. The foregoing sections survey some of the

30. See, for example, Susan Moller Okin, "Reason and Feeling in Thinking about Justice," *Ethics* 99 (1989): 229–249 (also in *Feminism and Political Theory*, ed. Cass Sunstein [Chicago: University of Chicago Press, 1990], pp. 15–36).
31. For an overview of approaches, see Janet Strayer, "Affective and Cognitive Perspectives on Empathy," in *Empathy and Its Development*, ed. Nancy Eisenberg and Janet Strayer (Cambridge: Cambridge University Press, 1987), pp. 218–244; for an attempt to integrate the cognitive and the affective, see Lawrence Blum, "Particularity and Responsiveness," in *The Emergence of Morality in Young Children*, ed. Jerome Kagan and Sharon Lamb (Chicago: University of Chicago Press, 1987), pp. 306–337.
32. Sidney Callahan, *In Good Conscience: Reason and Emotion in Moral Decision Making* (San Francisco: Harper, 1991), pp. 129–131. An example of such a case is found in Huckleberry Finn's decision not to turn in the runaway slave Jim; see Jonathan Bennett, "The Conscience of Huckleberry Finn," *Philosophy* 49 (1974): 123–134; see also Martin L. Hoffman, "The Contribution of Empathy to Justice and Moral Theory," in *Empathy*, ed. Eisenberg and Strayer, pp. 47–80.

most important issues confronting a plausible neo-Kantian moral theory today. I want to bring discourse ethics to bear on these issues with a systematic intent, however, and so I shall begin this study with the central claim of discourse ethics. This claim can be found in the discourse-ethical principle of universalization (U). Only when we have gotten a clear idea of this principle and eliminated certain potential misunderstandings can we hope to deal with the current challenges.

In Part One, then, I explicate the discourse-ethical principle of universalization as an idealized, argumentation-theoretic account of the moral point of view. This principle represents Habermas's attempt to get beyond his earlier notion of an "ideal speech situation." The latter idea gave rise to a number of problems and misunderstandings, and, not surprisingly, (U) has received its share of criticism as well. To render discourse ethics plausible one must at least deflect such criticisms. Since the strongest objections concern the derivation of (U), it will help to structure the discussion around that derivation. I shall not pretend to establish a definitive "proof" here. One can at most clarify the ideas behind (U) and render it plausible as an idealization. For this it is necessary, first, to have some idea of the methodology behind discourse ethics, as well as the phenomena it seeks to explain and what burden of argument this involves. One also needs a sense of the specific problem context discourse ethics seeks to address: morality as conflict adjudication in pluralist circumstances. All this I take up in Chapter 1. Next, one must understand the basic concepts employed in discourse ethics: the notions of norm, value, interest, consequences, etc., and how these enter into moral discourse. These concepts I elaborate in Chapter 2. The derivation itself occupies Chapter 3. I undertake the derivation not for the sake of an exercise in logic but to bring out the intersubjective concept of practical reason built into (U). This concept, I shall argue, is at once decisive for addressing contemporary debates and puzzling.

The intersubjective dimension of (U) decisively determines the significance of discourse ethics for the debates on practical reason sketched above. In a nutshell, all these debates turn on how one conceives the links that join the morally reflective individual with other individuals, be they very specific individuals enjoying special relationships or the broader community from which one receives a particular identity and culture. That is, beneath the various attacks on neo-Kantian moral theory one can, I suspect, uncover a challenge to the quasi-Cartesian assumption that in moral reflection the individual somehow frees herself—or ought to free herself, if she hopes to be impartial—from various "attachments":

attachments to a tradition, to a particular community, to particular friends and family members, to conceptions of the good, to emotions, and so on. To address this challenge, one must focus first and foremost on the conception of individual moral reflection. And it is precisely here, I think, that the discourse-ethical principle of universalization has something very interesting to say, for it conceives moral reflection in a way that potentially brings these various links into the very heart of such reflection.

Part One aims to bring out the intersubjective concept of practical insight inherent in (U). The derivation plays a central role here, for the specific concept of intersubjectivity at stake "falls out" of that derivation, so to speak: it results only from the *combination* of premises from which (U) is derived. Moreover, (U) equips the notion of intersubjectivity with systematic contours full of potential for the controversies outlined above. Even if these contours exist only in an embryonic form in (U) itself, they can be developed in subsequent chapters for the issues respectively at stake. As this process of development progresses, we shall see the outlines of a multilevel concept of solidarity emerge.

Hence, as I work through the various arguments in Parts Two and Three, I suggest an interpretation and extension of Habermas's concept of solidarity that allows discourse ethics to address communitarian and feminist concerns without falling behind the modern differentiations within practical reason—between right and good, abstract universal and concrete particular, society and community. Rather than reducing either side of these differentiations to the other, I attempt to acknowledge their complexity with a multilevel concept of solidarity that reconnects justice with the good at various levels.

Besides opening the door to solidarity, however, the intersubjectivity in (U) is also puzzling, for it would seemingly uproot practical insight from its ancestral home in the individual's head. In Part One I only indicate this puzzle; the Postscript takes it a step further, but still lets its real implications lie fallow. Only at the end of Part Three will I even begin to hint at these implications.

Before that, I turn in Part Two to the liberal-communitarian debate. Here my primary goal consists in elaborating a discourse-ethical treatment of the good, again simply at the level of a logic of argumentation. This involves a number of questions. In Chapter 4 I attend to the more straightforward ones: how to distinguish good from right, how goods enter into moral discourse, and how the right has priority over the good. This will allow us to see in what senses morality actually concerns substantive goods. Chapters 5 and 6 turn to the more difficult question of whether discourse ethics presupposes a particular concept of the good, i.e., whether something like mutual understanding or rational cooperation amounts to a good that "constitutes" discourse ethics. Here I shall take Charles Taylor as the protagonist of choice. In Chapter 5 I simply clarify the issues at stake. In Chapter 6 I draw on the intersubjective concept of practical insight in order to respond to Taylor.

In Part Three I turn to the challenges raised by the need to situate discourse ethics in concrete, particular contexts of moral decision making. The first challenge is that raised by the ethics of care. In Chapter 7, then, I attempt to show how discourse ethics can take account of particularity in the application of moral norms. Even if moral discourse can never become a matter of friendship, it must include an empathetic sensitivity to the concrete other, as well as an attention to the particularities of the concrete situation. This allows a conception of morality that overcomes an excessive orientation to general rules.

Chapter 8 carries the concretization of discourse ethics a step further. Prior to this chapter, I employ (U) as an idealizing conception of moral universalization. Given the abstract nature of the questions at issue in Chapters 2 through 7, one can plausibly work with idealizations. However, in the case of discourse ethics such idealizations appear especially demanding. If discourse ethics is not to be dismissed as an unrealistic moral theory, one must at some point indicate what relevance it has for real discourse and conflict resolution. Chapter 8 takes up this question. There I attempt to indicate how (U) informs real discourse in the legal and political spheres, and what the further extension of discourse ethics into other spheres would require. In part, I do this to render discourse ethics more plausible. More important, however, is the further systematic issue that arises here: the attempt to locate discourse-ethical idealizations in the muddy circuit of reality fully displays the paradoxical character of (U) indicated earlier in Part One. This consists in the fact that (U) takes back with one hand what it gives with another. On the one hand, it points beyond subject-centered notions of practical insight. On the other hand, in the final analysis (U) still locates insight in the individual. This suggests that discourse ethics will eventually have to go beyond (U), or perhaps more accurately, carry through the daring initiative adumbrated in (U). Before concluding Chapter 8, I hint at some possible ways of doing this.

A Theory of Intersubjective Moral Insight

Introduction to Part I

The debates in which discourse ethics currently finds itself embroiled are the result of certain metamorphoses in an earlier context of debate. In its original inspiration, discourse ethics represented a response to the value skepticism growing out of the scientistic contraction of reason to the scientific and technical domains.[1] To this extent thinkers such as Apel and Habermas belong in that stream of philosophers who refused to deliver ethical decision making to either an existentialist decisionism or a placid emotivism.[2] For discourse ethics, however, such efforts were motivated by the hope of supplying Critical Theory with foundations in a concept of rationality broad enough to escape the paradoxes endured by the earlier Frankfurt School.[3] In any case, the particular species of moral skepticism found in the earlier scientistic opponents have since been replaced at the philosophical level by forms of thought loosely grouped under the label of "postmodernism." Whatever foothold moral cognitivism gained

---

1. This is especially clear in Karl-Otto Apel, "The *a priori* of the Communication Community and the Foundations of Ethics," in *Towards a Transformation of Philosophy*, pp. 225–300; also by Apel, "Das Problem der Begründung einer Verantwortungsethik im Zeitalter der Wissenschaft," in *Wissenschaft und Ethik*, ed. Edmund Braun (New York: Peter Lang, 1986), pp. 11–52; esp. pp. 11–19. In Habermas, cf. DE, pp. 43–57.

2. One thinks here of Kurt Baier, Stephen Toulmin, R. M. Hare, each of whom attempted to refute noncognitivist ethical theories in the early fifties.

3. For surveys of this problem terrain, see Rick Roderick, *Habermas and the Foundations of Critical Theory* (New York: St. Martin's, 1986); and Helga Gripp, *Jürgen Habermas: Und es gibt sie doch—Zur kommunikationstheoretischen Begründung von Vernunft bei Jürgen Habermas* (Paderborn: Schöningh, 1984).

against a positivistic value skepticism is once again threatened by variants deriving from Nietzsche.

At the same time, the various species of moral cognitivism emergent in response to positivism have recently encountered a challenge from another direction: the attempts to revive more traditionalistic and contextualistic approaches to morality. The debates described in the Introduction form part of this challenge. In Part One I want to present a reasonably healthy-looking specimen of discourse ethics for inspection, one that will prove adequate to the demands of these debates. To begin with, though, some opening clarifications are necessary. In Chapter 1, then, I want to provide at least a rough idea of the object or moral phenomena discourse ethics seeks to explicate, the general method guiding its explication, and the rather ambitious aims such an explication involves. We can then turn to the heart of the discourse-ethical account of morality, its dialogical principle of universalization. In Chapter 2, I introduce this principle and explain the notion of moral discourse it harbors. In Chapter 3, I attempt to derive this principle; this will show how discourse ethics points toward an intersubjective notion of moral insight. More broadly, by the end of Part One I hope to have shown how discourse ethics presents a coherent account of practical argumentation that not only does justice to deontological and consequentialist insights, but also has reasonable prospects for meeting the challenges posed by communitarians and proponents of the ethics of care. Whether and how it meets these challenges I take up in Parts Two and Three.

CHAPTER ONE

The Object, Method, and Aim of Discourse Ethics

In this chapter I want to recall the kinds of everyday moral intuitions discourse ethics takes as the phenomena or object in need of explanation. I shall also say something about the general method discourse ethics employs in its explanation. I hope thereby to present the communication-theoretic analysis of validity as a reasonable site for further discourse-ethical undertakings (section I). I then want to say something about the burden of argument such an undertaking sets for itself, situating the present study in this broader context (section II).

I. A FORMAL PRAGMATICS OF MORAL INTERACTION

Jürgen Habermas's discourse ethics takes everyday moral intuitions—what we "always already" presuppose in making moral judgments—as its point of departure. Like Kant, he attempts to thematize or reconstruct what is implicit in ordinary moral thinking and judging. To do this, Habermas finds the contrast between moral norms and mere imperatives useful, for the "force" of the former does not derive from extrinsic considerations, as it does for simple imperatives.[1] Rather, we experience this force of the "ought," feel bound to respect its command, even when—perhaps especially when—it is not in our own interests, when no punitive

1. TCA 1:298–305; cf. also LC, pp. 102–105.

consequences will result from breaking the norm. Admittedly, one can ask about *who* this "we" is—but that is the task of later chapters. In any case, the point is that moral 'oughts', in contrast to simple imperatives, carry an internal force or motivating power within the command itself, a force that seems neither to depend on external threats and gratifications nor to express merely the speaker's contingent will.[2]

Where exactly does this "force" reside? Let's imagine I've done something you find morally reprehensible (in a broad sense of "moral"). In one way or another you let me know this: "Why did you *do* that?" or, "You ought not have done that!" or, if you happen to be on the scene and quick enough, "What do you think you're doing?" One can imagine a number of possible responses to such accusations. I might deny having done the action altogether, or insist that you misunderstood what I did. I might feel a certain remorse and simply apologize, or I might explain my behavior by reference to circumstances beyond my control: I did not really intend the action; I was not aware of what I did; I was overcome by rage, etc. But suppose I respond with a defense that my action was morally right, or appropriate. I could say, "What's wrong with such an action?" or, alternatively, "Normally I wouldn't do that, but in this case it was the lesser of two evils." This is not meant to be an exhaustive list, although I hope to have at least suggested the major kinds of response.[3] The examples are meant to indicate several things. First, one should note how the force of such accusations is such as to call for a response on the part of the accused. Second, this can lead to a dispute involving the give-and-take of reasons; in fact, when it does not lead to such a dispute it is quite likely because the agent has admitted a certain (temporary) lack of rational responsibility.[4] Third, the various moves involved in such interactions can appear in a wide variety of social contexts: from a teenage girl arguing with her parents over curfews and use of automobiles, to the

2. It should be noted that imperatives in fact display a range of forms; cf. Habermas's corrections to TCA's analysis of imperatives in the Foreword to the Third Edition of *Theorie des kommunikativen Handelns* (Frankfurt: Suhrkamp, 1988), pp. 4–6; also his "Reply," *Communicative Action: Essays on Jürgen Habermas's "The Theory of Communicative Action,"* ed. Axel Honneth and Hans Joas, trans. Jeremy Gaines and Doris L. Jones (Cambridge: Polity, 1991), pp. 238–240.

3. In fact the typology of such interactions has been extensively researched; see, for example, Monika Keller, "Rechtfertigungen: Zur Entwicklung praktischer Erklärungen," in *Soziale Interaktion und soziales Verstehen: Beiträge zur Entwicklung der Interaktionskompetenz,* ed. Wolfgang Edelstein and Jürgen Habermas (Frankfurt: Suhrkamp, 1984), pp. 253–299; also Marvin B. Scott and Stanford M. Lyman, "Accounts," *American Sociological Review* 33(1968): 46–62.

4. The classic piece spelling out these moves is P. F. Strawson's "Freedom and Resentment," in *Freedom and Resentment,* pp. 1–25.

government official who defends duplicity by referring to the overriding consideration of national security. Discourse ethics proceeds on the assumption that a reconstruction of the everyday intuitions guiding such moves can serve as a heuristic device for the further analysis of the range of forms (and pathologies) of interaction through which a society organizes itself.[5]

We can continue with the above list of considerations and pull them together with a fourth point: what is at stake in such interactions, in various ways—that on which the above examples turn and what accounts for the normative force the agents either acknowledge, dispute, attempt to deflect, or whatnot—are shared behavioral expectations formulatable as norms that have currency within a given social group. In some cases the general norm itself is the object of challenge; in others the point at issue goes no further than whether a particular action in fact violates a norm. In the next chapter I will spell out the notion of social norm more fully; here the point is to get at its status as a *validity claim*, i.e., as something claiming to hold transsubjectively and thus open to the give-and-take of reasons. The accusation presumes that the violated norm holds not just for you but also for me; the apology recognizes this and attempts to make amends; the excuse absolves the norm-breaker of immediate responsibility for the violation; and the accused's defense, finally, either challenges the accuser to give reasons for the validity of the norm, or attempts to give reasons for its situational inappropriateness.

Explicit or tacit references to normative validity claims, then, account for the *internal* motivating power (or illocutionary force) experienced in interactions such as those above. In assuming or raising such claims the speaker refers the hearer to a social world of shared expectations about how the members of that world *ought* to behave. This sort of expectation, of course, differs from an empirical prediction (although one might attempt such predictions once one knows what normative expectations hold within a group). In making empirical predictions one assumes the position of an observer opposite an external world describable in terms of initial conditions, lawlike generalities, and predictable outcomes. Normative expectations, by contrast, can be experienced and

5. See Habermas's criticism of Toulmin's rejection of a universalistic reconstruction in TCA 1:31–42; p. 40 for the view that an analysis of everyday speech "remains a heuristically productive starting point for systematizing validity claims . . ." For his attempt to display the everyday occurrence and intuitive force of everyday 'oughts', see DE, pp. 55–60. For a further discourse-ethical "phenomenology of moral consciousness" see Lutz Wingert, "Gemeinsinn und Moral: Elemente einer intersubjektivistischen Konzeption der Moral," diss., University of Frankfurt, 1990 (forthcoming, Suhrkamp, 1993).

held only *within* a social world where one can experience demands of
the sort, "I have a right to expect this of you," or "You have no right to
expect me to do that," and so on; a world, that is, where one can be
disappointed in an expectation *not* because one mistook the general law
or a crucial initial condition, but precisely because a free agency allows
the other to violate existing norms.[6] Hence in order to reconstruct the
force of normative validity claims we must refer to intuitions operative
when we take the "performative attitude" of participants in social interactions.

How exactly is a reconstruction of such expectations to proceed? At
least some remarks on the general communication-theoretic project and
its method are in order here, inasmuch as this determines the overall direction of discourse ethics and thus provides a presupposed basis for the
present study. Here we shall have to do with broad strokes; if necessary,
finer details can be supplied as the need arises within specific contexts.

Methodologically, then, the communication-theoretic reconstruction
of validity makes use of a *formal-pragmatic* analysis to lay out the meaning such validity claims have for participants. According to this method
of analysis, the sense of a claim to truth, for example, is revealed by examining the practices connected with making and defending truth
claims: one understands the meaning of "truth," as we use it in everyday
parlance, when one can describe the rules for using the term.[7] Because
these rules are not nomological generalizations made from an observer's
point of view but are rather reconstructions of the intuitive "know how"
of competent speakers, formal pragmatics distinguishes itself from empirical pragmatics.[8] It requires the theorist to take the attitude of a participant in communication and make explicit the rules speakers tacitly
rely on for making themselves understood and for reaching agreement.

The formal nature of this approach lies in the attempt to get at those
competences or "pragmatic universals" constituting the very meaning of

---

6. Cf. TCA 1:85; this is the point of Strawson's "Freedom and Resentment."
7. The underlying assumption here is the collapse of correspondence theories of truth
which depend on an unmediated, extralinguistic access to facts. For a thorough discussion
of the background debates around this approach to truth, see Herbert Scheit, *Wahrheit,
Diskurs, Demokratie: Studien zur "Konsensustheorie der Wahrheit"* (Freiburg: Karl Alber,
1987).
8. See TCA 1:321–323, 328–331; in fact, Habermas's formal pragmatics draws on a
number of approaches in communication theory: structural semiotics, symbolic interac-
tionist, phenomenological, and rule-governed approaches (Wittgenstein, speech act theory); for an overview of these approaches, see Stephen W. Littlejohn, *Theories of Human
Communication*, 3d ed. (Belmont, Calif.: Wadsworth, 1989).

claims to truth, rightness, and so forth—that without which such terms would lose their place in a form of life. We shall see later how this limits discourse ethics to being a formal-proceduralist moral theory. Here I simply want to note how ambitious a project this is, for it requires the theorist to isolate those features of human interaction or "basic modes of language use" holding across all cultures.[9] In aiming at a *universalist* account of interaction, formal pragmatics abstracts from given institutional arrangements and the "generalized social contexts" studied by sociolinguistics, without going so far as to abstract from speech situations altogether and focus simply on grammatically well-formed sentences as linguistic analysis does.[10] I have already tried to suggest the plausibility of this strategy by referring above to the heuristic value of such analyses. In fact, a failure to achieve conceptual clarity at this level of abstraction can lead to further biases in one's social analysis.[11] The opposite danger, of course, is that empirical phenomena become so much sand to be poured into pregiven categorical boxes.

In any case, the point of this methodology is to locate the force of a validity claim by spelling out the communicative practices competent speakers find intuitively appropriate in any context where the given type of validity is at stake. The give-and-take of reasons associated with the above examples has already led us to speak of such validity as a trans-subjective phenomenon. More precisely, such practices seem to call for a *cognitivist* analysis of normative validity inasmuch as the force of the norm (or the immediate claim based on the norm) varies in proportion to the reasons that can be given pro and con. It is precisely in view of this that the accused, or hearer, may ask the speaker for reasons ("What's wrong with what I did?") or may supply counterreasons of his own ("I'm old enough now to stay out past ten o'clock!"). Discourse ethics thus distinguishes itself from subjectivistic ethical analyses, such as that of emotivism, by taking such reason giving seriously. At the same time, it does

9. TCA 1:331f; for a discussion of the aims and problems of universal pragmatics, see Thomas McCarthy, *The Critical Theory of Jürgen Habermas* (Cambridge: MIT Press, 1978), pp. 272–291; and Roderick, *Habermas*, pp. 74–81; for a readable overview of Habermas's communication-theoretic project, see David Ingram, *Habermas and the Dialectic of Reason* (New Haven: Yale University Press, 1987).

10. See Jürgen Habermas, "Vorlesungen zu einer sprachtheoretischen Grundlegung der Soziologie," in his *Vorstudien und Ergänzungen zur Theorie des kommunikativen Handelns*, 2d ed. (Frankfurt: Suhrkamp, 1986), esp. pp. 83–104; also his "What Is Universal Pragmatics?" in CES, esp. pp. 26–34.

11. See Habermas's criticisms of Toulmin and Austin in TCA 1:31–42 and 291f, resp. In Habermas's view both thinkers tie their analyses too directly to institutions, decisions which ultimately undermine the critical potential of those analyses.

not assume that moral objectivity can be assimilated to that of true factual statements.[12]

Let us return to the notion of validity now and render our earlier intuitive observations more precise. According to Habermas's analysis, the force of tacit and explicit validity claims lies in their claiming that a given norm or specific course of action *deserves* intersubjective recognition. Hence in making such a claim one at once (a) opens one's claim to an objective evaluation and thereby to others' criticism, and (b) maintains that what is claimed can withstand such evaluation. In these features Habermas finds his notion of rationality: validity claims are "rational" in being at once criticizable and groundable.[13] This then leads to a notion of "rational motivation" as explaining the force of validity claims: the speaker's validity claim exercises a "motivating force" on the hearer precisely because the claim refers the hearer to the "fact" that there are good reasons for accepting the claim. This does not mean that the speaker actually has to list those reasons, but rather that such reasons *could* be given if necessary (and if not by the speaker, then by someone other than the speaker):

> A speaker can *rationally motivate* a hearer to accept his speech act offer because—on the basis of an internal connection between validity, validity claim, and redemption of a validity claim—he can assume the *warranty* [*Gewähr*] for providing, if necessary, convincing reasons that would stand up to a hearer's criticism of the validity claim.[14]

Note that the above text refers us to yet a further precision in the analysis by distinguishing between validity, validity claim, and redemption of validity claim. This deserves some attention. What the speaker *claims* is that the conditions for the statement's validity *are in fact satisfied* (that the statement is true, right, etc.).[15] What internally motivates the speaker to make this claim—assuming he has not made it arbitrarily—is the confidence that the claimed proposition can *be supported* by convincing reasons. This distinction is necessary if one is not to conflate, for example, the truth or rightness one might claim for a proposition with the actual (fallible) justification backing the proposition. What this validity itself—i.e., the satisfaction of validity conditions for a statement—consists in I shall save for later; here I simply want to draw at-

12. DE, pp. 50–62.
13. TCA 1:8–22.
14. TCA 1:302.
15. Cf. TCA 1:38: "A *validity claim* is equivalent to the assertion that the *conditions for the validity* of an utterance are fulfilled."

tention to the distinction between (a) a speaker's actual *claim* to validity, raised at a particular time and place, (b) the *validity* as such (truth, rightness, etc.) which is claimed, and (c) the backing for the claim, or its *redemption* (or vindication).

In need of further explication here is the *connection* between the claim and one's confidence in its defensibility. At this point I simply want to note that our three-way distinction allows us to locate the force of a validity claim more precisely in this connection itself, as that which accounts for the rationally motivating power of the validity claim. Confidence in a proposition's defensibility motivates one to claim validity for it, and in raising the claim the speaker conveys to the hearer his confidence in the proposition's rational supportability or, as Habermas puts it, assumes the "warranty" that convincing reasons can be provided, thereby also (possibly) motivating the hearer to accept the proposition as valid.

At this point it seems to me one has a choice in how to pursue further the analysis of moral validity. One path—which Habermas chooses— aims to account for the intersubjective binding force of norms in terms of their potential for convincing reasons. This path leads directly to a theory of argumentation: although Habermas attempts to distinguish between the basic types of validity claim at several levels,[16] one must ultimately turn to the practices of argument by which the claim is redeemed.[17] In defending formal pragmatics against the semantic approach to meaning analysis, Habermas argues that understanding the meaning of a validity claim ultimately forces one to consider the pragmatics of its redemption:

> In this debate we are not concerned with questions of territorial boundaries or of nominal definitions but with whether *the concept of the validity of a sentence* can be explicated independently of *the concept of redeeming the va-*

16. See TCA 1:38: "a considerable burden of proof is placed upon the theory of argumentation; it has to be in a position to specify a *system of validity claims*." Habermas goes on, pp. 38–40, to distinguish types of validity claim according to what it is the hearer is invited to take a position on; this typology he then confirms in two further ways, through a semantic analysis of the corresponding sentence forms and a pragmatic analysis of the different kinds of grounding each type calls for. This recourse to several approaches suggests that Habermas's argument relies on the overall coherence of several analyses.

17. A more recent statement seems to temper this claim: "The presuppositions of action oriented to reaching understanding are more easily seen in processes of argumentation. This advantage as a research strategy does not signify any ontological distinction, as if argumentation were more important or even more fundamental than conversation or the everyday communicative practice that, constituted as a lifeworld, forms the most encompassing horizon. In this sense, the analysis of speech acts likewise enjoys only a heuristic advantage." *Texte und Kontexte* (Frankfurt: Suhrkamp, 1991), p. 146.

lidity claim raised through the utterance of the sentence. I am defending the thesis that this is not possible. Semantic investigations of descriptive, expressive, and normative sentences, if only they are carried through consistently enough, force us to change the level of analysis. The very analysis of the conditions of the validity of sentences *itself* compels us to analyze the conditions for the intersubjective recognition of corresponding validity claims.[18]

If the force of moral claims rests on the confidence that they can be supported by good reasons, then one can understand the specific type of claim by understanding how supportive reasons are produced—and confidence generated—through argument.[19]

For future reference, however, a second path should be noticed here: an analysis directly focusing on the confidence itself. After all, in many if not most situations people agree simply on the basis of such confidence, without insisting on the actual grounding of validity claims—although we do not normally accept "guarantees" just from anyone about anything. Habermas's analysis of validity also places *trust* at the heart of rational motivation and thus calls for a differentiated social and institutional analysis of such trust as a component in the force of moral validity claims. For the moment let it suffice simply to note this path. We shall come across it again at the end of our journey, in Chapter 8.

II. THE DISCOURSE ETHICS ENTERPRISE

We turn now to discourse ethics itself. Habermas summarizes its basic intentions in the Principle of Discourse (D): "only those norms can claim to be valid that meet (or could meet) with the approval of all affected in their capacity *as participants in a practical discourse*."[20] Although Habermas originally introduced (D) as the leading principle of his moral theory, he has recently given it a broader interpretation. As it stands, (D) simply explicates "the point of view from which action norms can be *im-*

18. TCA 1:316.
19. Hence the central claim of Habermas's theory of meaning: "We understand a speech act when we know what makes it acceptable"; TCA 1:297.
20. DE, p. 66; a number of recent works attempt to situate discourse ethics in broader contexts: see, for example, Seyla Benhabib, *Critique, Norm and Utopia: A Study of the Foundations of Critical Theory* (New York: Columbia University Press, 1986); Stephen K. White, *The Recent Work of Jürgen Habermas: Reason, Justice and Modernity* (Cambridge: Cambridge University Press, 1989); David M. Rasmussen, *Reading Habermas* (Cambridge, Mass.: Blackwell, 1990); Tony Smith, *The Role of Ethics in Social Theory: Essays from a Habermasian Perspective* (Albany: SUNY Press, 1991); Jane Braaten, *Habermas's Critical Theory of Society* (Albany: SUNY Press, 1991); Kenneth Baynes, *The Normative Grounds of Social Criticism: Kant, Rawls, and Habermas* (Albany: SUNY Press, 1992).

partially grounded."[21] Assuming that not all forms of normative behavioral regulation can be analyzed solely in moral terms—think, for example, of legal norms—(D) is both more and less than a moral principle. It is more in that it covers more areas of social action, less in that it does not tell us what distinguishes the validity of moral norms from that of other kinds of action norm. In the last chapter this point will take on greater significance when we turn to the relation between law and morality. Here it is important to see what (D) does tell us about moral validity, and how it provides a more definite direction to the lines of analysis already projected in the opening remarks.

To begin with, (D) falls in line with *deontological* moral theories insofar as it points toward a reconstruction of the intersubjectively binding character of 'ought' claims such as those illustrated above, where the issues involve legitimate interpersonal expectations. Like Kant's account of moral obligation, however, (D) issues in a *formal* moral theory, providing only a decision procedure for reaching valid norms. Continuing the above discussed emphasis on everyday reason giving, (D) locates this procedure in practical discourse striving for consensus, thereby setting out on a *cognitivist* explanation of the moral 'ought.' Finally, insofar as such formal procedures undercut any particular set of conventional or local norms and reconstruct features of any meaningful human cooperation, discourse ethics promises a potentially *universalist* account of morality. These four characteristics mark discourse ethics as fundamentally Kantian in its orientation; for this reason it is all the more important to notice that it significantly diverges from Kant insofar as it links normative validity with the real consensus of all those affected by a norm. The task of Part One is to lend this account of morality at least a prima facie plausibility, primarily through an explication of the discourse-ethical notion of practical discourse.

Before we can do this, however, a more basic question pointing to the larger context of investigation deserves some attention. Namely, why discourse ethics at all? In other words, why should one even consider it as a moral theory? On the face of it, (D) in no way disappoints the ambitions already evident in formal pragmatics. After all, it aspires to no less than a theory of normative validity in general that will accept nothing less than general validity. In view of the unfriendly environment for such ambitions, it is not surprising that some find it more palatable to

---

21. FG, p. 140; for the translation of this text, see Jürgen Habermas, *Between Facts and Norms: Contributions to a Discourse Theory of Law and Democracy*, trans. William Rehg (Cambridge: MIT Press, forthcoming).

back off from the strong claims Habermas makes for discourse ethics as
a full-blown account of morality, and simply point to its suitability as a
"public morality," i.e., a morality of citizenship, or one presupposed by
democratic political practices.[22] Although I too am sympathetic with
such a political reading, I would like to make a slight adjustment in keeping with the Introduction's focus on the problem of social cooperation.
That is, I would like to examine discourse ethics as it pertains to fair
conflict resolution. This adjustment attempts to steer a middle course,
neither jumping immediately into a specific social domain such as politics, nor attempting to define the moral domain *tout court*. Rather, it
requires us to look at moral norms only insofar as they resolve actual or
potential conflicts. For this we need only assume that there are conflicts
of interest the resolution of which involves a moral dimension—specifically, a justice or fairness aspect.[23] In this way we can temporarily
bracket Habermas's strong *identification* of morality with conflict adjudication, while nonetheless sticking closely to the basic approach guiding this identification, namely, Habermas's concern with the conditions
of social order.

From this point of view, then, social norms are primarily of interest
for their role in social coordination.[24] Here it is important to notice Habermas's distinction between two forms of coordination, "social integration" and "system integration." The cooperation structured by consensus on norms, be it a background consensus or a consciously achieved
one, represents a mechanism of social integration. System integration refers to the coordination that comes about through the intended and un-
intended consequences of actions. This latter mechanism is salient in
market processes, for example, which rely on the steering medium of
money to effect the efficient distribution of goods and services. Of
course, economic processes are also normatively regulated. However, the
difficulties attending this distinction need not detain us here; I simply

---

22. This is the approach suggested by Bruce Ackerman in "Why Dialogue?" *Journal
of Philosophy* 86 (1989): 6–8, and favored by Jean Cohen, "Discourse Ethics and Civil
Society," *Philosophy and Social Criticism* 14 (1988): 315–337, here p. 318.

23. Interest conflicts should not be limited to conflicts over the distribution of wealth,
as is the wont of liberal social theorists. See TCA 2:392; for Habermas's critique of Rawls
on this point, see CES, pp. 197–198.

24. One can trace this back at least to Hobbes; more recently see Kurt Baier, *The Moral
Point of View* (Ithaca, N.Y.: Cornell University Press, 1958), p. 190: "For morality is de-
signed to apply in just such cases, namely, those where interests conflict." In Habermas, see
"Vorlesungen," in *Vorstudien*, pp. 11–126; DE, pp. 66f; also helpful on this point is White,
Recent Work, pp. 28–47.

want to point out that moral norms do not bear the entire burden of social coordination in modern societies.[25] In what follows I shall use the term "moral" under these qualifications, unless noted otherwise.

This narrowing of the moral domain, however, does not dispel the relevance of our basic question, even if it restricts its scope somewhat. Why look to a proceduralist moral theory for an account of just conflict resolution? At one level an answer to this would take us into a theory of modernity, for discourse ethics aims to recover moral objectivity in a posttraditional world no longer able to look to an overarching moral authority agreeable to all. The presumption here is that no vantage point other than discourse itself can provide the objectivity once grounded in religious authority and metaphysical worldviews. The slight shift just introduced renders this point even more convincing, in my opinion, for the issue now takes on a yet more timely form: instead of moral objectivity as such, what is at stake is the possibility of conflict resolutions and modes of consensual cooperation perceived as fair (thus as normatively valid) in an increasingly interdependent world whose member nations are in turn subject to intensifying internal diversity. Once one frames the issue in terms of cooperation and conflict, the prima facie desirability of a discourse ethics is considerably unburdened of a *theory* of modernity—the need for consensuality today is all too evident. This is not to deny that such an approach would eventually have to come to terms with diverging views of modernity. Rather, I only want to cast the issue in a way that highlights the initial advantages of taking a discourse-theoretic approach.

Still, the basic question persists: granted that some theory of consensus formation would be interesting, perhaps useful, why should we peg such consensus on something so rationalistic as "practical discourse"? A ready answer to this might move directly from the formal-pragmatic account of validity to discourse ethics: after all, did not that account directly link the force of validity claims to a confidence that such claims can be supported with good reasons? To the extent that the very meaning of a moral validity claim, and in particular its illocutionary force, can be understood only in terms of the give-and-take of reasons supporting the claim—thus only in terms of practical discourse—then (D) would seem just a short step further, suggesting that discourse ethics is somehow implicit in our everyday moral claims—hence by extension implicit in

25. See TCA 2:117–197; "Reply," pp. 250–260.

claims that a given mode of cooperation is fair to those involved. Must not anyone who even *understands* the meaning of the normative claims he makes (or assumes as valid) accept some principle like (D)?

Although this is ultimately the argument Habermas wants to make, so direct a move would in fact be too quick.[26] True, discourse ethics attempts to thematize the intuitions behind "ought" claims by spelling out the kind of reason giving that leads one to accept or reject such a claim. To this extent it presents itself as implicit in everyday interaction. Yet this already presupposes an account of isolable normative validity claims that can be put up for open debate.[27] Perhaps such an account comes more easily when cast in terms of the need for social cooperation. In any case, linking the validity of norms with their justifiability does not yet answer the following more general, complex question: *who* gets to justify *which norms* on the basis of *what kinds* of reasons? Habermas himself has argued for the historical variability of the answers to this question.[28] Moreover, as current debates in moral theory indicate, there are ongoing controversies around the definition of various normative domains, who has a say in justifying their respective norms, and what sorts of justifications are acceptable—not to mention technocratic doubts about whether social decision making should rest on discursive consensus at all. The answers discourse ethics gives on these issues are not exactly controversy-free, and in Part Two I shall examine one such controversy in greater detail. For the moment suffice it to note that a convincing support for (D) must take the opening communication-theoretic account of validity considerably deeper, in the end tying this account to a theory of modernity as well.[29]

---

26. Cf. DE, pp. 100, 101: "there is no form of sociocultural life that is not at least implicitly geared to maintaining communicative action by means of argument, be the actual form of argumentation ever so rudimentary and the institutionalization of discursive consensus building ever so inchoate. Once argumentation is conceived as a special form of rule-governed action, it reveals itself to be a reflective form of action oriented toward reaching an understanding. . . . the concept of communicative action is . . . a concept of rationality strong enough to *extend* the transcendental-pragmatic derivation of the moral principle to the basis of validity of action oriented toward reaching an understanding." Cf. also DE, pp. 66f. This move is discussed at length in Gripp, *Habermas*, pp. 39–55; also see McCarthy, *Critical Theory*, pp. 317–325.

27. DE, pp. 57f: "The attempt to ground ethics in the form of a logic of moral argumentation has no chance of success unless we can identify a special type of validity claim connected with commands and norms and can identify it on the level on which moral dilemmas initially emerge within the horizon of the lifeworld. . . ."

28. CES, pp. 103–106, 178–188; for Habermas the shift from traditional to modern justifications involves a change in the *type* of reasoning; ibid., p. 185.

29. Hence Habermas's complex argument constituting the whole of TCA. Probably it is most accurate to characterize this argument not so much in terms of a single line of dependencies as a coherent network of supporting arguments (communication theory, theory of modernity, critique of competing accounts, and so on).

Not only this, one would also have to defend a demanding notion of personal autonomy that considerably outstrips our opening analysis of normative validity. That analysis suggested that normative validity claims, as expressing legitimate behavior expectations, only have force among individuals who consider themselves accountable—and to that extent autonomous—persons. To be sure, this accountability involves the exchange of reasons, making it plausible to infer that a normed expectation is an expectation one can *justify* to those subject to it: members may be expected to observe the norm precisely because its validity can be made evident to their reason.[30] Strictly speaking, however, our analysis tied the motivating force of the validity claim to the *confidence* that reasons *could* be given. Actors would be accountable, then, so long as they could refer to some authority they believe could ground their norms. In fact, this more limited accountability is probably the more typical basis of cooperation.[31] In calling for a real discourse leading to a consensus of all the affected parties, however, discourse ethics would seem to demand a much higher standard of personal enlightenment and responsibility. The strong discourse-ethical notion of autonomy requires subjects to question even pregiven legitimating frameworks and authorities. Validity can then be redeemed only on the basis of the formal properties of argumentation.[32]

Clearly, neither the discourse-ethical account of autonomy nor the broader communication-theoretic grounding of discourse ethics can get off the ground without working out the specific notion of practical discourse that (D) projects in regard to moral questions. Thus the plausibility of discourse ethics depends on the theory of moral argumentation that lays out the notion of a rationally motivated agree-

30. See MC, p. 155; DE, pp. 66f; particularly eye opening is "Vorlesungen," in *Vorstudien*, pp. 123f: there Habermas starts with the innocuous notion: "To the extent that we *want* to treat him as a subject at all, we *must* assume the other opposite us *could* say why he behaves in a given situation this way and not that" (p. 123). He then breaks this supposition down into (a) the assumption that the other acts with intentionality and (b) the expectation "that acting subjects only follow norms that appear to them as justified" (p. 124).

31. To cite a recent example, U.S. soldiers in Saudi Arabia felt their presence there justified without being able to provide full justifications themselves. More typical were responses such as, "If the President of the United States felt it was necessary for us to be here, that's 100 percent enough for me." Quoted by James LeMoyne, "Troops in Gulf Talk of War, and of Vietnam and Respect," *New York Times*, 30 September 1990, natl. ed.: A1.

32. A traditional authoritarian view would challenge precisely the assumption that everyone is qualified to question at the level of frameworks, arguing instead that the correct understanding at this level depends on certain experiences or other privileges which not everyone can be expected to have.

ment.[33] Such an account must for its part be not only internally coherent but also show how rational agreement is at least possible in principle on the basis of its idealizations. Moreover, it must provide for a feasible relation to practice. Precisely this underlying account of moral reasoning—the "idea of a discourse ethics"—constitutes the focus of the present study. Let us turn to that account.

33. See DE, p. 66: "This principle of discourse ethics (D) . . . already *presupposes* that we *can* justify our choice of a norm." As we shall see, it is precisely the analysis of argumentation summarized in the (U) principle that shows how such justification is possible.

CHAPTER TWO

Elements of Moral Discourse

The plausibility of discourse ethics crucially depends on an account of rational consensus formation through practical discourse. This account must go beyond the rather vague formulations in Chapter 1 about reason giving and tell us what convincing or rationally motivating reason giving involves. We find Habermas's most succinct answer to this challenge in the rule of argument given by the principle of universalization (U). This principle represents an attempt to explicate the moral point of view in terms of the impartial justification of general moral norms; as we shall see later, however, this does not imply that morality, taken in a broad sense, is exhausted by the idea of impartiality or by general norms. One must also bear in mind that, taken by itself, (U) simply delineates a logic of justification—the ideal structures informing serious attempts at discourse. In this and the following chapters I am primarily concerned with elucidating the various implications this logic has for moral theory; only in the last chapter can I confront the further complications that make real discourses less than ideal. This approach is in line with what I said in chapter 1 about formal pragmatics. By starting with ideal structures one has a better chance of keeping one's bearings—and a critical perspective—when one examines existing institutions and practices of discourse. In any case, in the present chapter I shall draw on a number of texts, both of Habermas and others, in order to clarify the notion of moral discourse that (U) entails.[1] I shall proceed as follows. After briefly introducing the basic intuition behind (U) and some of the questions it raises (section I), I shall turn to Habermas's article "Wahrheitstheorien" for the first clues to answering these questions (section II). By further pursuing these hints in other sources it will be possible to elaborate the various elements and terms in the formulation of (U); these can be organized around a concept of social norm (section III). Only after such preparation can we then go on and examine, in Chapter 3, Habermas's proposal for deriving (U)— a proposal that, if carried out, calls for a new, intersubjective basis for moral cognitivism.

I. BEYOND OVERLAPPING CONSENSUS

What does a rationally motivating exchange of reasons involve? Habermas summarizes his answer to this question as a principle of universalization (U), according to which a norm is valid only if:

> *All* affected can accept the consequences and the side effects its *general* observance can be anticipated to have for the satisfaction of *everyone's* interests (and these consequences are preferred to those of known alternative possibilities).[2]

Like Kant's Categorical Imperative, (U) specifies a rule for the impartial testing of norms for their moral worthiness. It thus represents the heart of Habermas's attempt to reconstruct the objectivity of the moral point of view. As already mentioned above, however, Habermas ties moral validity to what "all affected" persons can accept as participants in rational discourse, thereby giving us a dialogical principle finding adequate employment only in a real discourse. Nor more than (D) does (U) allow the solitary theorist to speak for all rational persons and churn out universally valid moral norms as Kant thought he could with the Categorical Imperative. Rather, it amounts to a rule of argument which should allow the participants in a discourse over moral norms to reach a rationally binding consensus. As we shall see, this rule is a highly demanding standard of rationality but, according to Habermas, participants in discourse must at least believe they have approximately satisfied it if they are to consider the outcome of their discourse as probably justified.

---

1. This and the next chapter expand an argument I originally presented in "Discourse and the Moral Point of View: Deriving a Dialogical Principle of Universalization," *Inquiry* 34 (1991): 27–48.
2. DE, p. 65.

In any case, the basic idea behind (U) is actually quite straightforward: assuming a willingness and ability to engage in the effort to understand others, if everyone knows what his or her real interests are and gets an equal opportunity to express those interests—i.e., an equal chance to argue for norm proposals that express those interests and argue against norm proposals that damage those interests—then, *if* an acceptable norm emerges from discourse at all, it must embody in some way a general interest.[3]

Some broad clarifications should be noted at the start. The "discursive will-formation" resulting from such an argumentation process should not be limited to the discovery of overlapping areas among private interests. On the one hand, (U)-governed discourse should not only discover already existing but unrecognized common interests—it should also allow for their *creation*: participants should be able to learn from one another that some interests are generaliz*able*, even if not previously de facto general.[4] On the other hand, limitation of (U) to mere discovery would remain too much within the bounds of compromise formation, for which no moral argumentation is necessary, but only the clarification of interest positions and the agreement to mutual limitation—here overlapping goals are merely happy coincidences where limitation happens not to be necessary.[5] (U), by way of contrast, picks up on Mead's notion of ideal perspective-taking and demands that participants take an interest in each other's interests, insofar as *all* have to accept the norm in view of its consequences *for each*.[6] This acceptance, moreover, must be a rational one, based solely on the convincing power of the better argument.

3. Habermas had earlier spelled this out in LC, p. 108: "Since all those affected have, in principle, at least the chance to participate in the practical deliberation, the 'rationality' of the discursively formed will consists in the fact that the reciprocal behavioral expectations raised to normative status afford validity to a *common* interest ascertained *without deception*. The interest is common because the constraint-free consensus permits only what *all* can want; it is free of deception because even the interpretations of needs in which *each individual* must be able to recognize what he wants become the object of discursive will-formation."

4. See McCarthy, *Critical Theory*, pp. 326–327; Jürgen Habermas, "A Postscript to *Knowledge and Human Interests*," *Philosophy of the Social Sciences* 3 (1973): 177; LC, p. 108.

5. See Herbert Scheit, *Wahrheit, Diskurs, Demokratie*, pp. 33–37; in Habermas, see W, p. 173.

6. Cf. Klaus Günther, *Der Sinn für Angemessenheit: Anwendungsdiskurse in Moral und Recht* (Frankfurt: Suhrkamp, 1988), p. 48 (an English translation of this work is now available under the title *The Sense of Appropriateness: Application Discourses in Morality and Law*, trans. David Farrell [Albany: SUNY Press, 1993]); for the connection with Mead see TCA 2:92–111. For the purposes of this exposition I shall assume that this reciprocal acceptability of foreseeable consequences is functionally equivalent to Habermas's other formulation, "equally good for all."

A good deal still remains to be explained in the above sketch. Without the introduction of something like moral perspective-taking it would be difficult to distinguish (U) from the strategic considerations underlying marriages of convenience, hardly a palatable result in any moral theory, least of all in a neo-Kantian one. But how is this move to a moral perspective grounded? And how are individual interests related to the general interest reached at the end of discourse if not by mere overlap? If not by overlap, how are these relevant at all as moral considerations? After all, Kant sharply separated moral considerations from individuals' empirical interests. The notion of "consequences and side effects" as well needs explanation if (U) is to be distinguished from rule utilitarianism. Finally, what grounds the universality affirmed in (U), i.e., its requirement that "all affected" take part in the discourse? In this and the next chapter I hope to provide some plausible answers to these questions.

In order to answer such questions we must ultimately come to grips with Habermas's proposed justification of (U). That is, Habermas suggested one could "derive" (U) by material implication from two not uncomplicated premises. The first referred to "what it means to discuss hypothetically whether norms of action ought to be adopted."[7] The second summarized the pragmatically unavoidable presuppositions of argumentation, as Alexy had spelled these out.[8] I shall save detailed consideration of these for later; what should be noticed here is that Habermas himself did not actually carry out this derivation—thus it is not surprising that both (U) and its justification met with a good deal of skepticism.[9] Benhabib, for example, argued that Habermas had not

7. DE, p. 92; this is a revision of the original formulation (which one might translate as follows: "by 'justified norms' we mean norms that regulate social matters in the common interest of all those possibly affected," in J. Habermas, *Moralbewußtsein und kommunikatives Handeln*, 1st ed. [Frankfurt: Suhrkamp, 1983], p. 103). The revision was necessary to avoid begging the question; cf. Benhabib, *Critique, Norm, and Utopia*, pp. 303–309.

8. DE, p. 89, which cites Robert Alexy, "A Theory of Practical Discourse," in *The Communicative Ethics Controversy*, ed. Seyla Benhabib and Fred Dallmayr (Cambridge: MIT Press, 1990), pp. 166–167; note that I will adjust Alexy's numbering for my own purposes; Alexy is more thorough in his *A Theory of Legal Argumentation: The Theory of Rational Discourse as Theory of Legal Justification*, trans. Ruth Adler and Neil MacCormick (Oxford: Clarendon, 1989): see not only pp. 130f but also pp. 187–208, where the presuppositions are limited by further rules, e.g., burden of argument and rules for introducing claims, etc. (hereafter cited as *Legal Argumentation*).

9. See, for example, Albrecht Wellmer, "Ethics and Dialogue: Elements of Moral Judgement in Kant and Discourse Ethics," in *The Persistence of Modernity: Essays on Aesthetics, Ethics, and Postmodernism*, trans. David Midgley (Cambridge: MIT Press, 1991), pp. 145–188; Seyla Benhabib, "In the Shadow of Aristotle and Hegel: Communicative Ethics and Current Controversies in Practical Philosophy," *Philosophical Forum* 21 (Fall-

justified the strong enlightenment ideal of universality built into (U). To shore up discourse ethics against objections such as this and show how (U) represents a plausible idealization of the aspirations informing any serious attempt to reach reasoned consensus, we must get clear about such terms as "norm," "consequences and side effects," and "interests." Rather than approach these terms directly, though, it helps first to situate them in Habermas's structural analysis of practical argument. Thus we turn first to the article "Wahrheitstheorien."

II. THE STRUCTURE OF RATIONAL CONVICTION

In "Wahrheitstheorien," Habermas presents a suggestive analysis of the structure of practical reasoning. The import of that analysis for our purposes lies in its attention to the role of *language* in argument. This is where we first find an indication of the links between universalization and items such as interests (in the form of needs and wants) and consequences.

"Wahrheitstheorien" relies heavily on Stephen Toulmin's theory of argument.[10] According to Toulmin, the objectivity, or intersubjective force, of singular moral judgments depends in the first instance on an appeal to particular situational facts which call for the judgment in question. Thus, if I say to you, "You ought to pay M. back by next week," I will, if I am challenged and am ready to argue the matter, first of all point out that "You borrowed the money from M. on the condition that you'd pay him back by next week." This move from particular facts to moral judgment is possible in virtue of a general warrant, in this case the moral norm, "If one has borrowed money, one ought to pay it back within the specified time." Moral discourse proper begins once you challenge me

Winter 1989–1990): 4–13 (a revised version of this article is now available in Benhabib's *Situating the Self: Gender, Community and Postmodernism in Contemporary Ethics* [New York: Routledge, 1992], pp. 23–67); Seyla Benhabib, *Critique, Norm and Utopia*, pp. 303–309; Anton Leist, "Diesseits der 'Transzendental-pragmatik': Gibt es sprachpragmatische Argumente für Moral?" *Zeitschrift für philosophische Forschung* 43 (1989): 301–317; Agnes Heller, *Beyond Justice* (Oxford: Blackwell, 1987), pp. 234–244.

10. "Wahrheitstheorien" first appeared in H. Fahrenbach, ed., *Wirklichkeit und Reflexion* (Pfullingen: Neske, 1973), pp. 211–266; I shall cite the edition in *Vorstudien*, pp. 127–183, referring to the article as W. It drew heavily on Stephen F. Toulmin, *The Uses of Argument* (Cambridge: Cambridge University Press, 1964), esp. pp. 94–145, which first appeared in 1958; in W, cf. esp. pp. 159–174; also quite helpful is McCarthy, *Critical Theory*, pp. 312–333; and Thomas McCarthy, "A Theory of Communicative Competence," *Philosophy of the Social Sciences* 3 (1973): 135–156.

further and I appeal to such a norm, i.e., once the participants in the dispute identify the normative validity claim at stake.[11]

The discourse proper concerns the backing or theoretical justification for the normative warrant. Given that moral arguments are, in Toulmin's terms, substantial rather than analytic, the move from backing to norm does not follow deductively. It is rather casuistic and inductive in nature: in coming up with a general norm one grasps the unity, that which is generalizable, in a host of observations about values, interests, consequences, and so on. Precisely in this move from particular and manifold to a general rule we find a principle of universalization:

> Like induction, universalization plays the role of a bridge principle which should explain why we can make a proposed norm of action plausible by referring to consequences and side effects of the norm application for accepted needs. This transition is evident if the casuistic evidence can support itself on *generally* accepted needs and wants.[12]

But why should this generalizing move attend precisely to needs and consequences? In order to follow Habermas's path to the above formulation we must first attend to his more general question: What makes such an inductive move at all cogent? His response is that the cogency or "consensus-generating force" of a theoretical justification of a norm partly depends on the appropriateness of the language system or conceptual framework employed in the justification—unless the discussants agree at this level, their arguments will pass one another like ships in the night and a rational agreement will not be possible. On the one hand, the language system fixes the basic concepts that allow the judgment to follow from the norm and the situational data; on the other, these same basic concepts make it possible for the backing or justification to motivate each participant to accept the norm.[13] How exactly is this motivation brought about? This question leads us to Habermas's next step, a definition of the material dealt with in moral argumentation: "Norms

11. Here the particular challenge is one of justification, i.e., the hearer grants the speaker's description of the situation but contests the presumption that such a situation generally calls for such a response; it would lead to a discourse of application if the hearer challenged the description of the situation; cf. Günther, *Sinn.*

12. W, p. 173; "needs and wants" renders the German *Bedürfnisse*, which in turn refers to the notion of *Bedürfnisnatur*, a term I shall render as "appetitive structures." The notion is a broad one, including both affective (wishes and inclinations) and perceptive (moods and feelings) dimensions; see Jürgen Habermas, "Intention, Konvention und sprachliche Interaktion," *Vorstudien*, pp. 307–331, esp. 317–320; cf. also "Postscript," pp. 170–171, 187 n40; and TCA 1:92.

13. W, pp. 165–166.

regulate legitimate chances for the satisfaction of needs and wants; and interpreted needs/wants are a piece of inner nature to which each subject, to the extent it is truthful with itself, has privileged access."[14] It would then seem to follow that one's acceptance of a general norm (or warrant) should be motivated by precisely that casuistic evidence whose language resonates with one's need interpretation, i.e., self-understanding.

If we may now understand "consequences" as referring to the foreseeable "chances" one would have to meet one's needs (or satisfy one's desires) in situations defined by the proposed norm, the above-cited formulation of universalization is at hand. It implies that a persuasive argument for a norm must tie the norm to a language of needs/wants and projected consequences for needs in such a way as to appeal to subjects' self-understanding of their needs and interest in satisfying those needs. For example, an argument against theft would quite likely convince established landowners to the extent it was based on the "right" (read "need") to private property regulated by contracts, etc. By contrast, the disenfranchised would probably find a general norm against theft more convincing only if it was so formulated as to elevate the need for adequate living conditions above written contracts.

One might legitimately ask at this point how the above account should be squared with practical reasoning based on appeals to authority, or sacred texts, and so on. Fortunately, for our purposes it suffices to establish the plausibility of Habermas's account for contemporary pluralistic situations where participants cannot convince each other by appeals such as those just indicated. Thus I want to emphasize how well this analysis *does* square with the common experience of haggling over terminology: clearly, the language or conceptual system one uses in an argument is anything but unproblematic, and the terms by which one describes consequences and needs are anything but exempt from challenge. At least today, any effort to persuade must strive to find just those terms which all those expected to accept the norm find appropriate. This suggests that rational acceptance of a norm must presume that one has been free to change any inappropriate or distortive aspects of the language system. Such freedom would seemingly have to include not only a freedom from external coercion or manipulation but from internal compulsions and self-deceptions as well.

In his initial formulations (and even in TCA) Habermas defined such

14. W, p. 172.

conceptual appropriateness in terms of "self-transparency," a term he has since dropped.[15] On this earlier view, an appropriate conceptual framework for the expression of needs does not distort individuals' understanding of their needs, thus allowing for a "self-transparent" relation-to-self. While it is easy to see how the above line of analysis could lead in this direction, it is far from clear that something like self-transparency can even be coherently defined for anything but angels and God. If linguistic self-transparency is incoherent at a human level, then more cautious counterfactual formulations of appropriateness must also be avoided. It will not do, for example, to call that language system "appropriate" each of whose terms *would* stand up to discursive examination, for such examination would be incoherent in principle, and not simply empirically impossible. Dispensing with the notion of linguistic-conceptual appropriateness altogether, however, would run counter to the daily experience of disputes over terminology. Hence I would like to propose a cautious formulation going something like this: in being rationally persuaded by an argument one must suppose that the language (terms, concepts, and so on) in which the argument is cast has been open to the examination and change of any perceptibly inappropriate expressions; in addition, one must suppose that any subsequent examination and change of terminology will not reveal self-deceptions that would undermine the consensus, had they been recognized at the start. The term "perceptibly" does the work of bringing "linguistic appropriateness" down to the ambiguous ground of human existence, where one can only deal with one's huge network of background assumptions in a piecemeal fashion, as this or that term begins to chafe and thus emerges as in need of examination. Conversely, to withhold one's acceptance of an argument on the grounds that every single term and its implications had not been thematized and grounded would be an *irrational* way of going about things. At the same time, the meaning of one's claim to rightness implies that the subsequent emergence of inappropriate terms would not be so radical that those agreeing to the original norm would later have to say, "We were self-deceived or misled in such an important way that our norm was never right."

In this formulation participants presuppose some self-knowledge but not complete self-transparency. The point is that one can be rationally

15. W, pp. 173, 178; TCA 2:145; in *Discourse*, p. 298, and NR, p. 131, Habermas rejects such formulations; for a criticism of this notion of transparency, see Adi Ophir, "The Ideal Speech Situation: Neo-Kantian Ethics in Habermas and Apel," in *Kant's Practical Philosophy Reconsidered*, ed. Y. Yovel (New York: Kluwer, 1989), p. 229.

motivated to accept a norm without presuming one has the infallible self-knowledge that self-transparency would seem to suggest. It is enough, rather, that at the time of their consensus the participants were rationally motivated to raise a *fallible* (i.e., probable) claim. At the same time, in raising a *claim* to normative rightness they are betting—on the basis of the self-knowledge they believe themselves to have—that subsequent self-discovery and changes in self-understanding will not lead them to reject the norm as altogether mistaken.

Note further that by dispensing with self-transparency one does justice to the prethematic status of background knowledge in rational consensus. That is, what one presupposes about one's background is not that it would withstand a term-by-term counterfactual testing, but that it forms, *as a whole*, an adequate resource for explicit, morally valid consensus on the particular norm at issue.

The above account admittedly calls for still further refinement. For example, the demarcation between moral argumentation and forms of evaluative discourse remains yet to be drawn.[16] We cannot address this, however, without delving further into the notion of moral norm and its internal links with items such as needs, interests, and consequences. In the next section, then, we must examine more closely the suggestions broached in "Wahrheitstheorien."

III. THE CONTENT OF PRACTICAL ARGUMENTATION: NORMS OF ACTION

The standpoint from which Habermas defines social norms is that of social coordination—the classic question of how social order is possible—and thus, at least derivatively, that of potential conflict resolution.[17] In this section I want to argue that this point of departure already contains a certain semantics linking norms to consequences and interests, though not in an unduly consequentialist or utilitarian fashion. Although I suspect this account could be generalized across a variety of sociocultural forms of life, I am interested here only in its relevance for modern social cooperation.

We can start by getting an intuitive sense of social norms from Toulmin's analysis, which views a community in terms of the normed coor-

---

16. See TCA 1:15–23, 40–42, where Habermas defines "therapeutic critique" and "aesthetic criticism"; only later, in PV, does he develop a concept of evaluative discourse proper.
17. Thus he sees communicative action in general as a mechanism for action coordination; cf. CES, p. 88; *Vorstudien*, pp. 571ff; also TCA 1:88–89; DE, pp. 66f.

dination of its members' desires, interests, and actions.[18] It is precisely the
community's background consensus on a set of norms that makes such
coordination possible: in situations where desires conflict or actions
threaten to cross each other up, an appeal to the relevant norm restores
harmony insofar as it calls up shared expectations which constrain actions and the fulfillment of needs in a coordinated fashion.[19] Such situations where cooperation has to be restored make up merely the tip of a
much larger iceberg of assumed cooperative relations that are noticed
only when they threaten to fall apart.[20]

This suggests that at one level a norm actually *defines* consequences
for the satisfaction of interests in potential conflict situations insofar as
it sets constraints to such satisfaction and, at least implicitly, determines
which interests are most relevant. Although this admittedly stretches the
term "consequences" somewhat, the first kind of "consequences of a
norm's general observance" are those patterns of interaction and role
expectations directly defined in the norm's content. Habermas has referred to these as the consequences that the acceptance of a validity claim
would have for further interaction: "As soon as the hearer accepts the
guarantee offered by the speaker, obligations are assumed that have consequences for the interaction, obligations that are contained in the
meaning of what was said."[21] In the case of general norms—warrants in
Toulmin's scheme of argument—we have to do with validity claims the
illocutionary force of which flows directly from the norm's general content.[22] An example can make this clearer. Suppose one of two business
partners comes up with a scheme for quick profits, to which the other
rejoins, "But wouldn't that amount to theft?" The first partner, uncom-
fortable, finds the charge difficult to elude. He cannot help but recognize

18. Stephen E. Toulmin, *An Examination of the Place of Reason in Ethics* (1950; Cambridge: Cambridge University Press, 1970), pp. 135, 136: "In all communities . . . people
control their behavior so as to have regard for one another's interests. . . . The concept of
'duty', in short, is inextricable from the 'mechanics' of social life, and from the practices
adopted by different communities in order to make living together in proximity tolerable
or even possible."

19. Cf. TCA 2:121–126.

20. Ethnomethodological studies have confirmed this in a striking fashion; see, for example, Harold Garfinkel, "A Conception of, and Experiments with, 'Trust' as a Condition
of Stable Concerted Actions," *Motivation and Social Interaction*, ed. O. J. Harvey (New
York: Ronald Press, 1963), pp. 187–238; also the summary in John Heritage, *Garfinkel
and Ethnomethodology* (Cambridge: Polity, 1984), chap. 5.

21. DE, p. 59; cf. also TCA 1:297–302.

22. As opposed, for example, to cases where the exceptional status of the particular
affected individual is highlighted, e.g., cases where one might say, "Normally that norm
applies but, considering your situation . . ."

that the general term, "theft," fairly clearly covers the situation projected in his scheme. He has, in effect, already accepted a general norm against theft and now finds that his background acceptance has obligated him in a certain way, a way that has consequences for his interest in profits. The point here is that these "defining consequences" follow simply from the general meaning or content of the norm against theft and its extension to the situation involving a certain interest. To take this a step further, one can say that in this case the norm against theft structures the very situation in which interaction occurs, constraining the pursuit of interests along certain lines.

To avoid overly utilitarian connotations I shall call such consequences the "action constraints" of a norm. They can be further clarified through R. M. Hare's analysis of the semantics of 'ought' claims.[23] To recall the analysis quite briefly, moral 'oughts' always contain a general—hence universalizable—description of the relevant respects under which one is ready to prescribe the given action as something one ought to do. Thus if one adopts a norm as a moral principle of action, one "logically" commits oneself, simply in virtue of the semantics of such norms, to the action constraints as the norm describes them for *each* affected role. To return to the example of repaying loans, if I expect—on moral grounds— that my debtors repay me, then logical consistency requires me to admit that *I* ought to repay *my* creditors as well. The "consequences of a norm for the satisfaction of interests" is, at a semantic level, simply the action constraints defined by the norm, as these would affect one's interests without prejudice to which of the pertinent roles one occupied.[24] In some cases, at least, one may even speak of the norm as defining an entire practice or institution: after all, one can hardly imagine the practice of lending apart from a norm such as 'Creditors ought to be repaid'. In any case, by accepting a norm at this first level one accepts such constraints for every role and situation coming under the norm. Such a notion of consequences is a quite general one, which we do not have to associate exclusively with consequentialism or utilitarianism. In fact, it was the hallmark of deontological ethics to focus on these action constraints to the exclusion of the broader impacts of a norm's observance.

23. See R. M. Hare, *Freedom and Reason* (Oxford: Clarendon, 1963), esp. pp. 7–49, 86–95.
24. Hare, *Freedom*, pp. 91–94; cf. also J. L. Mackie, *Ethics: Inventing Right and Wrong* (New York: Penguin, 1977), pp. 83–102; Mackie argues that Hare's talk of the "logic" of "ought" is too strong.

Normative constraints, then, harbor a rich store of interrelationships, which the above only begins to open up. What I want to underline for now is its rather direct, participant-level focus on specific, value-laden role expectations defined by the norm itself. But this hardly exhausts the "consequences" of norms. One must, with utilitarians, recognize that a norm not only defines consequences but also, in a broader sense, *has* "consequences and side effects" insofar as its general observance has a variety of direct and indirect effects—more or less foreseeable on the basis of empirical knowledge—on the form and degree of social order. Following Hegel's (as well as Weber's) critique of Kant's *Gesinnungsethik*, Habermas takes such consequences as morally relevant.[25] I will thus interpret the reference in (U) to "consequences" as a reference both to defining "constraints" and to extrinsic consequences (which we might call "impacts") relevant for the satisfaction of interests.[26]

Under "impacts," then, I include all the effects of a norm's observance that extend beyond the pattern of interaction and role expectations directly defined in the norm's "descriptive" content. While action constraints can be garnered for the most part directly from the norm's content, which projects certain roles and typical situations covered by the norm, a grasp of a norm's impacts requires one to ask further questions about the empirical and contingent effects a general observance of the norm might have for various groups in a social body, for the environment, for social reproduction, and so on. A classic example of this distinction is found in Marx's critique of capitalism. If one focuses directly on the exchange between owner and worker, that exchange might appear to embody an acceptable value of equality. However, by asking how this exchange contributes to a certain social order—effects extrinsic to the exchange itself, strictly speaking—Marx was able to call the norms of capitalist exchange into question. What looks like a perfectly reasonable expectation at the participant level ends up generating endemic misery and inequality. This consequence is seen, however, only by stepping back from the immediate exchange and taking up the more distanced gaze of an observer of society. This suggests that this second level corresponds to that of functionalist theory and the broader kinds of consequences typ-

25. See Jürgen Habermas, "Labor and Interaction: Remarks on Hegel's Jena *Philosophy of Mind*," in *Theory and Practice*, trans. John Viertel (Boston: Beacon, 1973), pp. 151–152; more recently, ME, pp. 205–206.
26. This is also how Alexy takes the term "consequence" in *Legal Argumentation*, p. 203, n76—the source that Habermas relies on for his formulation of (U).

ically emphasized by utilitarianism, where the fundamental perspective is more that of an observer than a participant.[27]

However, the above does not yet explain the internal connection Habermas makes between norms and interests when he speaks of norms *incorporating* interests. Does not such a use of the term "interest" appear as an interloper on territory that Kant originally set aside for noumenal absolutes alone? That norms have consequences for what we want and need—enjoining or allowing their pursuit in some cases, forbidding or restricting them in others—does not yet establish the relevance of such interests for moral argumentation. Again one need only recall Kant. If we reject Kant's two-world doctrine, however, an intrinsic connection between norms and interests becomes more plausible. The relevant distinction then is not that between empirical desires, feelings, and needs, on the one hand, and the a priori interest in a noumenalized freedom on the other. Moral claims must rather draw all their material from *within* empirically given appetitive structures (*Bedürfnisnatur*), linguistically transforming just such material into an interest worthy of general recognition. To explain this, something must be said about the relation between needs, interests, and cultural values.

Habermas's analysis of this interrelationship actually presents a spectrum of potential moral contents ranging from the more particular to the more universal. At its most subjective and particularistic, appetitive structures include the various desires, feelings and needs of an individual. Even to express these to oneself, however, one must have recourse to evaluative terms in a shared language. This means that appetitive structures find expression, in an *interest* understandable to others, only through cultural values deposited in traditions of need interpretations. For example, I can make my interest in owning a house in the country understandable to others by appealing to the values of "peace and quiet," freedom from the city's congestion, environmental beauty, and so on. Employed in this fashion, however, such values still do not claim universal validity, that is, the interest they explain is not put in the form of a universally binding norm such as, 'Everyone ought to have (or be able to have) a house in the country'. Nonetheless, at least some values are potential candidates for incorporation in norms claiming universal validity. The clearest examples are the fundamental values connected with the satisfaction of basic bodily needs, the basic freedoms to act and de-

27. Cf. Habermas's two-level interpretation of Marx in TCA 2:334–343.

cide, and so on. The relevant question then becomes whether a given feeling or desire—which already, as interpreting a need through a shared cultural value, is understandable to others—can be transformed into a moral judgment.[28] It is precisely moral norms which provide the warrant for such a transformation.

This connection is perhaps most readily exemplified in the relation between feelings and norms. Suppose I find out someone has lied to me. The anger this evokes in me I can express in the form of the moral judgment, "You should have told me the truth," in virtue of the general norm, 'One ought not lie'. On the basis of its relation to the norm the feeling of anger is a *moral* feeling, a "righteous indignation." By way of contrast, the liar's feeling of discomfort at acknowledging an embarrassing truth is understandable but not capable of transformation into a corresponding normative expectation. Consider, for example, the case of lying about one's health in order to obtain a job in which health is an important consideration. We can certainly understand that the nature of the health problem might be embarrassing in itself, just as we can understand the person's interest in obtaining the job. Neither the feeling of embarrassment nor the desire for a job, however, translate into a norm permitting one to lie in this case (though they may in other cases, say where the nature of the job does not warrant the employer's knowledge of the health problem). The liar's feeling of shame, however, *does* represent a moral feeling, for it signals his awareness of having violated a moral norm. This connection between moral norms and feelings can even effect a change in one's feelings. A girl who has just been appointed captain of the school softball team understandably experiences a certain pride until she realizes that someone else actually deserved the honor, an awareness that might spark in her the moral feelings of guilt or even indignation.[29] In fact, if someone does not experience the appropriate moral feeling in such cases, we often question that person's capacity for moral judgment.

The last point suggests that an internal relation exists between norms and certain kinds of feelings, which in turn suggests how norms incorporate needs and interests. For feelings represent just one dimension of complex, perceptual-volitional appetitive structures that also include

---

28. DE, p. 104; see also "Intention," in *Vorstudien*, pp. 317–328, esp. 326: need interpretations presuppose a language community sharing evaluative expressions and a tradition of cultural values; also TCA 1:15–17, 20, 88–90, 92.

29. See DE, pp. 55–64; EzD, p. 143; also Toulmin, *Reason in Ethics*, pp. 138–139, 146.

moods, inclinations, and desires.[30] To say that norms "incorporate" needs and interests, then, is to posit an internal relation between norms and appetitive structures. Inasmuch as these structures of feeling and desire find articulation only through evaluative terms, norms bear a relation to need interpretations and therefore to cultural values. The associations here are admittedly a bit loose. Moreover, the notion of value remains somewhat vague—but therein lies its usefulness in an analysis of conflict and discourse. In an emotional argument over conflicting interests and expectations it is often difficult to identify where more particular attachments and passions leave off and morally normed expectations begin. This is understandable, however, if norms, including universal moral norms, represent one type of value mixed in with a whole spectrum of values and interests ranging from the more particular to the more universal, all of which contribute to one's affectively charged interpretation of situations. I do not mean to deny that one can differentiate norms and values in terms of their different semantic structures. But one can hardly assume this distinction *going into* a moral discourse meant to first establish what counts as a moral norm in a given case. It is important, to begin with, to see that norms are embedded in an ambiguous way in value-charged need interpretations.

To further illustrate this in the above examples, my indignation at being deceived, the lying applicant's uneasy conscience, and the captain's guilt indicate that the recognition of a general norm engages one's need interpretation at more than a strategic level. That is, such feelings show that the actors are not related to the norms at issue simply as constraints whose consequences externally impinge on their various personal interests. The norms also positively *engage* the actors' need interpretations and self-understandings—thereby stimulating the various moral feelings—precisely because they have been internalized as parts of those need interpretations and self-understandings.

If there is an important difference between norms and values prior to moral discourse, then it lies in the fact that the needs and interests incorporated in norms take the form of *expectations* regarding the action constraints set by a norm. To this extent, at least, normative values differ from values expressing mere preferences. Moral indignation at deception, for example, results not simply from an interest or preference that

30. Habermas takes feelings (along with moods) as perceptual: "feelings 'perceive' situations in the light of possible need satisfaction." TCA 1:92. Desires and inclinations represent the volitional side of need interpretation.

one know the truth but from the expectation that one deserves to be told the truth. Not to put too fine a point on it, we might summarize the above reflections by saying that one of the action constraints of a norm is its selection of a given need as a shared value that members of the given community can expect each other to act upon or respect.[31] Thus the captain's guilt points to a violated shared expectation that only the most deserving should be captain; the lying job applicant has disregarded expectations based on the values of honesty and workplace safety. The perspective from which such implications appear is that of the participant involved in interpersonal relationships. As already pointed out, such expectations are not, in the final analysis, anticipations of empirical regularities but rather affectively charged perceptions leading to the judgment that one is legitimately entitled to, or obligated to, certain modes of behavior.[32] In other words, the expectation at issue here is first of all accessible through the performative attitude one takes to a second person (a "you") deemed a responsible agent—thus it is not to be confused with expectation in the sense of an observer's empirical prediction.

This should allow us to see how norms might incorporate common interests. To begin with, note that there is a heuristic advantage to rephrasing our earlier question (whether a feeling or desire can be transformed into a moral judgment) in the language of interests, inasmuch as normed expectations always appear concretely as interests: A's expectation of B that B act in a certain way is, at the level of their direct interaction, not only an appeal to a shared value but also A's (understandable) interest or will. Hence the question for the A-B interaction is whether A's *understandable* interest in B's acting thus and so is also a *common* or *general* interest. In putting the issue this way, one maintains an awareness of how some very specific groups stand to benefit from a given value. Thus we might say a norm embodies a "common interest" in upholding the given value as one enjoying a certain priority for action: whatever else one does, this value is to be preserved. Here "common" means no more than "mutually expectable" on the basis of shared worldview or need interpretation, which is to say that members of the group sharing this worldview expect each other to uphold the same value, each according to his or her role. At any rate, the value-become-norm deter-

31. The term "action constraint" may seem a bit strained here, unless one sees it as encompassing both overt behavioral rules as such and their evaluative dimension. Note, too, that we need not assume here that a one-to-one correlation always obtains between a given norm and some value: a norm may incorporate several values and a single value may be embodied in a set of norms.

32. TCA 1:85.

mines in cases of conflict of interest which interest has priority, or at least regulates how conflicting interests can be coordinated. In accepting the value of honesty as a general norm 'Thou shalt not lie', for example, one gives the interest in truthful answers a certain prima facie priority over other particular interests, such as hiding embarrassing facts, when these interests conflict. I shall save a more precise specification of such priority for later.

In his reading of Mead, Habermas reconstructs the emergence of such interests through stages of socialization.[33] An interest first appears to the child as its parents' arbitrary will, given as an imperative and enforced by sanctions. In learning to obey such imperatives the child comes to expect that through the parents' care its needs will be satisfied in return, hence that both child and parents "satisfy each other's interests."[34] As the child realizes this concrete reciprocity represents a generalized behavior pattern, it comes to see that the interests involved express a "general will," that they are "interests of the group as a whole." The child only acquires a normative consciousness proper once it can grasp these generalized behavior patterns in terms of complementary, role-connected entitlements and obligations.[35] In any case, this shows that a notion of common interest need not beg the question in favor of a postconventional morality, so long as we understand it in the above sense of that generalized will found across a broad range of ways of understanding norms.[36] One could, for example, apply this model to a traditional notion of norm such as that found in the Torah, where the Ten Commandments are embedded in a worldview which connects the observance of the commandments with the common interest of the Jewish people.

The above considerations have primarily focused on the relation between values and normative constraints. But values are also at stake in the impacts of a norm's general observance. That is, which consequences and side effects one *selects* as relevant and how one *assesses* these depend on evaluations. We can thus broaden our idea of how norms incorporate needs and interests accordingly: insofar as a norm defines shared action constraints, it has an internal relation to a value (or set of values) through

33. TCA 2:31–42.
34. TCA 2:34; at this level the child's expectation is based on empirical regularity.
35. TCA 2:36, 37.
36. At a rudimentary level a norm "refers to the collective regulation of the choices of participants in interaction who are coordinating their actions via sanctioned imperatives and the reciprocal satisfaction of interests"; at the next level of *internalized* role expectations, the norm "simultaneously *entitles* group members to expect certain actions from one another in certain situations and *obligates* them to fulfill the legitimate expectations of others"; TCA 2:37.

which individuals interpret appetitive structures as needs and interests. Insofar as a norm's general observance produces a variety of further consequences, it has an external relation to the values through which individuals notice and assess such consequences in light of their interests.[37]

This account considerably complicates the relation between norms, values, and appetitive structures, especially in view of the fact that for any given norm, more than one value will often be at stake even at the level of constraints. What is more, my account draws the language of need evaluation even more deeply into moral discourse. If I may anticipate Chapter 4, one would expect such evaluations to center on notions of the good life and on self-understandings, which apparently bodes ill for Habermas's attempt to single out moral questions as those that admit of universally binding solutions *across* differences in conceptions of the good life:

> Thus the development of the moral point of view goes hand in hand with a differentiation within the practical into *moral questions* and *evaluative questions*. Moral questions can in principle be decided rationally, i.e., in terms of *justice*. . . . Evaluative questions present themselves at the most general level as issues of the *good life* (or of self-realization).[38]

In other words, the moral principle of universalization (U) guiding moral discourse can lead to consensus only if participants can narrow the conflict down to a justice issue at some point, leaving aside differences in their conceptions of the good. This is not to say that such conceptions cannot be rationally discussed at all, but only that the rationality of such evaluative issues must be sought in the context of a particular life history or group tradition. What is good for me, or what is good for a particular group, depends on the specifics of my own life and identity, or on the group's particular traditions and collective self-understanding. As we shall see, such questions have a different structure from moral (i.e., justice) questions, and they are properly the subject, not of moral, but of "ethical-existential" or "ethical-political" discourses, depending on whether an individual's or a group's good is at issue. In what follows, I will use the term "ethical discourse" (or in some contexts, "ethical-hermeneutical discourse") to cover both forms of discourse about the

37. See also the discussion of these relations in Thomas McCarthy, "Practical Discourse and the Relation between Morality and Politics," *Ideals and Illusions: On Reconstruction and Deconstruction in Contemporary Critical Theory* (Cambridge: MIT Press, 1990), pp. 181–199.

38. DE, p. 108; Habermas at first did not consider evaluative issues to be objects of discourse proper; see TCA 1:20; he has since developed a notion of ethical discourse, a notion I shall define more fully in Chapter 4.

good, while moral discourse will continue to refer to the justification of general norms regulating interpersonal relations.

Given the close connections between need interpretations and ideas of the good, however, the relevance of such interpretations to moral discourse seems to endanger the distinction between moral and ethical discourse, and with it Habermas's entire moral-universalist project. To be sure, the discourse-ethical notion of needs and interests, and their relation to moral norms, is much in need of further analysis.[39] At the very least, though, moral discourses would seem to depend on the results of ethical discourses in which participants get clear about their needs and interests.[40] Moreover, the fact that needs and wants are up for discussion and possible transformation is important for valid moral consensus.[41] I hope to further clarify such issues in Chapter 4; for the moment let the following summary of the link between norms, needs, and interests suffice: whether one finds the constraints and impacts of a norm's general observance acceptable or not depends on how one understands certain interests, which in turn depends on one's need interpretations. This means that moral argumentation cannot avoid at least drawing its terms from such interpretations, or using terms which occupy certain positions in such interpretations. As far as the norm itself goes, if it is to resolve conflicts between interests, it seemingly must give priority to an "interest-regulating" value or values—i.e., a value-laden means of specifying limits to the pursuit of more particular interests and deciding which interests in cases of conflict have priority or make a legitimate claim on those involved. In order to specify this last point further, we must turn to the justification of (U).

---

39. For an impressive step in this direction, see Nancy Fraser, "Talking about Needs: Interpretive Contests as Political Conflicts in Welfare-State Societies," *Ethics* 99 (1989): 291–313.

40. "Reply," p. 226.

41. I.C, p. 108; CES, pp. 88–90.

CHAPTER THREE

Deriving a Dialogical Principle of Universalization

In the foregoing analysis I have been concerned to provide some initial sense of the basic idea behind Habermas's notion of practical reasoning. I have, moreover, attempted to specify the key conceptual complex this basic idea involves: the notion of social norm and its language-mediated relation to needs, values, and interests. There we saw that norms have consequences for such interests, which suggests how (U) might incorporate consequentialist insights without being unduly utilitarian. With this notion of norm in hand we can now complete the answer to our leading question: What exactly must reason giving involve if it is to issue in a rational consensus over moral norms? In order to indicate how (U) might provide a plausible answer to this question, it will be necessary first to specify the context in which (U) is most at home (section I). We can then move to Habermas's proposed argument for (U), beginning with a clarification of the two premises (section II). I shall then take an objection raised by Seyla Benhabib as an occasion to show how (U) results from the combination of these premises (section III). The next section will then flesh out the perspective taking built into (U) (section IV). Finally, I want to draw attention to some of the implications of this reading of (U), especially those that call for an intersubjective notion of moral insight—the real point and power of (U) (section V).

I. CONFLICT AS CONTEXT

The discourse-ethical account of rational consensus has the most plausibility for situations where the resolution of conflicts of interest turn on the general validity of a moral 'ought'. Here I simply want to note this context; in Part Two it will deserve a closer examination. Thus, keeping with the restriction noted in Chapter 1, section II, I shall focus specifically on modern conflicts of interest, for I do not intend to establish the transhistorical validity of a general theory of morality. This also implies two further qualifications. First, in examining the moral dimension of conflict resolution I do not imply that such resolution only involves moral considerations or that it must in all cases involve explicit discourse. How much one can rely on strategic considerations and established institutional patterns of coordination that relieve the need for explicit consensus is a much broader question that cannot be answered in the following analysis (in Chapters 6 and 8, however, I shall at least touch on this issue). Second, I shall not be examining here the kind of reason giving surrounding disputes over the application of general norms to concrete situations (where collisions between norms are possible, and the interpretation of the situation is at stake). This admittedly leaves out of consideration a large area of morally significant conflict. It does not imply, however, that a discourse-ethical analysis of application is impossible, an issue Chapter 7 will take up.

II. PREMISES

On what basis does Habermas arrive at the account of rational argumentation in (U)? As an answer to our leading question, we might restate (U) as follows: the general moral norms regulating "fair" (i.e., just or morally valid) patterns of cooperation and conflict resolution must be able to satisfy the condition that

> all those affected by the norm's general observance can accept the consequences and the side effects that observance can be anticipated to have for the satisfaction of everyone's interests.

What I take to be the central aspect about (U) in need of justification—especially if it is to contribute to the current Anglo-American debates—is its linking moral validity to a real consensus based on universal perspective taking. Everyone affected is allowed into the discourse and must be able to accept the norm's consequences for *each* affected person. Even aside from the ambitiously counterfactual nature of this notion of discourse—a point we shall have to return to—how does one reach it simply as an idealization? To answer this we must first clarify the premises of (U). One of these has to do with the material or content of practical discourse (subsection 1), while the other states the rules of discourse (subsection 2).

I.

As already noted, Habermas proposed that (U) follows by "material implication" from two premises.[1] One of these refers to our shared sense of "what it means to discuss hypothetically whether norms of action ought to be adopted." This premise must contain both a definition of "norm of action" and say something about discourse over norms so defined, though without going so far as to specify pragmatic rules of discourse. Since this premise primarily concerns the content at issue in a moral discourse, let us call it the "content premise" or (CP). Now if a group is attempting to settle a conflict of interest by appealing to a norm, and if norms settle such conflicts (or establish conditions of cooperation in potential conflict situations) in virtue of their action constraints, i.e., by laying down role expectations in such a way as to regulate and delimit the pursuit of interests, then it would seem that the content at issue in the justification of a norm must include both these constraints and the participants' affected interests. The participants in a moral discourse would have to ask themselves, "Are the constraints defined by norm N such that, generally observed, N will acceptably regulate our various interests in the potential conflict situation at issue?" They might also—though it is less clear that they would have to do so—appeal to the foreseeable extrinsic consequences and side effects, for society as a whole, resulting from the general observance of the norm. If the norm ended up creating more conflicts and problems than it solved, the participants would have reason to look for a better alternative. If this analysis is not mistaken, then, (CP) accounts for the idea in (U) that moral discourse must attend to "consequences and side effects the norm's general observance can be anticipated to have for the satisfaction of interests."

(CP), however, does not clearly indicate at what depth or breadth the various interests should be considered. To get at this issue we can start

1. DE, p. 97.

with a simple extreme. Suppose one appeals to a norm that enshrines a certain value as so absolute that it overrides any interest that could possibly conflict with it. This value would thus set certain inviolable constraints to the pursuit of all other interests; anyone who could formulate his or her interest by linking it with this value would be the winner should that interest conflict with any others, irrespective of what those other interests might be or whose they might be. If Hare is correct, however, anyone who proposed to settle a conflict of interest by such an overriding moral appeal is committed to generalizing this 'ought' for all sufficiently similar situations and irrespective of role. This means that the norm may not function simply as a convenient way to absolutize the interests one happens to have as the occupant of a particular role. In other words, one cannot stop with the strategic consideration that the norm is favorable to the interests one has as occupying a particular role, but must argue that the norm enshrines a value overriding the interests attaching to each of the various roles defined by the norm. Yet this is just what a fanatic Nazi could sincerely maintain: that he is so committed to the Nazi ideal that he would accept the consequences of norms based on that ideal even should it be subsequently discovered that he himself has a Jewish ancestry. Although the Nazi in this well-known example finds the defining consequences of a norm's general observance quite acceptable for *all* interests attaching to roles defined by the norm, it is doubtful that those interests ever had much of a chance in the hypothetical testing of the norm.

The above example shows how the universalization based on the semantics of moral 'oughts' is limited in its depth: the values underlying a norm escape examination just because the procedure remains "monological," carried out by the individual without requiring actual intersubjective consensus. One might also ask about the breadth of such testing, i.e., whether such testing would have to consider at all the side effects a norm's observance by two parties, say A and B, has on the interests of a third party C. One could argue that in affirming a norm N for regulating a relationship defined by the roles R_1 and R_2 one makes no commitment whatever regarding contingent side effects on third parties not mentioned in the norm. "Side effects for the interests of third parties" thus presents a more complicated issue. In fact there are two problems here. The first is that third parties are indeed affected by the norm's general observance yet would not seem to be immediate addressees of the normative expectation itself inasmuch as they do not fall under the roles implicit in the norm's content. The second is that no discourse aiming at the justification of a general norm can possibly foresee all the consequences and side effects the norm's observance will have. In justification one must rather work with the typical situations the norm could regulate and, at most, the foreseeable consequences.[2]

Should we conclude that discourses of justification simply cannot address contingent side effects for third-party interests (as well as other consequences not mentioned in the norm itself)? In fact, linking the validity of norms with the acceptability of the impacts (consequences and side effects) beyond the norm's immediate constraints represents precisely the discourse-ethical advance over Kantian rigorism. I would like to suggest that the key to solving these difficulties within the bounds of (CP)—norm as general expectation—lies in the following intuition: insofar as A and B hold that their interaction is ruled by a moral 'ought', they tacitly expect C to *allow* them to follow this 'ought'. Part of such an expectation is a belief that the acceptance of N by A and B does not involve action constraints violating other moral norms accepted by all the parties. Permit me to tentatively propose two ways one might extend this idea so as to show why extrinsic impacts should be relevant to moral deliberation.

In one sense, (U)'s reference to "side effects" reflects an important proviso in one's acceptance of a norm as justified: the norm is valid only under the proviso, "other things being equal."[3] Here I must anticipate the discussion of application in Chapter 7. This proviso implies that, in affirming a norm N_1 to be valid, one is aware that unforeseeable circumstances may come about where one would have to concede, "Were this situation typical I would not call the norm valid as it stands," or "When I accepted the norm as valid I did not mean it to apply without further ado to *this* sort of situation." While the actual appraisal of such situations devolves on a discourse of application, the reference to "side effects" can be taken as installing in (U) a rebuttable presumption of typicality regarding the situational variables entering into the justification. Should this presumption prove false—when a situation arises with unacceptable side effects—one could challenge that justification not in general but *for this unique situation*, i.e., one could argue that the justified general norm is not situationally appropriate. Part of this inappropriateness could be the collision of N_1 with other norms N_x regulating one's

---

2. See Günther, *Sinn*, pp. 25–64; Habermas, PV, p. 114; interestingly, in his discussion of fanaticism Hare goes beyond his semantic analysis to imagine the course an actual discourse with the Nazi might take; see *Freedom and Reason*, pp. 159–185.

3. See Günther, *Sinn*, pp. 257ff.

interaction with persons not explicitly mentioned in N_1. For example, one can accept the general norm to keep promises but still find it morally appropriate to break a promise in a given situation if a more serious obligation unexpectedly arises. Here the norm to keep promises has collided with another norm that justifiably overrides it.

At this first "presumptive" level (CP) does not call for any direct prediction of all possible side effects in the general justification of a norm. But what about such impacts as are foreseeable in *typical* situations coming under the norm? These go beyond defining constraints only insofar as they direct one to circumstances one can expect to be typically present even though not explicitly mentioned in the norm. As I understand the intentions of discourse ethics, the inclusion of such effects likewise reflects a recognition of Hegel's critique of Kant. The point is that norms always function in empirical contexts involving more than is explicitly defined by the norm's content. Marx, for example, recognized how the bourgeois norms of equality and freedom were part of a larger set of *typical* patterns of social reproduction extending beyond the explicitly defined expectations governing the exchange relationship. These larger patterns can also tacitly assume the existence of certain typical roles for "third parties" affected by a norm's general observance. One might, for example, examine the explicit expectations holding between workers and their employers for their effects on the often unspoken roles occupied by homemakers. Even if not mentioned in workplace norms, the latter's compliance is not the less important for the functioning of those norms. By including such consequences in the justification of a norm one is forced to examine the broader unspoken expectations involved in a mode of cooperation one deems legitimate.

The above indicates that (CP) links the justification of norms to an acceptance of "consequences and side effects the norm's general observance can be anticipated to have for the satisfaction of *all* interests affected by that observance." This acceptance, however, need not be based on a dialogical consideration of those interests, for the semantics of "ought" would seem only to require that one be willing to accept—monologically—the norm irrespective of one's role or position vis-à-vis the norm's constraints and consequences. This is not yet the full-blown perspective taking required by (U).[4] To arrive at (U) we need a further

---

4. Cf. Mackie, *Ethics*, pp. 92ff; also quite excellent is David Wiggins, "Universality, Impartiality, Truth," in *Needs, Values, Truth: Essays in the Philosophy of Value*, Aristotelian Society Series, vol. 6 (Oxford: Blackwell, 1987), pp. 59–86. Wiggins takes all but the final step to a discourse ethics.

premise about the formal-pragmatic presuppositions of rational discourse.

2.

According to Robert Alexy, seriously engaging in argumentative discourse involves one in certain commitments, which Alexy describes as follows:

> Whoever gives justifying grounds for something at least pretends to accept the other as a speaking partner with equal rights, at least with respect to what concerns the justificatory process, and neither to practice coercion him or herself nor to rely on coercive means practiced by others. Furthermore, he or she claims to be able to vindicate his or her assertion to anyone at all.[5]

Alexy draws from this the three pragmatic presuppositions (or rules) of discourse, which Habermas enters as a premise in the derivation. Stated in full they are:

[Anyone who enters argumentation must make the following presuppositions:]

(a)   Every subject with the competence to speak and act is allowed to take part in a discourse.

(b)   i.   Everyone is allowed to question any assertion whatever.

     ii.   Everyone is allowed to introduce any assertion whatever into the discourse.

     iii. Everyone is allowed to express his attitudes, desires, and needs.

(c)   No speaker may be prevented, by internal or external coercion, from exercising his rights as laid down in (a) and (b) above.[6]

This premise, which states the rules of rational discourse, I shall call (RP). Important for our purposes is not so much Alexy's formulation as the general intention underlying it, namely to explicate what participants in a discourse must suppose of themselves if they are to consider their con-

---

5. Alexy, *Legal Argumentation*, p. 130.
6. DE, p. 89; EzD, p. 161; in the German edition of *Legal Argumentation* (*Theorie der juristischen Argumentation* [Frankfurt: Suhrkamp, 1983], p. 169), Alexy calls these demands for *Universalität*, *Gleichberechtigung*, and *Zwanglosigkeit*. He also notes that the second regulates the freedom of the discourse and further demands *Offenheit* of the participants.

sensus (should they reach one) rationally motivated. Thus I shall point out what seems to me the most plausible aspects of these rules for the present context, after which I shall say something about their idealizing status.

The first rule (RPa), which Habermas terms "publicity" (*Öffentlichkeit*) and Alexy, "universality," opens the discourse to all those with competence on the issue. As I read it, the point of this requirement, which goes back to Peirce's "ideal community of investigators," lies in this: one cannot very well claim that a solution one adopts is rationally persuasive and, at the same time, hold that other rational persons would refuse to accept it as reasonable, were they in the same situation in all relevant respects. This holds even in cases where one's position or problem is utterly unique—the scope of actual dialogue partners need not yet be at issue.[7] While it is true that even the very meaning one can attach to some general norm depends on a real community of speakers, the exact boundaries of this community do not seem to be specified by (RPa) itself. In other words, *who* one considers in fact "competent" or rational is a further question. In contrast to Benhabib, then, I prefer to read this rule as a rather formal one which leaves open which concrete persons, language groups, and cultures qualify as "competent speakers." As we shall see, only the connection with the semantics of norms allows one to get from this thin notion of universality to a more substantive enlightenment position.

The second requirement (RPb: the right to equal participation, *gleichberechtigte Teilnahme*) secures symmetrical chances at participation, while the third (RPc: uncoercedness, *Zwanglosigkeit*) requires conditions of communication ruling out repression, "be it ever so subtle or covert," of the rights accorded in the first two rules.[8] That the participants to a discussion should have symmetrical chances to introduce and challenge assertions, for example, reflects most rules of debate and parliamentary procedures. Conversely, one could hardly consider one's arguments for a norm *rationally* persuasive if certain objections were systematically excluded or neglected by restricting the chances one of the

7. On Peirce, see Karl-Otto Apel, *Charles S. Peirce: From Pragmatism to Pragmaticism*, trans. John Michael Krois (Amherst: University of Massachusetts Press, 1981), pp. 28–29ff; also by Apel, "Scientism or Transcendental Hermeneutics?" in *Transformation*, pp. 93–135; and "The *a priori* of the Communication Community," *Transformation*, pp. 256–263, 277–282; cf. also Chaim Perelman's notion of the "universal audience" implicit in attempts to convince; *The Realm of Rhetoric*, trans. William Kluback, Introduction by Carroll C. Arnold (Notre Dame: University of Notre Dame Press, 1982), pp. 13–20; also Alexy, *Legal Argumentation*, pp. 160–164.

8. DE, p. 89; I take Habermas's terminology for these rules from his EzD, p. 161.

parties had for presenting their arguments, raising objections, or suggesting alternatives. The point behind rules (b) and (c), then, is to ensure
that a consensus really issues from a cooperative effort to find the most
convincing solution to a problem. The presumption here is that such cooperation requires the discussants to respect each other as responsible
agents whose arguments and objections should be taken seriously.[9]

That participants should be allowed to express their needs and desires (rule b iii), and even be internally free to do so (if this is what the
lack of internal coercion implies in rule c), may appear implausible as
a general rule of argumentation as such, although one might argue that
competent speakers must have enough interior freedom to distinguish
arguments appealing to inner compulsions from more rational arguments. In a discourse aimed at justifying a normative regulation of a
(potential) conflict of interest, however, such requirements make more
sense. If such a justification aims to establish a claim that the various
interests ought to be regulated by norm N, one could hardly consider
the regulation justified if participants did not—at least by the end of the
discourse—have some sense of what constituted one another's affected
interests. Insofar as some participants were kept from expressing their
interests, either through internal or external coercion, the other participants could not be assured that their consensus rested on the better argument or that N did not run roughshod over someone's *morally* relevant interests.

What exactly is the status of these discourse rules? We can characterize it in this way: participants must at once *presume* these rules are sufficiently fulfilled (at least by the end of a discourse) yet can never assure
themselves they *in fact* have been fulfilled in any real consensus. In other
words, one can never be fully sure that one's assent in fact is a rational
one, for such certitude really would require an angelic "self-
transparency." The rules thus have the peculiar status of being at once
counterfactual—one proceeds *as if* they hold—and actually effective for
discourse—argumentation *is constituted* by their being presumed.[10]
Originally Habermas connected these rules with the "appearance [*Vor-
schein*] of a form of life."[11] He has since abandoned this formulation,
however, for idealized rules of discourse can never coalesce into a con-

---

9. See Wolfgang Kuhlmann, *Reflexive Letztbegründung: Untersuchungen zur Transzendentalpragmatik* (Freiburg/Munich: K. Alber, 1985), pp. 188–199.
10. W, pp. 179–182.
11. W, p. 181.

crete, empirically represented institution or form of life.[12] For this reason, Habermas now prefers not to call these "ideals." They are rather "idealizations" having somewhat the nature of regulative *ideas* (in the Kantian sense) one must rely upon to criticize empirically existing discourses and institutions. As constitutive of real discourse, however, they are also more than regulative ideas.[13]

Before moving on I would like to suggest that these rules still somewhat retain the aura of an "ideal." They are not only unavoidable idealizing suppositions of discourse but, at the same time, something participants *strive for*. This does not mean these suppositions would have to be empirically realizable: a fruitful ideal must simply make a positive difference for practice, either by guiding practice in a determinate direction or by providing a basis for criticizing practice. This does require, however, at least a partial realizability, the ability more or less to approximate the ideal in actual practice. Otherwise criticism on the basis of the ideal would be simply destructive: those criticized would not be able to respond to the criticism through changes in practice that, by meeting the critique, brought the practice closer to the ideal by reducing its vulnerability to critique. Naturally this process of approximation can never attain full realization or even the sense of being "close," something requiring some representation of what it would look like "to fully arrive"— in that sense "ideal" is a misleading term. For every approximation always remains in principle open to future criticism, and thus can never be known even to fulfill *sufficiently* the rules of discourse.

III. DERIVATION

In her constructive criticism of Habermas, Seyla Benhabib argues that with respect to discourse ethics (U) is "either redundant or inconsistent" as a universalizability principle.[14] In her view, discourse ethics is sufficiently equipped with its basic principle (D) and the pragmatic rules of argument. If one reads these rules, especially the universality requirement (RPa above), in a strong sense such that "all competent speakers" includes all natural language users, then linking this requirement about

12. See Jürgen Habermas, *Autonomy and Solidarity: Interviews*, ed. Peter Dews (London: Verso-New Left Review, 1986), p. 212; also his "Critics," pp. 227–228.
    13. On the status of these idealizations compare also EzD, pp. 157–166; Thomas McCarthy, "Philosophy and Social Practice: Avoiding the Ethnocentric Predicament," in *Philosophical Interventions*, ed. Honneth et al., p. 251.
    14. Benhabib, *Critique*, p. 308; cf. pp. 306–309, 325f.

discourse with the basic (D) principle—that normative validity must be established in discourse involving all concerned—leaves (U) nothing informative to add about moral validity.[15] But if one reads the universality requirement weakly, as I propose, then (U) is inconsistent insofar as one can reach it only by smuggling in a substantive notion of moral universality. Nor does the weak reading of the premises support a notion of universality distinct from any other, such as those of Rawls and Kant.

Benhabib also criticizes the consequentialist tinges in (U).[16] I have already tried to show that (U) does not entail any exclusive alignment with consequentialism; what consequentialism it does contain is simply an acknowledgment of Hegelian criticisms of Kant. Thus her real challenge concerns the *structure* of Habermas's argument. Her objection thus presents an occasion to get clear about that structure and how it leads to moral intersubjectivity. In response to Benhabib, then, I want to argue that it is precisely the *combination* of the two premises, in a modern context of commitment to argument, that leads to a notion of universality exceeding the content of either premise by itself.

As I reconstruct it, the argument hinges on linking the notion of norm as shared general behavior expectation with the idea that such expectations be established only in argument. If one assumes (1) a pluralistic group decides to resolve their conflicts of interest cooperatively by reaching argued agreement (as rational conviction) on a norm; and if (2) a commitment to argument means treating all the competent speakers on the issue as equal dialogue partners in this argument (RP); and finally, if (3) a social norm is a shared general expectation serving to resolve potential conflicts of interest by regulating the pursuit of those interests (CP);[17] then (4) every such moral expectation must rest on reasons all those subject to (and affected by) the expectation can accept in open debate, for otherwise the norm is not justified for those

15. Benhabib elaborates this strategy as a "weak justification program" in her "Liberal Dialogue versus a Critical Theory of Discursive Legitimation," in *Liberalism and the Moral Life*, ed. Rosenblum, pp. 143–156, esp. pp. 151–152; the program is "weak" insofar as it does not pretend to deduce its strong notion of moral universality from foundations of some sort.

16. See her "Shadow of Aristotle," pp. 11, 12.

17. A normative expectation is "shared" in the sense that two parties A and B both expect at least one of the parties to act in a certain way in a certain situation. Beyond this, an expectation would also be "reciprocal" if those involved in the (potential) conflict situation expect certain behaviors *of each other*; it need not be completely reciprocal (or "mutual," if you will), for the expected behaviors of each may be different. This terminological suggestion I owe to Thomas McCarthy.

subject to it, and thus its observance may not be expected of them (nor may the noninterference of other affected parties be expected).[18]

This is the basic structure of the argument for (U). In step (1) we already find something looking quite close to (D), for (1) highlights the intuition behind those tendencies to give reasons when disputes arise about what should or should not be done. That any group or society *ought* to decide to carry out such "tendencies" to the point of argued agreement—that a commitment to discourse is somehow most rational or most in concert with the structures of lifeworld communication, or that it is the result of a moral learning process—such claims can only be grounded outside the theory of argumentation, i.e., in a theory of communicative action together with a theory of modernity. The derivation of (U), however, moves within the theory of argumentation and cannot do any better than assume such a commitment. Given such a commitment as point of departure, Habermas's justification of (U) spells out what reason giving taken "to the point of argued agreement" must involve to be rationally motivating.

To a large extent, steps (2) and (3) simply explicate the commitment expressed in (1). Step (1) specifies the situation as involving at least potential conflicts of interest in need of regulation; this regulation will be sought through argument aimed at reaching rational agreement on a norm. What does such argumentation involve? Step (2) holds that it must include all competent speakers on the issue. Although the notion of "competence" remains open to further specification, (2) delineates the structures of inclusion as those of an egalitarian reciprocity. Only if such reciprocity characterizes the discourse does the argued agreement deserve the appellation "rational"; only on this condition have those involved "been convinced," as opposed to merely "being talked into" something. This means that all those expected to agree to the norm must do so freely, for (2) rules out basing such agreement on noncooperative measures such as the use of overpowering external incentives, force, or manipulation. Rather, each person expected to comply with the norm must agree after being convinced as an equal partner in a real dialogue. As an argued agreement, moreover, appeals to authority or tradition—if not ruled out altogether—cannot be such as to overrule

18. Here one can see the difficulties discourse ethics will have accounting for the moral character of relations mature human adults have with children, etc., where a complete mutuality cannot hold; just this makes it appealing to limit discourse-ethical claims to capture the moral sphere as a whole.

the participants' own expression of interests and questioning of pre-given interpretations.

What is the exact range of "competent speakers" in need of convincing? According to (3) a norm procures cooperation (and settles conflicts) by establishing shared expectations, which suggests that each person expected to comply with the norm—each one whose expectations must be patterned in a way that secures cooperation—must be able to agree it is right. So far this hardly adds anything to (1). The real step (3) takes beyond (1) is given with the semantics of the moral 'ought'. Following the results of our earlier analysis of norms, normative expectations must be seen as extending to anyone who could possibly come under the roles defined in the norm. If the suggestions regarding broader consequences and side effects are not mistaken, we can further extend this to include "all those affected by its general observance."[19]

This result is then expressed in (4), which represents the basic idea behind (U). Note that the broad sweep of (4) does not rule out as irrational every conflict resolution based on something less than universally valid norms. Certainly there are cases where it is rational for the members of a given group to base their internal cooperation on more particularistic points of agreement, such as a shared religious worldview, or a prior commitment to some particular goal. Rather the point of the four-step argument given here is that *if* a group recurs to general moral 'oughts' for the basis of cooperation, there is an intrinsic commitment to the ambitious reason giving envisioned in (4). Why and how such commitments take "priority" over more particularistic concerns I shall address in the next chapter.

It cannot be denied that the four-step justification given above shares much in common with Benhabib's "weak justification program." This is especially clear in the commitment to argued agreement spelled out in (1), a commitment whose extent and viability depend heavily on a society's development of an enlightenment consciousness. In contrast to Benhabib, however, I have tried to show how one can save Habermas's

---

19. This answers Charles Larmore's question, Why should we bother to dialogue with those who are "weak" or "strange," i.e., those with whom we neither need nor desire to cooperate? See his *Patterns of Complexity* (Cambridge: Cambridge University Press, 1987), pp. 59–66. Larmore too argues that a discourse ethics requires a fairly strong notion of respect for persons as having their own perspective on an issue. The discourse ethics I present here, however, can only answer Larmore's question by combining the kind of respect one accords a "competent speaker"—a category from which strangers might be excluded—with the general extension of the moral 'ought': as soon as we extend our normative expectations to strangers they fall under the discourse-ethical obligation of inclusion in dialogue.

proposed justification program as an argumentation-theoretic explication of the commitment given in (1). Now it may well be that the notion of argumentation in (RP) and the notion of norm in (CP) import
modern views. Nonetheless, the rules of rational discourse (RP) need
not imply a universal attribution of moral personality any more than
scientists have to assume that all human beings are competent counterparts in a scientific discourse. Nor can such a strong notion of universality be drawn solely from (CP), which remains bound to a monological perspective. Rather, the "dialogical universality" of (U) results
from the interaction of context (1), a formal notion of "competent
speaker" (2), and a largely semantic analysis of moral 'oughts' (3). Insofar as the analyses given in (CP) and (RP) are not altogether implausible explications of modern intuitions about morally valid consensus,
the crucial questions shift to the context and commitment given in (1):
what makes it so rational to base all normative expectations on such
consensus? To what extent can or ought we turn to consensual conflict
resolution, given the uncommon degree of personal moral autonomy
this seemingly requires? Before such questions can be answered—an inquiry that ultimately goes beyond the scope of this study—it is indispensable that we have a clear sense of the intersubjective character of
such autonomy. In section IV, then, I shall complete the derivation of
(U) by fleshing out the demand for real perspective taking implicit in
(U); section V will then note some of the further implications of this
dialogical understanding of universalization, in particular the intersubjective notion of moral insight it implies.

IV. THE DIALOGICAL INTERSUBJECTIVITY OF (U)

Albrecht Wellmer has recently suggested that the plausibility of Kant's
Categorical Imperative, monologically employed, lies in the fact that if *I*
cannot will a maxim to be a universal law, then neither can *we*.[20] Yet even
this formulation, he argues, expresses no more than a provisional assumption, inasmuch as my judgment about what I can or cannot will as
universal law depends on my grasp of others' needs and values, something to be had only in real dialogue.[21] In this section I shall show how
this opening to real dialogue flows from the argument in section III, leading finally to the intersubjective notion of moral conviction contained in

20. Wellmer, "Ethics and Dialogue," p. 135; cf. also pp. 121–126.
21. Wellmer, "Ethics and Dialogue," pp. 140–141.

(U). Such intersubjectivity, I shall argue, is given with the kind of perspective taking argumentation requires.

Let us start by recapping the progress so far, only in a more concrete way. Suppose the cooperation between an employer A and her employee B is threatened by a conflict: A expects B to relocate to a different city, but B objects on the grounds that no decent employer may expect this of employees. B contests A's expectation not just for a particular situation—although certainly B's particular relocation is at stake—but in general. B is thus questioning the general moral validity of a certain norm N regulating the interaction between *any* employer and employee, *ceteris paribus*. This, of course, is an ambitious claim, and if B is serious about making it effective he will probably have to put up with being dismissed for insubordination and take the matter to court. That he might enlist the press, start a campaign to revise existing laws, and so on, is not an entirely farfetched scenario.

Bringing suit and changing laws involve more than moral discourse. The important point here is that such campaigns can and often do involve moral battles, as any number of moral-legal crusades in the United States have shown. Of course, B will more likely settle for an attempt to appeal simply to A's own moral decency, and then, if A is not convinced and the law is not on B's side, settle for grudging compliance or change jobs. I sketched the more ambitious scenario, however, as preparation for the discourse-ethical point that a conflict about the general validity of a normative expectation actually goes far beyond the individual disputants. In locating their conflict at the level of general validity, A and B are not simply disputing whether this particular employer A may expect action *a* of this particular employee B in this individual situation S. Rather, the dispute concerns whether any employer may expect *a*-type actions of any employee in similar circumstances. Now if this is to be an *arguable* expectation, any rational person in those circumstances should be able to be convinced that the expectation is justified. In arguing about the matter, therefore, A and B commit themselves to find an argument any rational person could accept, which is to say they seek reasons anyone could accept as good after the open, unhindered debate defined in (RP). Following the discussion in section III, "any rational person" includes all those affected by the norm's observance.

The crucial point I want to establish here is that in choosing to argue, each party commits itself not just to its own rational conviction but to that of *others* as well. This is the kernel of intersubjectivity in (U). More specifically, the commitment to rational conviction must involve something like taking an interest in others' interests, both in proposing (or rejecting) a norm in argument and in accepting a norm at the moment of reaching agreement.

To get at this we can start with the minimum of each individual's monological reaction to the contested norm. Inasmuch as a general norm is at stake, these reactions produce reasons that turn on the action constraints given with observing the norm. B, for example, finds it unacceptable that an employer have so much power over an employee. Thus he contests the relationship or role definitions intrinsic to the norm that regulates relocation. B might also think of foreseeable impacts of such a norm ("Think of workplace morale!"), including its broader side effects ("This would lead to a fragmentation of neighborhoods"). In rehearsing these various reasons B also *evaluates* the norm's constraints and impacts in some sense, connecting these with aspects of a need interpretation. One can see in the above arguments, for example, references to the values or disvalues of freedom/power, workplace morale, neighborhood stability. A, by contrast, might find that without an employer "right" to relocate employees a business could not perform efficiently. Thus A's evaluation appeals to the values of efficiency and business success.

How such morally relevant values should be characterized in general we must postpone to a discussion of the relation between the right and the good. For the moment it is enough to see what happens when A and B bring their privately rehearsed reasons to open debate in order to propose or argue against a norm. In that case each hopes to convince the other by appeal to such values. Continuing with our minimalist approach, suppose that each at least argues in light of his or her own needs and wants. Thus B argues that the constraints and impacts of the norm are unacceptable for his interests, say his interest in freedom to choose where to live, or in a workplace and neighborhood not disrupted by sudden changes, respectively, in personnel and neighbors. In arguing like this, B must assume not only that A understands the values he appeals to. He must in addition hope that A finds these values convincing in some fashion. This hope can easily be dashed, of course. A might, for example, believe that a workplace not punctuated by periodic upheavals in personnel is too complacent to be really efficient. Or she might consider a "happy workplace" an irrelevant consideration. Thus in order to convince A that the norm is wrong, it would seem B must either draw on those values A herself accepts or convince her to accept values that would in turn support his rejection of the norm.[22] In one fashion or another B must find or create a bridge to A's interests, and to this extent "take an interest in A's interests."

If this conclusion seems a bit rash, we can scale back our example to a yet thinner scenario. Suppose that A, after hearing B's arguments, proposes an alternative norm with the claim, "You want x and I want y, and norm N_{xy} arranges it so both of us can pursue these without restriction." A believes she has found a way to harmonize each one's individualistic pursuit of private interests such that neither interest interferes with the other. This would seem to involve even less concern for the details of the other's interests—each can simply live and let live. Yet even here A has to take some minimal interest in B's interests: simply to propose N_{xy}, A must have at least *understood* B's interests enough to see that N_{xy} has consequences B will probably consider favorable. What is more, even if A finds B's values disgusting, she must have at least such familiarity with them as would allow her to *evaluate* the norm's consequences as favorable from B's standpoint. Hence even on this still quite minimalist account, for A to make an *argument* to B she must not only evaluate the norm's consequences in the light of her own interests and values but also in the light of B's. Anything less than this would seem simply to be a guess and not an argument.[23]

Suppose, now, that B actually accepts A's norm proposal. If both parties are to consider their mutual acceptance as grounding a moral norm, then—at the very least—A must suppose of both herself *and* B (just as B must suppose of himself and A) that their acceptance is on both sides *rationally motivated*, i.e., based on an insight into the better argument. This supposition, whose conditions the pragmatic presuppositions of argument attempt to elucidate, means that each supposes him- or herself as well as the other free to argue and question, clarify interests, and so forth to the point of reaching as much clarity as possible over the acceptability of the norm's constraints and impacts. It means, further, that each is willing to submit his or her understanding and description of the other's interests to revision in the light of such questioning and interest

22. This would take us into Benhabib's notion of "moral-transformatory" discourse; see her *Critique*, pp. 311–314.
23. That is, if A simply throws out a proposal in the blind hope that B will accept it, the cognitive aspect of arguing that B ought to accept the proposal disappears. The situation would then seem to be that of negotiating a compromise, where one seeks only to get others to agree to terms as favorable as possible to one's own interests—leaving the *others* to look out for their interests. Consider, for example, haggling over prices in a marketplace: here the buyer usually is not interested in a fair price but in the lowest possible price.

clarification. Recalling "Wahrheitstheorien," we can see this means that each must have had the chance to react to and replace any terms that appear inappropriate, at least insofar as they affect the crucial arguments. That is, for A to consider the argument for N_{xy} cogent she must not only be convinced *for herself* that this argument appropriately describes B's interests (as well as her own); she must in addition have grounds for supposing that B *himself* accepts the argument in terms *he* finds appropriate. Conversely, B must suppose the same of A.

In short, each cannot rest secure in his or her own apprehension of the other's interests, but must open that apprehension to the other's questioning, modification, and confirmation—in short, to real dialogue. The commitment to the other's rational conviction behind this openness to dialogue takes the interest in the other's interests even further than that involved in proposing a norm, for at the moment of consensus the other's bare acceptance of my proposal does not suffice. I must in addition have grounds to suppose this acceptance is not distorted, i.e., that it rests solely on an insight into the better argument. To the extent that this does not hold, our norm does not rest on argued agreement and hence is not valid. Thus if the other unquestioningly accepts my norm proposal, there is reason for *my* cross-examination of that very acceptance.

Now the particular example (especially the imagined solution, N_{xy}) attempted to present a conflict resolution based on argumentation for a normative expectation in which only the most minimal restriction of interests needed to be established. Each party is claiming it ought to be allowed to pursue certain interests (or that the other ought not infringe on these interests) and, happily, a norm is available allowing both to do just that. But this rather harmonious (as well as individualistic) account of conflict adjudication is more likely the exception than the rule. It would allow both parties to arrive at a *modus vivendi* in which neither had to grapple with the much more difficult question concerning the legitimate claim raised by another's values. If *all* social conflicts of interest could be reduced to such harmonization, solving them would be largely a matter of cleverness—in fact, one could hardly claim there *were* any conflicts of *interest*. But if not all conflicts are so easily resolved, then their adjudication will require those involved to argue about how much one party's interest makes a legitimate claim on another, so that the manner and extent to which conflicting values and interests allow of normative regulation can be determined. Such decisions would seem to involve moral discourse even more deeply in the language of need interpretation and value. The point of the example, however, is that *even* in this most felicitous case a rational consensus must involve real mutual perspective taking as a basis for confidence in the rationality of the agreement.

For those less harmonious cases an even more demanding perspective taking is required. This is further heightened if we remove the assumption silently simplifying the scenario, namely that only A and B need agree. In fact, since they are arguing over a general norm, each must suppose his or her reasons are good enough to convince all those possibly affected by the norm's observance. Even if A convinces B to give up his normative expectation she cannot on that basis alone claim that this expectation has been shown to be unjustified. "Good reasons" are those which all possibly affected persons could accept. If such reasons not only harmonize but also in many cases restrict competing interests, then this suggests that the evaluation of the norm's constraints and impacts must somehow be mediated by values that all can *positively accept* in some way.

We can assign a preliminary meaning to such "positive acceptance" by turning to the notion of "generalizable interest" that Habermas connects with valid moral norms. Two points are decisive: (1) that in arguing for a norm one is evaluating it in terms of its impact on various interests (one's own and others'); and (2) that in at least some cases not all affected interests can be equally satisfied, so that the participants must agree on which interests make legitimate claims on all (and which do not) in the potential conflict situation in need of normative regulation. This harkens back to our earlier distinction between understandable and normative interests. A generalizable interest, then, is one with general suasive force in moral argumentation, i.e., an interest the appeal to which supports the acceptance of a norm for all those possibly affected by an issue. To return to our example, if A finds B's appeal to employee freedom (here specified as a right against forced relocation) a convincing ground for giving up her claim to employer relocation rights, then she accepts the interest in such freedom as generalizable for the employee-employer relation. All this means is that in the typical situations involving this relationship the interest in not being forced to relocate makes a legitimate claim over other understandable interests typically at work in such situations. *For this type of situation*, then, the value of freedom, suitably specified in terms of employee rights, has the ability to convince everyone to accept a certain norm upholding the interest expressed in terms of that value. It would seem that if such values and interests do not exist (or if they cannot be created), then conflict resolution must either discover a pre-existing harmony (or overlap) of particular interests—as in our minimalist scenario—or must resort to compromise.

It would be precipitous here to construe this as subordinating moral discourse to evaluative questions. In fact, practically nothing has been said here about what such values are or what their acceptance involves with respect to the participants' notions of the good life. Nor need the acceptance of such values be so complete and unqualified as the example suggests. It might be a qualified reciprocal acceptance, for example where A acknowledges the value of freedom and B, the value of business competitiveness, such that A and B can fashion a new norm doing justice to both perspectives. Or it may involve the creation of a third, overarching value or interest that each party can connect with his or her own, more particular, values. I mention these possibilities simply to indicate that agreement need not involve one party "winning the argument," intellectually forcing the other to see his or her value as exclusively overriding or as a concrete good the other must fully adopt as well, a move that would probably have to occur in an ethical discourse.

We can now reformulate (U) in a way that captures its intersubjective dimension, yet without making any too venturesome commitments about the relation to values, as follows:

(U)   A norm is reached on the basis of good reasons, and a rational consensus thereby attained, if and only if

(a) each of those affected can convince the others, in terms they hold appropriate for the perception of both their own and others' interests, that the constraints and impacts of a norm's general observance are acceptable for all; and

(b) each can be convinced by all, in terms she or he considers appropriate, that the constraints and impacts of a norm's general observance are acceptable for all.[24]

This conclusion, I suggest, expresses the basic intention of (U). In what follows I will explore the implications of this conclusion in greater detail.

24. The idea of each being "convinced by all" may sound a bit odd, but it simply expresses the flip-side of (Ua), taken from the perspective of one being convinced in one's own language system. Intuitively, (Ub) says that a group may not consider a norm valid unless each can be convinced, in terms he or she finds appropriate, of the validity of the norm.

V. IMPLICATIONS

In this final section of Chapter 3 I shall discuss some of the general implications of the above reading of (U). First, I would like to say a few things about the dialogical conception of the moral point of view contained in (U). Most significant in this regard is the notion of "insight into the better argument" bound up with this; here I shall merely introduce the possibility of an intersubjective notion of moral insight; in the Postscript to Part One I shall spell this out a bit more. Second, some of the advances over liberal notions of dialogue deserve brief mention. We can then, in a third section, turn to the problematic side of (U). The problems most relevant here have to do with the demanding concept of personal autonomy seemingly called for by (U).

I.

One of the most interesting clarifications the above explication provides has to do with the particular interpretation of the moral point of view provided by (U). Generally the moral point of view is seen as the individual subject's impartial standpoint toward the various interests and desires at stake in a conflict situation. (U) arrives at such impartiality *only by way of* a reciprocity defined in terms of the perspective taking given with the need to find arguments convincing in the language of the other participant.[25] The moral point of view is thereby "decentered," for the individual's weighing of interests and alternative norms no longer suffices to define impartiality. Individuals "take" the moral point of view precisely insofar as they give themselves over to such a process of dialogical interchange, to the give-and-take of opinions striving toward consensus.

The explication shows that such reciprocity has two complementary sides. On the one side, it allows each participant a certain autonomy with respect to need interpretation and self-understanding. At the very least, each participant is allowed to reject norms that would not do justice to his or her self-understanding. On a more positive note, I would suggest that rational consensus may not necessarily require participants to agree fully on a *single* conceptual framework. That is, (U) would seem to allow for the possibility in some cases that a single norm could be arrived at through a number of different frameworks (and need interpretations). Even if such agreement requires in principle the existence of a single more abstract framework, the integrity of thicker, more particular frameworks

25. See EzD, pp. 152–158.

could be preserved insofar as participants can mutually enter into one another's perspectives and argue directly for a common norm *from within* each perspective.[26] On the other side, this autonomy results from interaction with others, inasmuch as the individual's needs or interests become *normative* only if they find the assent of others. (Of course, how much commonality agreement on a moral norm requires, and how much difference it can tolerate, cannot be decided simply by pointing out these formal features of mutual understanding as given in (U); one must turn to hermeneutical theory for that. My point here is simply that (U) allows for a notion of mutual understanding that could include both sameness and difference.)

Habermas has expressed this dual character of moral reciprocity in terms of the inseparability of the principles of justice and solidarity.[27] Although a fuller exposition of these principles must await Part Two, we can already see that the above conclusion shows how the argumentation-theoretic kernel of justice and solidarity follows from the pragmatic presuppositions of argument. In (Ua) we find the principle of solidarity in the form of a demand that each individual's claim to moral objectivity must be submitted to intersubjective testing.[28] In (Ub) the principle of justice takes the form of the requirement that a valid consensus depends on the consent of each individual who, as autonomous, has the right to take a position in light of his or her interests.

This suggests, in turn, that the impartiality defining the moral point of view is likewise double-sided. The participants must be able to present their needs and interests in the language of others, a task that requires at once a degree of imaginative abstractive capability with respect to one's own need interpretations *and*, just as much, the ability to understand the other's position—something like empathy, only in a cognitive sense. This demanding empathic presupposition is often overlooked by criticisms of impartialist moral theories.[29]

Perhaps most interesting—and certainly quite puzzling—are the implications the conclusion holds for the notion of rational conviction or insight. The cognitive character of moral reciprocity consists in this: I can be rationally convinced of the worthiness of a norm only if I suppose that

---

26. Or, as Habermas puts it, this presupposes that "the languages and vocabularies in which we interpret our needs/wants and explicate our moral feelings must be porous to one another." EzD, p. 208.

27. See in particular JS, esp. pp. 243–249.

28. See JS, p. 247.

29. Susan Moller Okin, "Reason and Feeling," makes this point quite convincingly for Rawls's original position.

others are rationally convinced, which in turn depends on their supposing I am rationally convinced. If this is not to be a vicious circle, then rational conviction must be something we arrive at together. Insight and conviction must take up residence somehow *outside*, or perhaps better, *between* the individual subjects of discourse. In short, the argument announces a paradigm shift, a departure from the "philosophy of the subject" and its overprivileging of individual self-consciousness.[30]

It remains far from clear how such a notion of insight is to be explicated. One cannot deny it a certain aura of paradox. It looks like something that in principle cannot be attained, for if my insight depends on yours, and yours on mine, neither of us can be first at getting there—in which case, however, it would seem that neither of us can get there at all. This suggests that insight must be somehow reconceived as a process occurring in the public space defined by communication and dialogue. In the Postscript to Part One I will make an initial attempt at this reconception. But does this mean that an individual could never make a sound moral judgment without actually consulting those affected by the issue? If such consultation proves impossible in some case—for example, in decisions involving comatose persons—is a good moral decision altogether impossible? Such a conclusion would certainly be too strong. Rather, the logic of practical reasoning spelled out in (U) implies that the quality of such judgments depends on how well the individual has been able to carry out at least an imaginary dialogue with those affected, i.e., how well he has taken their perspectives and interests into account in an effort to arrive at a judgment they *would* approve, were they in the position to do so. This effort is easier when the judgment involves norms so basic and widely accepted that one can fairly safely presume their acceptance by others. Such cases do not, however, alter the central claim advanced in discourse ethics: that the rationality of an individual's imaginary dialogue depends on, or is in some sense a derivative form of, real discourse. Imaginary dialogues thus represent second-best substitutes, even if they are often necessary.

If this conclusion still seems paradoxical or radical, one should note that it did not require a metaphysical point of departure nor does it necessarily take us beyond our everyday experience. We reached it simply by submitting the notion of reciprocal behavior expectations to a logic of

---

30. On this theme see *Discourse*; also PT, esp. pp. 149–204; finally, Habermas's discussion of Humboldt in "Reply," pp. 215–222, 288 n10.

argumentation. And the destination is, I trust, not wholly unfamiliar: the experience of being given the right words, or being helped to see a point, by someone else whose own confidence depends in turn on one's own excited, "Yes, that's it—that's the solution we're looking for!"

2.

The advances, or potential advances, achieved by discourse ethics over more conventional models of the moral point of view have been discussed by a number of authors.[31] Here I only want to mention some of the more significant of these advances, simply for the sake of gaining a fuller understanding of discourse ethics.

To begin with, the dialogical character of discourse ethics brings significant advantages over moral theories emphasizing the individual's capacity for abstraction. In contrast to Kant's "pure" ethics of the will, for example, the real discourse envisioned by Habermas does not abstract even in part from the consequences and side effects of the general following of a norm. This renders discursively redeemed norms more relevant to real situations. Moreover, by acknowledging the essential intuition of consequentialist ethics, moral discourse can be informed by scientific expertise about such consequences in a way the lone individual could never be.[32] In addition, the dialogical definition of impartiality implies a structural reduction of perspectival bias in the projection of the expected consequences and side effects of a norm's observance.

One also finds an advantage over the Rawlsian form of abstraction. Like Habermas, Rawls is engaged in a project of capturing moral intuitions in a formal procedure that would allow for social consensus in a pluralistic society. Unlike Rawls, however, discourse ethics does not require its participants to abstract from their concrete interests in entering a fictive original position, so as to be subsequently forced by the conceptual structure of that position into particular institutional results. Discourse ethics does not involve an attempt to derive substantive results

31. See ME, pp. 203–209, for the contrast between discourse ethics and Kantian moral theory; for the contrast with Kant and Rawls, see Baynes, *Normative Grounds*; also Kenneth Baynes, "The Liberal/Communitarian Controversy and Communicative Ethics," *Philosophy and Social Criticism* 14 (1988): 293–313; Benhabib, "Liberal Dialogue," pp. 143–156.

32. This is emphasized by Karl-Otto Apel, "The Problem of a Macroethic of Responsibility to the Future in the Crisis of Technological Civilization: An Attempt to Come to Terms with Hans Jonas's 'Principle of Responsibility,'" trans. Wilson Brown, *Man and World* 20 (1987): 30–33.

from such a thought experiment of a hypothetical consensus. Rather, the actual interests of the participants make up precisely the matter under discursive examination, and the institutional shape of justice is left to the real results of such examination.[33]

The latter point is a significant one, for it moves practical discourse beyond liberal models of "neutral dialogue," which typically strike more controversial topics from discussion. Rawls, for example, restricts justice debates to the grammar of a particular set of "primary goods" which all rational agents can be presumed to share.[34] By contrast, the foregoing explication of discourse-ethical universalization suggests that no subject matter may be ruled out of discussion a priori. Although a full discussion of this point must await Part Two, I can indicate briefly how the inclusion of need interpretations in moral discourse takes one beyond the impasses communitarians have pointed out in liberal models of consensus formation.[35]

As we have seen, discourse ethics allows moral argumentation to consider the central concepts and need interpretations at stake in a norm. This permits it to respond to a charge brought against liberal models of decision making, that the liberal abstraction from a shared, thicker conception of the good of human life has fatal consequences for the rationality of contemporary social consensus. MacIntyre, for example, has argued that the material structure of justice conflicts involves incommensurabilities that preclude *rational* formal-procedural solutions as envisioned by liberal moral theories.[36] However problematic MacIntyre's own proposals, his objection makes the plausible point that rational conflict resolution is possible only if the participants can take the argument to an already agreed upon notion of the good of human life. Lacking such a prior shared understanding and acceptance of the common good, or human telos, social conflict resolution can rest on nothing more than the manipulation of subjective preferences and feelings—democratic procedures at best simply postpone the irresolvable differences characterizing a society that has taken leave of tradition-mediated agreement on the

33. For Habermas's discussion of Rawls, see JS, pp. 229–231; EzD, pp. 125–131.

34. See, by Rawls, "The Idea of an Overlapping Consensus"; and "The Priority of Right and Ideas of the Good"; by Ackerman, "Why Dialogue?"; and "What Is Neutral about Neutrality?"; these models of argumentation have been criticized by Baynes, "Liberal/Communitarian," pp. 301–303.

35. I have spelled out the following argument more fully in my "Discourse Ethics and the Communitarian Critique of Neo-Kantianism," *Philosophical Forum* 22 (1990): 120–138.

36. MacIntyre, *After Virtue* (2d ed.), e.g., pp. 51–61, 152–154, 202, 244–255; cf. also his *Whose Justice?*, pp. 106–107, 334–350.

common good.[37] MacIntyre tries to illustrate his point with the thought experiment of a debate between a liberal Rawlsian and a blue-collar Nozickian over redistributive taxation.[38] His basic point is that their debate must stop, still unresolved, as soon as it gets down to each party's divergent beliefs about the good of human life—beliefs that, as merely subjective preferences, present incommensurable differences not open to further discussion. Turning to democratic decision procedures for a settlement cannot make up for this fundamental rationality deficit.[39]

For discourse ethics, however, such differences are not to be excluded a priori from moral argumentation, but are rather open to discussion in an effort to arrive at a mutual understanding of different need interpretations, such that participants could agree on modes of cooperation within which different ideas of the good of human life can at least coexist. Our earlier discussion of (U) indicates that participants would have to agree to the consequences of the norm in light of interests describable in terms agreeable to each. Now this suggests, in response to MacIntyre, that differing conceptions of the good life need not be wholly disregarded in the effort to reach consensus, for each person must be able to satisfy the other that the norm's consequences would be compatible with those interests of the other—interests that presumably depend on a conception of the good life—which each can recognize as making a legitimate claim on all. How much of a common conceptual framework this requires admittedly remains an open question; we have already adverted to the possibility that the morally necessary level of agreement might be compatible with the integrity of more particular frameworks and need interpretations. Beyond these rather formal implications of the structure of (U) it is unlikely that one can make any a priori or general statements on this; one would rather have to examine specific conflicts. In any case, it is important to note in this regard that the search for a peaceful "coexistence" among diverse goods suggests that a recognition of a "legitimate claim" need not be a fully *substantive* endorsement of (or concrete pursuit of) the other's good. I can, for example, recognize your right to worship Allah without becoming myself a Muslim.[40]

---

37. For a somewhat more measured objection along similar lines, see Taylor's *Philosophy and the Human Sciences*, esp. "The Diversity of Goods" and "The Nature and Scope of Distributive Justice," pp. 230–247 and 289–317.

38. MacIntyre, *After Virtue*, pp. 244–251.

39. MacIntyre, *Whose Justice?*, pp. 343–344.

40. The moral relevance of just this kind of mutual understanding gets short shrift, it seems to me, in the account of cross-cultural understanding given in *Whose Justice?*. For Habermas's critique of this book, see EzD, pp. 209–218. As Habermas points out,

3.

We can summarize the foregoing considerations as follows: discourse
ethics takes a primarily Kantian approach considerably beyond the limits
traditionally assigned it, acknowledging the intrinsic relevance of foreseeable consequences and concrete interests for moral deliberation. The
above explication of (U), as well as the above contrasts in this section,
should at least indicate how discourse ethics brings consequentialist and
utilitarian insights within the gamut of a deontological morality. Beyond
this, the foregoing response to MacIntyre broaches the issue of how discourse ethics might also do justice to the teleological or eudaemonist intuitions championed by communitarians.

This latter issue, however, by far exceeds the response given above. As
already indicated in the Introduction, the issue between communitarianism and discourse ethics concerns the role notions of the human good
have in moral discourse. Now the analysis so far has shown that moral
norms display internal relations to need interpretations and values—precisely where one would also look for conceptions of the good life. Less
clear in the account so far is how, in the heat of debate, particular conceptions of the good and evaluative issues can be distinguished from
moral issues. More specifically, at what point does the evaluation of consequences for the other's interests stop? If rational consensus means that
I have to agree that your own perception of your interests is not distorted,
am I not thereby drawn into an evaluative or ethical discourse with you,
precisely in the midst of a moral discourse?

This requirement, which I have associated with the argumentation-
theoretic kernel of solidarity, would seem to make tremendous empathic
demands, for it enjoins each participant to inhabit the world of the other
discussion partners, at least enough to present and assess arguments
those partners could accept. This certainly requires a keen sense of the
other's interests, desires, and needs. What is more, the structure of (U)
requires that participants agree in principle about what each of them
considers his or her good—to be sure, without imposing a single substantive conception of the human good on all. That is, each must at least
be able to determine whether some interest of another makes a legitimate claim on everyone else. More precisely, the participants' joint
examination-assimilation-and-transformation of their various interests

---

MacIntyre's account reduces interpretation to an asymmetrical relation: one either assimilates the other to one's own tradition or is oneself converted to the other's tradition; EzD,
pp. 217f.

and values must be such as to arrive at a consensus about how conflicting interests should be regulated—they must together be willing to discuss and adjust their various interests and values enough to agree on a fair means of cooperation in satisfying those interests. Arguing for various adjustments, assessing whether a proposal is fair for each person's pursuit of the good life—all this requires a liberal quantity of mutual understanding. If we look at MacIntyre's analysis of what is involved in such understanding—the simultaneous inhabitance of two worlds[41]—(U) hardly appears promising for real conflict resolution, for it would seem to set the requirements altogether too high. Thus the highly idealized account of normative validity presented in Part One raises the question, Is discourse ethics at all feasible?

The remaining two parts of this study will address such issues. In Part Two I shall try to straighten out the complex relations between discourse ethics and the notion of good, showing in the process how discourse ethics acknowledges eudaemonist moral intuitions, at least to some extent. Part Three will then attempt to bring the still highly idealized account of discourse closer to actual practices; for this one has to show how discourse ethics can be feasibly situated in more concrete contexts.

41. MacIntyre, *Whose Justice?*, pp. 374–376.

Postscript to Part I

Insight as Intersubjective

The above derivation has need of a genuinely intersubjective notion of rational conviction or insight, by which that "intermediate domain of symbolic meanings" might take on "a dignity of its own."[1] But how does one describe, or even locate, such a notion? Is not insight precisely the accomplishment of the individual subject—however much that subject might rely on others for information and the materials in need of insightful coordination and synthesis? Do not the experiences of insight and conviction—of getting the point, of catching on to a solution, of hitting the target squarely with an answer—do not such experiences, after all, reside within the individual? A focus on the kind of problem solving employed in arriving at factual judgments, in scientific research, in mathematics, or even in solving crossword puzzles, encourages an affirmative answer to these questions. Nonetheless, even in such monologically inclined pursuits the presence of the intersubjective makes itself felt. One avenue by which we might approach this is that opened by Bernard Lonergan's extensive analysis of insight.[2] Despite Lonergan's focus on the individual thinker, his analysis provides a helpful entry into our problematic. My intention here is not to assimilate discourse ethics to a Lonerganian analysis, but rather simply to find in Lonergan some hints which would be compatible with discourse ethics. As we shall see, Lonergan's

1. PT, p. 7.
2. Bernard J. F. Lonergan, *Insight: A Study of Human Understanding*, 3d ed. (New York: Philosophical Library, 1970); first published in 1957, this is now available as vol. 3 of the *Collected Works of Bernard Lonergan*, ed. Frederick E. Crowe and Robert M. Doran (University of Toronto Press, 1992).

analysis of the reflective dimensions of insight helps break down its seemingly impenetrable immediacy.

Lonergan distinguishes two levels at which insights occur in the pursuit of truth. A direct insight meets the challenge of organizing data, of
synthesizing puzzling elements of experience, thereby rendering that data
or experience understandable. Strictly speaking, however, the product of
a direct insight is no more than a possible answer to a question or problem. Whether that answer or—in the realm of science, hypothesis—in
fact is correct calls for a further insight which Lonergan terms "reflective," insofar as one must take the prospective answer back to the conditions of its correctness and ask oneself to what extent those conditions
are fulfilled. Thus reflective insight grasps not the unity in a set of data
but rather the fact that the conditions for a prospective judgment are fulfilled. And the key to grasping the fulfillment of such conditions, hence
to distinguishing "mere bright ideas" from correct insights, lies in the
recognition that there are no "further, pertinent questions."[3] These levels
of insight interweave with one another in a dynamic learning process. In
fact, one is hard put to imagine direct insights without reflective insights,
inasmuch as the former arise precisely in response to pertinent questions.
That is, the synthesizing formulation of an idea must already involve a
"reflective" moment, since an idea, a prospective answer, impresses one
as worth entertaining only through its power to answer certain questions. Nonetheless, direct insights carry a reservation, a tentativeness, to
the extent that yet further questions remain unanswered.

The intersubjective currents in Lonergan's analysis can be detected in
the notion of "further pertinent questions," for these are not restricted
simply to "further questions for me"—typically they arise from others.[4]
In the realm of normative questions, however, the need for other people's
questions becomes not just typical, but *essential*. We can see this most
clearly if we contrast normative issues with the monological limit-cases
found in elementary mathematics or in crossword puzzles, where the
competent individual can more or less single-handedly master all the relevant data and pertinent questions and thus can equate his or her subjective certainty of having achieved the correct answer with an objective
certainty. Such an equation the normative realm excludes in principle.
There the single individual can never master all the relevant data or pertinent questions, simply because the correctness of moral norms—ac-

3. Lonergan, *Insight*, pp. 283–287.
4. Cf. *Insight*, pp. 284–285, and the example from modern physics, p. 302.

cording to discourse ethics—depends on the agreement of others, and that agreement can never be fully foreseen by the one advancing a norm proposal. The other, precisely as other, represents a partially hidden set of potential questions and further relevant data—questions that often come to light only in response to a concrete proposal calling the other to thematize further his or her own views.

This reference of norms to a public sphere affects the experience and nature of normative insights in such a way as to rule out even the subjective certainty one has in the more monological spheres of problem solving. However much I might feel that my proposal pulls together all the various considerations thus far come to light in a debate, the other represents an unknown undermining my confidence, however subtly. In moral argumentation the Archimedean "Eureka!" must ever be tinged with hesitation, an expectant awaiting of the other's "yes" or "no." At best the individual creatively exercises his or her linguistic competence to gain a partial insight into the current set of thematized public statements defining the normative problem. Yet far too much remains unthematized among the participants for individual creativity to yield, of itself, that rational conviction required by (U). Such conviction comes only with the others' "yes"—only then does one even have the *experience* that we, together, have had an insight, have hit the target squarely.

We can get at the same point if we start by defining the individual's "conviction" as that particular individual "not having any further questions." According to this definition, one has an insight when one's exercise of linguistic creativity answers one's questions and thereby grants one a rest from doubt—recall here Peirce's "fixation of belief." Once again, however, the nature of normative problems must undermine such "rest." As long as *you* have, or might have, a further question, then *I* also have got one since I cannot get you to accept my solution until I can say it in a way that gets rid of your question. Insofar as your acceptance partially *constitutes* the correctness of the norm, my doubt must persist so long as you doubt that the behavior defined by the norm may be expected of you.[5]

Where rest from doubt cannot be achieved by the individual alone, insight must be an intersubjective phenomenon. Intersubjective insight, as something occurring only within the interaction of several subjects,

---

5. In Lonergan's terms this definition focuses on reflective insight; direct insight might indeed remain in the province of the individual insofar as the individual's proposals represent attempts to unify positions. For Lonergan's own suggestions at moral theory see *Insight*, pp. 596ff; cf. in Habermas, "Reply," pp. 217f.

resides at the point where several things come together, i.e., where (a) creative individual exercises of linguistic competence meet over (b) a set of public statements thematizing a problem of social coordination, which are in turn set against (c) lifeworld background resources for solving the problem. In this framework a *partial group insight* occurs at the moment a formulation is put forward, against which none of the members of the group can think of objections or further questions. This formulation results from a *process* of argumentation in which the various individuals freely cooperate in the creative employment of their linguistic competences, working with their various background resources and thematized statements of the problem. The insight's *content* is a statement of a norm proposal, which coordinates the thematized constraints of the problem in such a way that none of the participants can think of further pertinent questions.[6] The insight itself is genuinely intersubjective in that no single individual has a rational conviction alone, but only at the moment that it becomes clear to all that no one has any further questions. This being ascertained, the group is *justified* in adopting the norm. The norm in fact is *right*, however, only if no possibly affected person could/can/will be able to think of a pertinent further question leading to the rejection of the norm.[7] The norm's present justifiability, i.e., its rational acceptability for a given group, gives that group the confidence that their *claim* that the norm is right will hold up over the long haul. By dealing with all the questions they can think up, they gain confidence that the norm will prove resistant to all later pertinent questions which other possibly affected persons can think up. At the same time, this group confidence is no absolute: it allows for the possibility that a single individual might think of reasons for rejecting the prevailing consensus. Such rejection, however, tacitly appeals to a future audience that will vindicate the individual's objections to the earlier consensus.

6. The notion of pertinence may, for the moment, be defined with Alexy in terms of rules for burden of argument; cf. his *Legal Argumentation*, pp. 187–208.

7. Certainly further questions will most likely arise. Rightness implies that such questions can be answered without rejecting the norm.

Solidarity: Discourse Ethics and the Good

Introduction to Part II

We cannot get around the question concerning the role of the good in moral discourse. In the first place, the analysis in Chapters 2 and 3 repeatedly caught sight of goods and values cropping up within moral discourse, so that the distinction Habermas wants to draw between moral and ethical discourse, between questions of justice and questions of the good life, remains muddy. In addition to this internal problem, however, there is also the context of debate within which we first situated discourse ethics. As the Introduction showed, how a moral theory situates itself in that context depends crucially upon the position it adopts vis-à-vis the good. Inasmuch as this issue arises as an element in the theory of practical reasoning, no account of discourse ethics as a theory of argumentation will be complete unless it addresses this question, if only in a preliminary fashion.

In fact, the systematic difficulty is closely intertwined with the polemical context. For example, we saw that discourse ethics could get around MacIntyre's objection that rational consensus requires prior agreement on a tradition-mediated notion of the common good. However, in anchoring rational consensus in agreement on the terms defining need interpretations, has not discourse ethics blurred the distinction between moral and ethical discourse, thereby committing itself—in some sense—to acknowledging the communitarian point that the good is prior to the right? The question here is this: if moral consensus depends on agreeing on the interpretation of needs, must not such consensus presuppose agreement on a common good, or must it not at least produce such agreement on the way to reaching consensus on a moral norm?[1] This question is best approached, I think, by turning immediately to the defining issue in the communitarian-liberal debate, whether the good or the right has priority. Admittedly, this question has been fairly well beaten to death in Anglo-American circles, especially in so blunt a form. Nonetheless, it can serve us as a tool for opening up the very sorts of complications pointing beyond such a simplistic dichotomy. In fact, the question's very simplicity allows us to see whether a discourse ethics can do justice to eudaemonist moral intuitions.

In Chapter 4, then, I shall begin by defining the discourse-ethical distinction between the right and the good—i.e., between moral questions and ethical ones—in order to show how this implies the priority of the right, at least in certain contexts. This will spell out how moral discourse is and is not about notions of the good life; specifically, I shall argue that moral and ethical discourses are indeed different in kind, but their distinction in practice is often more a matter of degree. I shall then connect the results of this discussion with Habermas's notion of solidarity in an attempt to show how that notion bridges the splits between justice and the good introduced by moral theories that focus on one side or the other of the communitarian-liberal divide. Chapters 5 and 6 then address a further challenge to the priority of right, the question of whether the commitment to moral discourse does not itself constitute or presuppose some unacknowledged notion of the good. In order to get around this objection, notably raised by Charles Taylor, Habermas's discourse ethics must advance rather ambitious claims. These claims, which I have already indicated in Chapter 1, cannot be fully established here. However, I can attempt to make them plausible in comparison to Taylor's counterclaims. Thus, after weighing the burdens of argument that Taylor and Habermas respectively confront (Chapter 5), I shall suggest some reasons for preferring Habermas's approach to morality (Chapter 6).

1. The notion of "good" is slippery enough to take in a number of the categories developed in Part One. To begin with, the objects of needs and wants are goods of various sorts; likewise, one has an "interest" precisely in achieving a good. Thus I take the notion "good" as analytically connected with needs/wants and interests. Value terms (or more loosely, values) have a similar relation, for one can only identify and talk about goods as such by reference to such terms. In the ensuing discussion, then, I shall take each of these terms as indicative of a relation between moral discourse and the good.

Moral Discourse and Conceptions of the Good Life

We may understand the distinction between moral and ethical issues best, I think, by holding to our argumentation-theoretic approach. This is in line with Habermas's general reliance on speech act theory, which leads him to distinguish object domains according to types of validity claims, themselves distinguished according to the types of reasons appropriate for their redemption. To begin with, then, I shall lay out the central semantic and pragmatic means of distinguishing questions of the good from moral questions. This will suggest how the two domains are different in kind (section I). Next, I shall show that this distinction implies the priority of right over good in the context of conflicts and their adjudication (section II). This will indicate how the same material can arise in both domains, such that a sharp separation between moral and ethical discourse cannot often be had in practice (section III). The chapter will close by connecting these results with Habermas's concept of solidarity, thereby fleshing out the rather sparse remarks on this in Chapter 3 (section IV).

I. THE DISTINCTION BETWEEN ETHICAL AND MORAL PERSPECTIVES

We can begin to give some further precision to our earlier, more intuitive separation of the moral and ethical domains by distinguishing these domains in terms of, first, the different *grammars*; second, the *questions* which form the respective points of departure and the different themes of debate; and, third, the *perspectives* from which the answer is obtained in each case.[1]

(1) To begin with the different grammars, although both ethical and moral claims can appear as 'oughts' or imperatives, Habermas defines them such that ethical claims have a teleological orientation to the realization of goods or values, while moral claims refer first of all to obligatory or prohibited actions, thus—if only at a further remove—to norms or rules which specify reciprocal behavior expectations (which are not necessarily symmetrical).[2] Some have suggested that if there are universally binding moral 'oughts', then it belongs to their very meaning that they override—have at least a prima facie priority over—other kinds of considerations, such as instrumental efficiency or satisfying some preference, even one important to one's happiness. A norm such as 'Thou shalt not kill', for example, sets limits to one's pursuit of one's ends. If this norm did not have such priority, if one could freely disregard it whenever some other purpose or desire came into conflict with it, then it would be hard to see how it could be called a *moral* 'ought', at least in the accepted understanding of moral 'ought'-claims as enjoying some kind of categorical character.[3]

Following this line, then, one can characterize norms as rules binding on all persons equally and absolutely, whereas values specify shared preferences or goods considered worth striving for. Norms are thus either valid or invalid, whereas values admit of degrees of acceptability.[4] One probably should not make too much of such grammatical differences, however. For one, they do not allow one to pick out valid moral norms at the start of a discourse. Nor can this distinction answer the communitarian challenge that norms tacitly rest on some kind of good or membership in a specific tradition. In fact, many norms, once they are tested beyond a given community, prove to express no more than the imperatives, values, and interests of a particular culture or group. All this is not

    1. Besides PV and EzD, one can see earlier traces of Habermas's analysis in TCA 1:15–22, 2:92–101; DE, p. 108; and JS, pp. 245–247. See also NR, pp. 118, 141.
    2. PV, p. 101; EzD, pp. 143f, 168–169. Before these recent texts Habermas had drawn the distinction between the moral and the ethical as one between normative judgments and value judgments, resp.; cf., for example, TCA 1:15–23, but also 38–42.
    3. E.g., R. M. Hare, *Moral Thinking: Its Levels, Method and Point* (Oxford: Clarendon, 1981), pp. 21–24, 55–61; but also in Habermas, cf. EzD, pp. 187f.
    4. See FG, pp. 310–312; also Bernard Peters, *Rationalität, Recht und Gesellschaft* (Frankfurt: Suhrkamp, 1991), pp. 81–89, 189–191.

to deny the widely accepted distinction[5] between norms and values, or between deontological and teleological imperatives, but only to note its limitations for a discourse-ethical analysis that would define moral validity in terms of the *pragmatics* of discourse. For our purposes, then, the differences in themes and perspectives are more useful.

(2) What then are the relevant questions and themes involved in discourses over these two sorts of issues? In Habermas's view, ethical discourses ultimately address the questions, Who am I? (or, Who are we?) and Who do I/we want to be? This ties the language of values and goods very closely to an individual's or group's identity—hence the goods at stake in ethical discourses are not simply surface preferences, but rather the deeper values informing one's self-understanding and sense of self-worth.[6] Thus ethical discourse generally looks back to the individual's or group's past history or tradition, in order to choose a future course in the light of existing possibilities. By contrast, the grammar of moral obligation suggests that the relevant question for a moral discourse would be something like, What behavior may we legitimately expect of one another? or, What norm or obligation can each person accept on the basis of good reasons? At least for a modern understanding of morality this boils down to the question, What rules governing our living together are equally good for all?

(3) Admittedly, the presence of the term "good" in the last-mentioned question indicates a certain degree of overlap between the themes of ethical and moral discourses. The latter must likewise at least take notice of the interests and self-understandings of its participants, as (U) suggests, a point I will pick up again below. But moral discourse does not require that participants be able to tell each other what identity each ought to assume, or what life goals each ought to pursue. This suggests there is a *difference in kind* between the two forms of discourse, which seems to lie in something like the angle at which interests are approached: while ethical discourses move *within* a life history or tradition, moral discourses seek both to discover and create potential connections and commonalities *across* the different self-understandings of the participants. In

5. For introductory overviews see William K. Frankena, *Ethics*, 2d ed. (Englewood Cliffs, N. J.: Prentice-Hall, 1973); Friedo Ricken, *Allgemeine Ethik* (Stuttgart: Kohlhammer, 1983), esp. pp. 54–66.

6. See Charles Taylor on "strong evaluations" in "What Is Human Agency?" in *Human Agency and Language*, vol. 1 of *Philosophical Papers* (Cambridge: Cambridge University Press, 1985), pp. 15–44; Taylor distinguishes such evaluation from the "simple weighing" of preferences as well as from a Sartrean notion of "radical choice."

fact, this difference in perspective is crucial for distinguishing ethical from moral discourses, as Habermas himself has made clear.[7] At their most basic level, ethical discourses seek agreement on which values should define one's self-understanding or identity in the light of one's life history or tradition. Thus the axis along which the discursive pragmatics of ethical 'oughts' lie is that of self-actualization and the perspective is an ego- or ethnocentric one (in the nonpejorative sense of a personal or group concern). By contrast, the moral perspective considers how the interests of *each* person will be affected by a given action or norm. In asking whether each person could freely accept the norm, the participants to a moral discourse must take a universalizing perspective leading them beyond the bounds of their particular tradition and institutions. Because of the role distance this move involves, and because it gives to each affected person, at least tacitly, a voice in the legitimacy of the behavior expected by the norm, Habermas aligns moral norms along the axis of self-determination: the mutual imputation of personal autonomy. That is, moral 'oughts' express what we may expect of each other as autonomous persons capable of orienting our action according to validity claims.[8]

II. THE PRIORITY OF RIGHT IN DISCOURSE ETHICS

The above distinction between two kinds of issues and perspectives has significant ramifications for the analysis of conflicts and their resolution, for it suggests that ethical questions are not likely to be rationally resolvable except within a particular form of life. The distinction singles out moral conflicts as admitting in principle of rationally binding solutions *across* differing traditions, life histories, and cultures. If, therefore, we inquire into the significance of Habermas's moral-ethical distinction for conflict adjudication—our guiding interest, in any case—the real motive behind the distinction begins to surface. The following text is enlightening:

> If we want to decide normative questions having to do with the elements of living together not by the direct or masked resort to force, by pressure, influence or by the power of the stronger interest, but rather by a nonviolent conviction based on a rationally motivated agreement, then we have to concentrate on the circle of questions accessible to an impartial evaluation. We

7. PV, pp. 105–107; NR, p. 118; in PV, p. 106f and NR, pp. 141–142, Habermas notes that "maxims of action" can be considered from both perspectives.
8. PV, pp. 109f, 112f; EzD, pp. 145f; MC, pp. 165–169, 193; also see TCA 2:94, 97.

should not expect a generally binding answer if we ask, what is good for me or good for us or good for her; for that we must rather ask, what is *equally good for all.* This "moral point of view" projects a sharp but narrow circle of light which throws into relief, against the mass of all evaluative questions, those action conflicts that can be *resolved* in relation to a universalizable interest: the questions of justice.[9]

The opening conditional reflects Habermas's concern with the conditions of social order. From this point of view, social—including moral—norms are internally related to social order, and thus are means for adjudicating among conflicting interests.[10] Given this way of posing the problem—in fact an entire research program—it makes sense to single out precisely those kinds of conflict admitting of a noncoercive resolution. The ensuing analysis of such conflicts would consequently provide a critical perspective on the normative bases of social cooperation, i.e., it would allow one to distinguish modes of normed cooperation in principle accessible to rational consent from those depending on direct or masked oppression.

But can the interest in conflict adjudication really explain the exact boundaries Habermas draws between the moral and the ethical or evaluative? That is, why is it that precisely the semantics and pragmatics of "good" happen to fall outside the scope of the universalizable (and hence rationally resolvable)? Is it so unreasonable to suppose that conceptions of the good life could converge—and by assuming they do not, does one not assume a rather individualistic approach to questions of the good life?

At one level Habermas takes it as a contemporary social fact that we live in a world populated by an irreducible variety of conceptions of the good life whose intersubjective binding force can no longer be grounded in a religious or metaphysical worldview acceptable to all. If this is our world, and if we still hope for a noncoercive form of social cooperation, it follows that moral norms must shoulder a much larger burden in the task of mutual understanding.

But such an argument lends an air of regret to the whole affair, as if it were simply a misfortune for modernity to have lost its sacred canopy. In fact, Habermas makes the much stronger claim that precisely a *rationalization* of traditional life forms—their becoming reflexive—leads to a postconventional separation of morality and ethics. It would be difficult enough simply to rehearse, let alone defend, the theory of modernity

9. NR, p. 118.
10. See chapter 1, section II.

backing this claim. The position can, however, be briefly stylized as follows. What individuals or groups perceive as their goods depend on their particular identities which emerge through concrete historical experiences. As soon as such identities—at a sufficient depth—encounter each other in the plural, the power any particular behavior expectation might have enjoyed within a group is relativized by the awareness of different expectations (for the issue at hand) existing within other groups. Hence if one is to base one's normative expectations about how members of the other groups should behave—to the extent of cooperating in a single society—on the rationally motivating force of validity claims, one can no longer appeal to conditions determining one's particular identity within a local group. In fact, this process works in *both* directions: if one cannot convince others that they ought to acknowledge some conception of the good life, it is difficult to maintain the initially unquestioned strength of one's own conviction—at least as a conviction having *moral* force. One is subsequently driven to relativize such convictions insofar as they turn out to be merely particular ideas. In argumentation-theoretic terms, claims based on particular conceptions of the good life simply cannot have the same kind of intersubjective force as claims finding universal assent. One has to distinguish between what is good for me (or my group) and what is (equally) good for all.[11]

Within a group, of course, ethical considerations will be relevant for noncoercive forms of social coordination. In fact, the above account does not rule out the possibility that even across diverse groups common substantive goods could emerge and play a role in intergroup cooperation—indeed, precisely as substantive *ethical* agreements on goals, i.e., agreements on what the two groups together want to become. Accordingly, Habermas now maintains that a full-blown analysis of rational consensus formation would have to pursue not only the moral dimensions of agreement but also ethical ones and, in addition, the elements of compromise most agreements involve. This holds especially for the analysis of political consensus formation in modern pluralist societies.[12] Nonetheless, the above analysis already entails a certain priority of moral con-

11. See EzD, pp. 206f; also FG, pp. 124–129. Note that I pass over Habermas's account of the learning processes leading to postmetaphysical thinking, as a result of which those kinds of validity claims still able to find universal assent have pulled apart from each other (into the separate spheres of science and morality) to such an extent that they can no longer support a single vision of the good life; cf. PT, pp. 3–53.
12. FG, chap. 4; EzD, pp. 200–201; also Jürgen Habermas, "Towards a Communication-Concept of Rational Collective Will-Formation: A Thought Experiment," *Ratio Juris* 2 (1989): 144–154.

siderations over ethical ones. To get at the essential point here, I will put things rather starkly: if our concern is settling conflicts (or regulating potential conflicts) so as to ensure a peaceful social cooperation, and if we need to settle such conflicts across varying conceptions of the good which cannot be ranked on a metaphysical basis, then we must reach these settlements on the basis of moral considerations. Moreover, if the individual and group pursuit of particular goods depends on others' cooperation, at least to the extent of noninterference, then such pursuit is possible (under conditions of rational cooperation) only insofar as moral considerations *allow* for it, i.e., only so far as the individual can bring his or her notion of the good into harmony with rules of cooperation acceptable to all.[13] It follows that the moral acceptability of the individual's pursuit of the good life is a condition for that pursuit.

From the standpoint of the theory of argument: if my pursuit of my own good depends on certain rules obligating your cooperation (at least your noninterference, but perhaps also your financial support in the way of taxes, etc.), then I can only get you to accept such rules rationally insofar as I can adduce arguments you find convincing. But, unless we happily agree on conceptions of the good, such arguments can only appeal to generalizable reasons, i.e., moral reasons. Such reasons might include arguments to the effect that, while most people do not share my good, my pursuit of it will make me a better member of society, and that therefore I ought to be supported in my pursuit (an argument claiming that my pursuit of my own good will at some point be equally good for all). Or I might argue that this good is essential to my identity, just as other goods are essential to yours, and human beings ought to be able to develop their identities. Note that the priority of moral considerations here follows only from a *dialogical* perspective: from the monological perspective of the single agent, moral considerations simply stand side-by-side with personal reasons as reasons for pursuing one course of action over another.[14] Once Kant's notion of the "good will" oriented by that which is absolutely good is no longer available, the priority of the moral has to be secured dialogically, in light of my need for your cooperation.

Two objections can be anticipated here. First, the above concept of

13. Note in this regard that insofar as social cooperation can be based on compromise, it must still refer, at least indirectly, to moral considerations governing the fairness of compromises; FG, pp. 204–207.

14. This is just the problem that Bernard Williams brings to the fore in his "Moral Luck," in *Moral Luck* (New York: Cambridge University Press, 1981), pp. 20–39; it lurks as well in Thomas Nagel, *The View from Nowhere* (New York: Oxford University Press, 1986).

morality might appear rather individualistic, its dialogicity notwithstanding. For it seems to suggest that each individual comes to moral
discourse with his or her conception of the good life, chosen in private
and from scratch, and then attempts to arrive at mutually constraining
rules of cooperation with other individuals who have likewise chosen
their goods privatistically. In response, we can note that the normative
issues moral discourse pulls out for direct thematization are originally
embedded in an entire network of tacit background expectations about
cooperation, in virtue of which alone individuals develop a sense of
themselves as individuals with an identity. Given the vulnerability of the
human creature, individuals develop identities and conceptions of the
good life only insofar as they can rely on each other for cooperation and
mutual recognition. Thus the above argumentation-theoretic account
should not be taken to imply that individuals achieve their identities
prior to any engagement in social cooperation. Rather, the variety of conceptions of the good life and identities have arisen only through pre-
existing structures of cooperation that have become threatened by conflict, however, and thus require explicitly discursive repair work.[15]

The second potential problem concerns the unconditional obligatory
character of moral norms. On the above account, it would appear that
a moral norm only obliges those who first choose social cooperation as
their good. This would make moral norms into hypothetical imperatives:
if in situation S you want to resolve conflicts peaceably and cooperate
with others, then follow norms X, Y, and Z, etc.[16] Granted, in dropping
Kant's rigid distinction between phenomenal and noumenal realms Habermas must relax the categorical quality of moral 'oughts'.[17] Nonetheless, the impression of conditionality painted above will have to be ad-
justed, a task I will take up in Chapter 6, when I address the question
whether a metagood of some sort underlies the entire discourse-ethical
enterprise. Before doing this, however, it is necessary to further clarify
the rather nuanced relationships moral discourse sets up vis-à-vis particular notions of the good life.

15. See JS, pp. 243–247; ME, pp. 199–202; for an image of individualistic discourse
attributed to Rawls, see Sandel, *Liberalism*, chap.1, for example.
16. This account thus falls short of *grounding* the moral point of view as prior, for it
would allow the "free rider" to take part in moral discourse simply to gain the strategic
advantages of cooperation. Conversely, it does not explain why we should worry about the
impact of our norms on others whose cooperation we do *not* require for our following of
the norm.
17. EzD, pp. 170–171.

III. THE RELEVANCE OF GOODS IN MORAL DISCOURSE

The above account implies that notions of the good life enter into moral discourse as *material*. Although in a moral discourse I do not argue that all ought to adopt my way of life or vision of the good, the degree and kind of cooperation I may expect of others as I pursue my good depends on the extent to which, and with what qualifications, others accept my pursuit of that good as making legitimate claims upon them. Conversely, in Chapter 3 we saw that the convincing justification of a norm must show that the norm will have acceptable consequences for the interests of each. In attempting to justify a norm to another, one must thus have a sense of the other's needs and wants, which is to say one must understand something of the other's notion of the good life. Moreover, in assessing the impact of a norm on those needs and wants one must appeal to values the other can accept as deserving recognition, indeed as having a certain priority in the type of situation falling under the norm. Only in terms of such values can one level legitimate claims on others' cooperation—if only to the extent of noninterference—in one's own pursuit of happiness.

Chapters 2 and 3 also indicated that, in taking notice of participants' interests and self-understandings, moral discourse may not impose any a priori restrictions on participants expressing their notions of the good life, or inquiring into the consequences of a norm for their own and others' good. Habermas actually insists on this point: "If the actors do not bring with them, and into their discourse, *their* individual life-histories, *their* identities, *their* needs and wants, *their* traditions, memberships, and so forth, practical discourse would at once be robbed of all content."[18] In fact, his formulation of (U) demands this lack of restriction: how else could participants determine that a norm was "equally good for all" or had "acceptable consequences for the satisfaction of *each* individual's interests" if each participant did not have some sense of the others' notions of the good life? Without this it would be impossible to evaluate whether a norm put someone else at a relative disadvantage. One can easily imagine, in the cases suggested earlier, that a participant might argue that a given norm proposal would have damaging consequences for her pursuit of the good life. If she proposed an alternative, she would have to convince others that this alternative did not wreak

18. "Critics," p. 255.

comparable damage on their pursuits and identities as the first norm proposed. If the situation in need of regulation was such that some detriment to interests could not be avoided, then the participants would have to enter into a joint assessment of the relative claims made by those interests. Such arguments and assessments could hardly convince if there were restrictions on the *material content* of moral argument.

The reference to such content, however, is not yet a specification of the substantive common good communitarians would like. Again, the participants are not primarily concerned that everyone else concretely adopt their own goals. Nonetheless, the fact that both moral and ethical discourses can involve the same material content certainly gives rise to ambiguities—in the heat of debate it is not so easy to distinguish moral and ethical questions. Thus it often occurs that one of the contested issues in a discourse turns on whether an issue is a moral one, with generally binding implications, or simply the particular perceptions of a single group presuming to speak for all. The difficult point at issue in such cases is the extent to which one can require cooperation of others in certain activities and pursuits, i.e., whether one's conception of a certain mode of social cooperation can be legitimately expected of others, or whether it expresses a merely particular conception of one's *own* good.

This difficulty recalls our earlier analysis of appetitive structures. We saw that moral norms have an internal relation to individual need interpretations, such that the values by which those norms are expressed—in terms of which they are internalized as "needs"—lie along a continuum of values stretching from the more particular to the more universal. Whereas our foregoing analysis of norms as conditions for cooperation highlighted their difference in kind vis-à-vis goods, here the term "continuum" suggests merely a *difference in degree*. In fact, the distinction I drew above between questions of justice and questions of the good life—in effect, a distinction between the "formal" and the "substantive"—is not so clear in practice as the analysis in section II of this chapter might suggest. Habermas too seems to suggest a clear distinction of this sort when he asserts that justice pertains to "those structural aspects of the good life that can be distinguished from the concrete totality of specific forms of life."[19] Elsewhere he suggests that moral norms differ from notions of the good life in that such norms delineate the rational form or

19. ME, p. 203. Elsewhere, however, he emphasizes the difference in degree: "Moral judgments differ from ethical ones only in the degree to which they are independent of context"; EzD, p. 219.

the "*necessary* conditions for such a life."[20] Yet no concrete norm, be it ever so particular and culture-bound, comes with the label "For formal purposes only"—or what amounts to the same difficulty, just about all of them bill themselves as indispensably "necessary for rational living." For this reason it is usually only the *process* of discourse itself that separates moral from ethical claims, as those admitting of consensus from those able to find assent only within a particular tradition. When interests conflict, it is at first an open question whether each person can cast his or her interests in terms of values the others can affirm as normatively binding (even if only at a very abstract level). It can often happen that how one first describes one's interests involves values either unintelligible or unacceptable to others, but that dialogue shows one how the others' values can actually be used to express one's own interest, thereby opening the way to some kind of consensus.

This suggests that, from the standpoint of the competing interests and notions of the good life that underlie action conflicts, the distinguishing feature of *morally* relevant interests, values and goods (or the morally relevant aspect of these) is that they in some fashion permit the participants to *converge* on an action norm regulating the conditions of their pursuit. That is, participants are able to see in these goods and interests legitimate claims on their mutual cooperation. So long as the discursive process can distill out points of mutual recognition sufficient to ground common expectations about the "formal conditions" for each person's pursuit of happiness, moral discourse has a point. Such agreements leave each participant free to reconcile the explicit consensus with, and interpret it in terms of, his or her own "thicker" understanding of the good life. Here we can anticipate the kind of moral self-identity discourse ethics requires of participants in a moral discourse: a moral consensus requires that these thicker conceptual commitments and self-understandings—in short, need interpretations—be flexible enough to allow participants to adopt the moral point of view in a conflict situation, such that at least some aspects of their lifestyles and identities are open to a cooperative, discursive testing. Only if it can be shown that one's *entire* identity and outlook are *inflexibly* involved in each justice

20. Jürgen Habermas, "Questions and Counter-Questions," in *Habermas and Modernity*, ed. with an Introduction by Richard J. Bernstein (Cambridge: MIT Press, 1985), pp. 192–216; here p. 215; also see "Critics," pp. 262–263. In EzD, p. 174, Habermas appears to go even further when he claims that basic moral norms "regulate [*normieren*] precisely the necessary pragmatic presuppositions of communicative action . . ."

question will discourse ethics appear hopelessly quixotic.[21] Assuming some such flexibility, the real issue in a moral discourse then concerns the extent to which another's outlook and identity amount to a claim on one's own.

We can take the above reflections one step further by asking whether and in what sense moral discourse actually *fashions*, or requires participants to fashion, their interests and values. Even if, strictly speaking, it is not the business of moral discourse to decide what constitutes the good of human life, such discourse certainly affects each participant's pursuit of the good. If nothing else, moral norms limit what goals one may pursue and how one may pursue these. This means that moral discourse may well bump up against ethical issues and perhaps even require a move into an ethical discourse. (This would occur, for example, if either party thought the other to be deceived about its values and concept of the good life so grievously that it hindered reasonable cooperation.) As far as moral discourse as such is concerned, we might say that it *sets limits* to the pursuit of individual happiness in that it makes cooperation with others' pursuit of happiness a condition for the pursuit of one's own happiness. Insofar as such limits rest on a jointly affirmed value (or the mutual affirmation of one another's values), however, they contrast with mere compromise, as well as with consensus as *modus vivendi*. This point, which leads into a discussion of solidarity, is important enough to deserve some illustration.

Consider first the example of welfare legislation. Insofar as I accept such legislation as morally required, I accept reductions in my income (through redistributive taxation) so as to allow those less fortunate some chance at a decent life. No concrete specification of anyone's happiness need be accepted here, yet I limit my pursuit of some goods for the sake of cooperation with others' pursuit of their goods. (Of course, for some this might not be seen as a limitation at all, if contributing to the poor actually constitutes a good in itself for them.) At the same time, I positively endorse an overarching value to the point of considering it a requirement of justice: the value of each individual's having access to the minimum material conditions of life makes a justice claim on me. In *this* sense, then, one might say moral discourse refers to and even issues in something like a "common good"—à la Rawls's concept of "primary good," only without the a priori restriction to a definite list of goods. A more accurate description, however, would be something like "interest-

---

21. Cf. EzD, pp. 216–218.

regulating value," i.e., a value in connection with which each one's pursuit of his or her happiness or good can be endorsed by others. The role such values play in mediating rational consensus likewise recalls Rawls's idea of primary goods, for these constitute the basic terms of argument inside the original position.[22] Habermas refers to such values as "generalized values" or "abstract basic values."[23] We might also call them "moral values," to distinguish them from more particularistic cultural values. Moral values include, for example, the values connected with the satisfaction of basic needs, the exercise of basic freedoms, the development of one's human capacities, and so on. Such values allow one to give expression to generalizable interests, "interests it is . . . in everyone's interest that everyone should have."[24]

The welfare example suggests that the moral value at stake has a certain bite inasmuch as it may require some people to readjust their expectations about how freely they can pursue their own lifestyle. It is important to see here that such readjustment, as resting on the positive endorsement of such values, goes beyond that required by a *modus vivendi*.[25] This can be further illustrated with a rather classic example. Consider a religious group that believes its claim to truth so absolute as to justify the exclusion of nonadherents from full participation in society (e.g., from public office, teaching positions, and so on). Should it lack the political means of enforcing such exclusionary practices, this group might nonetheless tolerate an open society for the sake of broader social cooperation—thus as a *modus vivendi*. Its cooperation only becomes *moral* in the discourse-ethical sense, however, when it rests on a positive recognition of the nonadherents' religious freedom—the moral or "interest-regulating" value that then *positively shapes* the religious group's pursuit of its interest in evangelization. Such a recognition probably could not occur without some adjustment in this group's self-understanding.[26]

22. See Rawls, "Priority," pp. 255–258.
23. *Discourse*, pp. 344, 345.
24. Braaten, *Habermas's Critical Theory*, p. 34.
25. Cf., for example, the discussion of *modus vivendi* in Larmore, *Patterns of Moral Complexity*, pp. 70–77, where it is understood as a means of political accommodation that does not require a change in one's personal ideals.
26. Precisely this shift, from a view of religious freedom as a "second best" solution to an intrinsic value, was accomplished in the Roman Catholic Church during the 1950s and 1960s, primarily through the writings of John Courtney Murray; it is doubtful that the shift could have occurred without painstaking efforts on Murray's part to argue for a new understanding of the Catholic tradition on this issue; see J. Leon Hooper, *The Ethics of Discourse: The Social Philosophy of John Courtney Murray* (Washington, D.C.: Georgetown University Press, 1986).

If endorsement of such moral values, however, does not amount to agreement on a substantive conception of the good life (or substantive common good), neither does it automatically specify a concrete moral norm. There may be a few exceptions to this. The values of human life and physical integrity, for example, seem immediately connected to the very abstract norms 'Thou shalt not kill' and 'Do harm to no one'— though these norms hardly exhaust the content of the values they incor- porate. In any case, a cautionary note is necessary here as a corrective to the above account. So far I have cast the consensus problem primarily as one of agreeing on those values the appeal to which will convince each person a proposed norm of definite content is justified. Normally this appeal to values is itself quite complex; perhaps more often the values are embedded in the assessment of a norm's consequences for interests. Values come into play both in the assessment itself and in the selection and description of interests. However, one could turn the problem around, supposing that the participants agreed in principle on the values at stake but could not settle on how those values were best incorporated in a concrete norm. Even abstract norms such as those just mentioned admit of many historically specific variations, such that participants in a historically situated discourse might agree to the abstract norm yet re- main vehemently at odds over the question, say, of capital punishment. By moral value, then, I mean values at once too abstract to spell out a substantive common good and too underdetermined to specify any one particular norm (at least beyond a certain point of abstraction). In Chap- ter 8 I shall discuss the ramifications such underdetermination might have for reaching consensus under time limitations.

IV. SOLIDARITY AND MORAL VALUES

The upshot of the foregoing discussion is that the endorsement of a moral value (or values) mediates consensus on a moral norm. While such en- dorsement might be spoken of as an agreement on a common good, it does not necessarily prescribe substantive notions of the good life for all participants. Now one use of the term "solidarity" suggests just such pos- itive concern for someone's welfare on the part of those who do not nec- essarily concretely pursue those same goods in their own lives. Those "in solidarity" with some other person or group may be quite removed in terms of the actual concrete goods and interests shaping their own lives; the Manhattan office worker, for example, may have very little imme- diately at stake in the Salvadoran peasants' struggle for land or a decent

wage. The office worker is neither a farmer nor interested in foreign ag-
ricultural investment; moreover, the success of the peasants' struggle may
even lead to increases in the office worker's cost of living. At the same
time, the office worker may go beyond a merely wishful sympathy, actually supporting the Salvadorans by efforts to affect U.S. policy. In this
sense, being in solidarity may involve a certain active support of the other's pursuit of happiness, so that one does in some sense share the other's
good.

Hence there is indeed good reason to believe that "discourse ethics,
though organized around a concept of procedure, can be expected to say
something relevant about substance as well and . . . about the hidden
link between justice and the common good."[27] We have already pointed
out the argumentation-theoretic roots of solidarity in the principle of universalization (U). There solidarity appeared in a rather thin form as the
demand that the individual submit his or her moral reflections to all
those affected. The point was that my own formation of a moral will
cannot remain solely within the confines of my own conscience, but must
be an intersubjective result. In the present section I shall attempt to flesh
this out a bit in light of the foregoing analysis. Inasmuch as Habermas
proposes the concept of solidarity as his response to communitarian and
feminist critiques of deontological moral theory,[28] we should expect to
find links with our own analysis.

Habermas calls on the notion of solidarity to argue that the discourse-
ethical concept of justice actually includes references to individual welfare and the common good. In doing so, he emphasizes that solidarity is
not something additional to justice, but is rather "its reverse side."[29] The
reformulation of (U) in Chapter 3 clearly highlights this two-sided character of the moral point of view: there we saw that rational consensus on
a norm requires that (a) each of those affected can convince the others,
in terms they hold appropriate, that the norm is acceptable for all; and
(b) each can be convinced by all, in terms she or he considers appropriate,
that the norm is acceptable for all. The analysis showed that *both* moments are indivisibly joined in the notion of rational conviction. But then
how does this square with Habermas's suggestion that *three* items are
tacit in moral discourse: respect for individual autonomy; concern for
the welfare of the individual; and concern for the integrity of the shared
lifeworld? That is, Habermas understands solidarity as bidirectional, so

27. ME, p. 202.
28. See ME and JS.
29. JS, p. 244.

to speak, for it encompasses both a concern for a (thin) common good
(or group/lifeworld integrity) and a concern for the individual's good.[30]
Thus far, however, we have explicated the argumentation-theoretic core
of solidarity simply in terms of the demand that each individual submit
his or her proposals for the consideration of all.

A concern for individual welfare can be seen in the empathetic character of solidarity. Habermas links such empathy with justice as follows:

> The agreement made possible by discourse depends on two things: the indi-
> vidual's inalienable right to say yes or no and his overcoming of his egocentric
> viewpoint. Without the individual's uninfringeable freedom to respond with
> a "yes" or "no" to criticizable validity claims, consent is merely factual rather
> than truly universal. Conversely, without the empathetic sensitivity by each
> person to everyone else, no solution deserving universal consent will result
> from the deliberation. These two aspects—the autonomy of inalienable in-
> dividuals and their embeddedness in an intersubjectively shared web of rela-
> tions—are internally connected, and it is this link that the procedure of dis-
> cursive decision making takes into account.[31]

We saw in Chapter 3 that rational conviction requires not simply the bare
agreement of all, but their rationally motivated agreement, and in such
a way that my consent cannot be rationally motivated as long as I lack
the confidence that yours is rationally motivated. This ties rational consent to "empathetic sensitivity," i.e., to an understanding of the other sufficient to allow an insight into the rationality of the other's consent. As
we have seen, such sensitivity involves an understanding of and concern
for the other's needs and wants—in short, the welfare of each individual
one hopes to convince of the validity of a norm. Moreover, such concern
is only analytically distinct from the moment of justice, for it is precisely
each *individual's* rationally motivated agreement that one seeks in fashioning empathetically sensitive arguments. If justice can be defined in
terms of the individual's rights and dignity, then its argumentation-
theoretic core consists in the fact that each individual enjoys an equal
right to adopt a yes- or no-position to a proposed norm.

In order to get at the further connection between justice and solidarity
as concern for the common good, Habermas turns to the dual anthropological function of morality:

> Since moralities are tailored to suit the fragility of human beings individuated
> through socialization, they must always solve *two* tasks at *once*. They must
> emphasize the inviolability of the individual by postulating equal respect for

30. See ME, p. 200, for example.
31. ME, p. 202.

the dignity of each individual. But they must also protect the web of inter-subjective relations of mutual recognition by which these individuals survive as members of a community.[32]

This takes us beyond our focus on the theory of argument. Suffice it to note here that the individual only develops a secure identity, or self-understanding, in virtue of *others'* recognition.[33] The self, then, depends on others, is vulnerable before others. Modern "justice" moralities have traditionally served to protect the vulnerable individual by carving out a space within which the individual may freely act as a possessor of rights. This approach emphasizes negative duties as those restrictions necessary to preserve an equal freedom for each.[34] Because such moralities often took the isolated, sovereign subject as their point of departure, however, the solidaristic moment could only enter in a second, subordinate stage, when individuals freely chose by contract to enter a community or polity.[35] This makes such one-sided justice moralities vulnerable to Sandel's criticism that they employ an untenable notion of the human being as an "antecedently individuated" self. Habermas's notion of solidarity addresses just this problem, for it brings out the *prior* social ties that were present all along but overlooked by subject-centered justice moralities. The point is that individuals only possess their autonomy, are only able to make rights claims and enter into contracts, in virtue of their prior mutual recognition of one another. Such "relations of mutual recognition" involve both a concern for one another's welfare as individuals and a reliance on a social network within which such recognition alone makes sense. Therefore, protecting individual freedom must also include the protection of individual welfare and the broader social bonds that make up the lifeworld.

Unfortunately, pointing out this anthropological function does not show how such concern for the common good is reflected in rational conviction itself. Nor is this question addressed when Habermas writes that solidarity "is rooted in the realization that each person must take responsibility for the other because as consociates all must have an interest in the integrity of their shared life context in the same way."[36] While this explicitly links concern for individual welfare and concern for group integrity, it must move outside the theory of argument to do so. But

32. ME, p. 200.
33. See PT, pp. 169ff.
34. Habermas makes this point in EzD, pp. 167f.
35. This is quite clear in Locke, *An Essay Concerning the True Original, Extent, and End of Civil Government* II 4, 6, 14, 15; for example, in *The English Philosophers from Bacon to Mill*, ed. Edwin A. Burtt (New York: Modern Library, 1967), pp. 403–503.
36. JS, p. 244.

how is such concern for a common good already implicit in the argumentation-theoretic core of solidarity?

The answer to this should be clear from the previous section. There we saw that moral consensus depends on the positive endorsement of certain basic values. As values that mediate the common recognition of certain interests (or goods) as making a legitimate claim on all, as well as mediating the acceptability of a norm's consequences for those interests, they represent a kind of abstract agreement on what is "equally good for all." They thus allow each to see a norm as incorporating a general interest. In this sense one can speak of a "common good" in the norm itself. This points to the very close connection between individual welfare and the common good, for the norm (if observed) preserves cooperation in a lifeworld around the recognition of values in connection with which each individual's welfare becomes the concern of all. Moreover, in thus undergirding the norms that structure a common lifeworld, these basic moral values are socially reproduced and personally internalized insofar as the norms are obeyed.

A second problem is potentially more troublesome. By defining solidarity in terms of the relations of mutual recognition that preserve the identity of a form of life, Habermas does not always adequately distinguish specifically *moral* solidarities from the more substantive, prereflective lifeworld solidarities that do not extend beyond this or that particular group.[37] What I have said so far recommends a distinction in terms of the relative abstractness or scope of the relevant values. Particularistic lifeworld solidarities bind together families, social classes, consociates at various kinds of work and play, and even national and ethnic groups. (Here one should probably not look for more than "family resemblances" among the various ways in which the different kinds of groups cohere.) The shared values binding the members of such groups are embedded in particular goals, experiences, and traditions shared by members but not necessarily by others. The basic values constituting moral solidarities, however, overreach such limits, at least in principle. To be sure, any given group will have come by its moral values through historically particular learning processes, and often such values first reside in particular traditions alongside less generalizable values. But the validity of moral values ultimately outstrips their genesis, and their force for preserving cooperation extends beyond group boundaries.

---

37. Habermas does draw the distinction, though without the labels I will give it, in *Discourse*, pp. 344–345.

We can thus distinguish between *concrete lifeworld solidarities* on the one hand and *specific moral solidarities* on the other—"specific" in that they coalesce around determinate moral values. The latter are no less observable for being moral or "abstract." They exercise their force as often as one accords basic rights to persons outside one's social class or ethnic group, as often as one displays civility and a willingness to cooperate with strangers, or as often as one willingly contributes to those in need.

To summarize, then, the discourse-ethical concept of rational consensus harbors at least three elements. First, a rational consensus requires *each* participant's rational conviction, which makes each participant's uncoerced, autonomous "yes" indispensable. This represents the rational core of justice, understood as regard for the equal freedom of each individual. Second, in seeking to convince another, a participant must be concerned that the other's conviction rests on arguments whose terms are appropriate to the other's need interpretation, i.e., arguments that do not distort the perception of the other's welfare. Third, however, participants can neither recognize each other's needs and wants, nor argue that a norm's observance has acceptable consequences for those needs and wants, unless they recognize values in terms of which each one's welfare becomes the concern of all, i.e., a generalizable interest calling for and structuring social cooperation. These last two elements constitute the kernel of solidarity. In solidarity, then, the empathetic concern for the individual's welfare is inseparable from justice, the normative basis of group cooperation.

This account of solidarity raises two questions. First, if individual welfare becomes a concern only insofar as it can be connected with quite general values and norms structuring cooperation in a lifeworld as a whole, the suspicion arises that discourse ethics is susceptible to a rigoristic disregard for particular context and the goods of particular relationships. Like other neo-Kantian and liberal moral-political theories, discourse ethics too remains bound, so it seems, to an impartialism that must level out and ultimately disregard the unique differences between individuals. This question, which calls for a lengthier investigation of the current debate between the ethics of care and neo-Kantianism, I shall take up in Part Three (Chapter 7). Still to be addressed in this part (Chapters 5 and 6) is the question whether the suggested anthropological functions of morality indicate that a notion of the good of human life underlies discourse ethics after all.

Discourse Ethics and the Good

We opened Part Two by asking about the relation between justice and the good in discourse ethics. After noting a difference in kind between justice questions and questions of the good life, we saw that the latter, though properly the subject of ethical discourse, are nonetheless relevant to moral discourses about justice issues. By probing this relevance we discovered that one can actually speak of moral discourse shaping a thin common good insofar as agreement on norms depends on the positive endorsement of certain, perhaps quite abstract, values that shape cooperation in a common lifeworld. At the same time, one must still speak of a priority of "right" in discourse ethics insofar as individuals' pursuit of their particular conceptions of the good life was set within bounds of cooperation agreed to in moral discourse, i.e., a cooperation each could affirm as just.

In this chapter I want to raise once again the question of such priority, only in a different sense. I take the question above all from Charles Taylor: does discourse ethics as a whole presuppose or amount to a theory of the good? To answer this, we must move across entire argumentative strategies in a single swoop, so as to get a bird's-eye view of their overall significance and structure. We have already done something like this in Chapter 1. Here the point is not so much to determine whether this or that argument in fact works as to understand what it intends and how it bears on Taylor's question. All the same, even this much will prove an ambitious undertaking, since it in effect requires us to assess and compare entire research programs. In addition, it requires us to discern the deeper sources, the often unthematized, quickly executed moves lying at the edges of explicit argumentation. Difficult as this appears, I do not see how it can be avoided, if some response to Taylor is to be made. I want to start by distinguishing the relevant question of priority from a number of other ways in which it can be posed (section I). We can then turn to Charles Taylor for one of the more forceful arguments for the view that the good is prior to the right for discourse ethics as a whole (section II). In order to prepare the ground for a discourse-ethical response to this challenge, a brief excursus into Rawls's treatment of the issue will be made. This will help us to appreciate the programmatic intentions of Habermas's project, and how it goes beyond Rawls's (section III).

I. QUESTIONS OF PRIORITY

One of the difficulties plaguing current debates in moral and political theory lies in the many senses in which one can ask whether the good or the right has primacy. I have already attempted to differentiate some of these senses in the Introduction, albeit against a somewhat broader background. It will be helpful here to specify these for the particular context.

In the previous chapter we have actually addressed two forms of this question. One of these we might describe as having to do with the relation between two practical questions. In situations where one's own pursuit of happiness affects others and thus harbors a conflict potential, a Kantian notion of moral obligation or duty constrains or subordinates that pursuit by the consideration of what all those affected can rationally accept. That is, in considering whether to pursue a particular course of action in such situations, one must first answer the question, Will this action adversely affect others? *before* one asks, Will it make me happy? The priority here is practical-logical, not temporal. It refers to the overriding character of moral (justice) considerations in cases where moral and ethical considerations conflict. As Allen Buchanan has pointed out, communitarian attempts to contravene the prima facie priority of justice considerations at this level have a regressive appearance, since they appear to open the door to totalitarianism. A more relevant question would focus on whether concrete cases could call for exceptions to the priority of justice, an issue I shall address in Chapter 7.[1]

1. See Buchanan, "Assessing the Communitarian Critique of Liberalism."

The other notion of priority addressed in Chapter 4 was contained in something like the following question: before participants to a moral discourse agree to a given norm N, must they first have agreed to a given good G? For example, before they can agree that taking innocent life is wrong, must they not agree that innocent life is a good? Or before they can accept a norm against stealing, must they not agree that property is good? Now our discussion of moral values and the thin common good contained in the discourse-ethical concept of solidarity indicates that, in a rather qualified sense, the good is prior to justice here. For, as we saw, fashioning convincing arguments for a norm depends on the participants' ability to agree that certain interests make a legitimate claim on all, and agreement on this has to be mediated by value terms. Insofar as such values mediate one's concern for the other's welfare, as well as one's assent to the norms that structure cooperation in a common lifeworld, one might say that they represent "abstract goods," assent to which underlies consensus on a norm. While this does not mean that one can argue directly from a good to a norm, something like a qualified priority of good is implicit in (U) itself, which bases normative validity on the participants' ability to accept the consequences of a norm as "equally good for all." Norms against murder and stealing are thus acceptable precisely insofar as they have the "consequence" of protecting goods all can recognize as important.

Now as I have tried to indicate, this last point does not justify any hasty inference to the claim that moral consensus presupposes a prior "thick" consensus on substantive goods. It may well be the case, of course, that such a consensus will facilitate a real discourse. In principle, however, the specific goods and values participants attend to in fashioning arguments are open to debate, and—at least insofar as they represent *moral* values capable of incorporation in generally binding norms—are as much created as discovered.[2] Thus the more difficult priority question lies at a different level.

To get at this level notice that both of the above ways of posing the priority question make important assumptions. The first assumes that one accepts a Kantian account of practical reasoning and morality, the second, that people are willing to enter a moral discourse. Hence one can reframe the priority question at a higher level by asking whether these prior acceptances (of Kantian morality, of the discourse-ethical proce-

---

2. Habermas makes this point in terms of generalizable interests, "A Postscript to *Knowledge and Human Interests*," p. 177.

dure) do not presuppose the acceptance of some good. The acceptance of Kantian morality is challenged by the classic question, Why be moral? The acceptance of discourse ethics can be challenged by the question, Must one's rational acceptance of discourse ethics presuppose that one first accepts some conception of the good of human life or society? Framed in this way, the latter question addresses the theoretical basis of discourse ethics. One could also reframe the question in more praxis-oriented, or motivational, terms as follows: What are the presuppositions for people actually accepting and carrying out discourse-ethical procedures for conflict resolution? I shall say something about this issue in Chapter 8. To better appreciate the force of such questions, let us turn to Charles Taylor.

II. CHARLES TAYLOR: THE PRIORITY OF GOOD

In his recent *Sources of the Self* Charles Taylor begins by drawing our attention to those background frameworks that constitute human agency and personhood. Such frameworks provide one with that sense of identity indispensable to, and at stake in, moral deliberation: "My identity is defined by the commitments and identifications which provide the frame or horizon within which I can try to determine from case to case what is good, or valuable, or what ought to be done, or what I endorse or oppose."[3] What is more, the self-understanding or sense of identity bound up with such frameworks provides practical orientation only in virtue of the "strong evaluations" or "strongly valued goods" making up the framework. According to Taylor, the fact that one must have a sense of such identity-defining goods and be able to locate where one stands in relation to them amounts to a "transcendental" condition of practical deliberation.[4] Even those who object to the language of transcendentality can admit that a mature self-understanding and capacity for moral choice must involve something like constitutive background languages and the ability to articulate one's choices and goals—"life plans," to use Rawls's term—in relation to the goods such languages delineate.

Taylor distinguishes such strongly valued goods, or "life goods," from merely arbitrary and subjective preferences.[5] Contrary to utilitarians

3. Taylor, *Sources of the Self*, p. 27.
4. Taylor, *Sources*, pp. 29–44; the cited terms are found on pp. 29 and 32, resp., while Taylor uses the term "transcendental" on pp. 32, 38.
5. See Taylor's "What Is Human Agency?"

such as Hare who attempt to distinguish the properly evaluative (or "prescriptive") aspect of such goods from their descriptive aspect, Taylor argues that one cannot separate the descriptive grasp of such goods from an understanding of the evaluation they contain. At the level of pure description, one cannot distinguish the class of courageous acts from foolhardy ones, for example, if one does not already grasp the evaluative point of "courage." This grasp involves two things: an understanding of the kind of "social interchange" at stake in the evaluation and a perception of the good at stake. To understand the point of courage, then, one must have a sense of the requirements of those risky situations in which one might act courageously; and one must see the good involved in selflessly risking one's own life in order to preserve the lives of others.[6]

Up to this point, Taylor's analysis does not necessarily compete with that of Habermas, and could even help to elaborate the latter's notion of ethical-hermeneutical discourse. Even when strong evaluations pertain to justice issues, Taylor's analysis of the internal relation between description and evaluation does not differ radically from our own account of the internal link between moral norms and values. Rather, we have to follow Taylor a step further to see his real challenge to discourse ethics.

This challenge arises when Taylor argues that morality as a whole depends on a certain conception of the good. Precisely in its attempt to define the moral domain in terms of justice and then give this domain priority over questions of the good life, modern moral theory, discourse ethics included, actually ends up giving certain life goods an overriding priority. Those life goods that attain such "unique importance" Taylor terms "'hypergoods', i.e., goods which not only are incomparably more important than others but provide the standpoint from which these must be weighed, judged, decided about."[7] To press this point further, he goes on to ask whether modern moral theory not only elevates certain life goods but, even more radically, depends on an unacknowledged "constitutive good" that first constitutes its life goods as such. Some historical examples can illustrate what Taylor means by such a good. For Plato the Idea of the Good was the constitutive reality in terms of which alone any other thing or action could acquire the designation "good." For Christian Platonists, God occupied this spot. Such a constitutive good not only

6. Taylor, *Sources*, pp. 53–55; Taylor does not actually introduce the term "life good" until p. 93.
7. Taylor, *Sources*, p. 63; cf. also pp. 88 and 93, where Taylor calls the goods underlying modern moral theory (freedom, altruism, universalism) first "hypergoods" (p. 88), then "life goods" (p. 93).

constitutes other goods in a theoretical sense, but also is their motivational "moral source," in that love of it "empowers us to do and be good."[8]

Modern moral theory is no exception, despite its repudiation of the good. Kant, for example, simply internalized the constitutive good in rational agency. To be sure, this is not the only possible basis of modern morality; some forms of modern humanism depend on something like the good of maintaining a "courageous disengagement" before a meaningless universe.[9] In any case, for any given moral theory some good of this sort constitutes the other values and goods prominent in the theory (such as freedom, universal justice, and so on), as well as motivating adherence to that theory. Only by articulating this good can one answer the question, Why be moral? And it is precisely because modern moral theory is inarticulate about its moral sources that it cannot answer this question—with the result that moral action appears as just one choice or good among others. To rephrase the question for discourse ethics, one can ask, Why adopt the goal of mutual understanding to begin with? As Taylor puts it, "I nevertheless also have other aims, other interests. Why then should I prefer rational mutual understanding? Why should precisely this aim occupy a special position?" To answer this, one must show "why it is I attach a value to rational understanding so great that it *should* be preferred to all other purposes."[10] Precisely in the attempt to abstract from such goods in the search for a generally binding decision procedure, however, modern moral theories such as discourse ethics "leave us with nothing to say to someone who asks why he should be moral or strive to the 'maturity' of a 'post-conventional' ethic."[11]

In short, Taylor proposes the thesis that both moral norms and life goods are set within an *evaluative* framework that alone determines the

8. Taylor, *Sources*, pp. 92–94; the citation is found on p. 93; cf. also pp. 307ff. The relation between hypergoods and constitutive goods is not altogether clear, since constitutive goods seem both to ground hypergoods (insofar as the latter are taken from a range of life goods) and to overlap with hypergoods (Plato's Good is both a hypergood and a constitutive good; cf. pp. 70, 93). In his "Comments and Replies" to criticisms of *Sources*, the important distinction seems to be that between life goods and constitutive goods; see *Inquiry* 34 (1991): 237–254, esp. p. 243.

9. Taylor, *Sources*, p. 94; also pp. 75–87, 404–413. This critique of modern moral theory also appeared earlier in Taylor's "Justice after Virtue."

10. Charles Taylor, "Language and Society," in *Communicative Action*, ed. Honneth and Joas, p. 31. At certain points I have amended the English translation of Taylor's article (a translation not made by Taylor himself) according to the original version, "Sprache und Gesellschaft," in *Kommunikatives Handeln: Beiträge zu Jürgen Habermas' "Theorie des kommunikativen Handelns,"* ed. Axel Honneth and Hans Joas (Frankfurt: Suhrkamp, 1986), pp. 32–52.

11. Taylor, *Sources*, p. 87.

point of such norms and goods. Hence he sets the moral domain firmly *within* the ethical, to use Habermas's terminology.[12] Now as I read Taylor, the considerations in Chapter 4 do not suffice to respond to such a challenge. In Chapter 4 we assumed the need for or value of rational conflict resolution; here precisely the grounds of this value—and hence of the very definition of the moral domain—are at stake. Taylor's thesis thus calls for a separate investigation.

There are actually two sides to his thesis, or rather two approaches to it, one more theoretical, the other more practical and motivational. Although one cannot ultimately separate these, I want to take a theoretical approach here, regarding Taylor's claim as a thesis about what the proponent of discourse ethics must presuppose in an attempt to argue for discourse ethics, i.e., to ground the rational acceptance of a discourse-ethical approach to conflict resolution.[13] We would misconstrue Taylor's question and sever theory from motivation, however, if we were to understand him as claiming that such evaluative frameworks and underlying goods amount to more "basic reasons," the appeal to which could "prove" a given moral theory. That being said, however, Taylor does hold that articulating such goods and frameworks shows why certain moral intuitions "command assent."[14] For a theory of rational consensus that rejects deductivistic models of argumentation, the conditions for such assent can hardly be swept aside as factors external to a rational reconstruction of such consensus. In any case, we can formulate the theoretical problem as the following: if accepting a discourse-ethical procedure depends on the prior acceptance of some hypergood or constitutive conception of the good of human life, then it would seem that discourse ethics depends on prematurely settling a competition among conceptions of the good. In that case discourse ethics either presupposes as settled precisely the kind of issue it claims one cannot settle in universally binding terms, or it presupposes as indisputable precisely the kind of thin conception of the common good which it claims should be the *result* of moral discourse.

According to Taylor, this problem surfaces as a "strange pragmatic

12. Cf. Taylor, *Sources*, pp. 532f n66, where Taylor considers the neo-Kantian domain distinction to be "based on a deep misapprehension about the nature of morality."
13. Taylor, "Language," p. 33, notes this close connection between the theoretical and the practical; ibid., p. 30, poses the theoretical question as one of justification; Taylor highlights the practical side of the question in his "Cross-Purposes: The Liberal-Communitarian Debate," in *Liberalism and the Moral Life*, ed. Roseblum, pp. 159–182. For a discussion of Taylor's practical critique as involving a claim about the social preconditions for liberalism, see Kymlicka, *Liberalism*, pp. 74–99.
14. Taylor, *Sources*, p. 87; also pp. 76–79.

contradiction" in attempts to abstract morality from questions of the good.[15] We can see this contradiction in the dilemmas facing proponents of liberal neutrality. In that context the question arises as to how one can "neutrally justify" liberal moral-political theories claiming to be neutral vis-à-vis competing conceptions of the good. A consistent neutrality theory, it seems, would undermine its very claim to neutrality if its justification rested on nonneutral grounds—for example, if it presupposed the acceptance of one of the competing conceptions of the good. In fact, it is generally recognized that wholly neutral justifications are impossible; even Charles Larmore's attempt at a "neutral justification of political neutrality" must draw on a commitment to dialogue and a fairly substantive notion of equal respect, as Larmore himself makes clear.[16] Without entangling ourselves in the issue of neutrality, we can see that an analogous difficulty faces anyone who proposes a discourse-ethical conflict resolution, should it turn out that discourse ethics depends on a limited conception of the good not shared by all those involved in the conflict. If, as Taylor suggests, discourse ethics tacitly selects just one hypergood among several influential hypergoods in Western culture, then it cannot ground rational consensus in cases where precisely such a conflict between hypergoods is at issue.[17] For in proposing that the parties to the conflict adopt a discourse-ethical procedure one would have already decided the outcome in relevant respects.

The above suggests that an issue in the justification or grounding of moral theory has serious implications for the analysis of rational conflict resolution. Precisely such implications bring out the real relevance of Taylor's analysis for the present study, which is concerned with the conditions of rational moral consensus. Does this mean that a reply to Taylor depends on a full and direct justification of the discourse ethics enterprise, i.e., on a formal-pragmatic analysis showing that the discourse principle (D) is implicit in everyday communicative action? If the answer to this question is yes, then a discourse-ethical rebuttal lies beyond the scope of this study. Nonetheless, we can ask whether Habermas's communications-theoretic approach, *should* it succeed, commits him to

---

15. Taylor, *Sources*, p. 88; cf. also his "Justice after Virtue," pp. 28f.

16. See Larmore, *Patterns of Moral Complexity*, pp. 53–65; for an overview of debates on the neutrality issue, see Richardson, "The Problem of Liberalism and the Good," pp. 15–20; for a critical perspective, see Reiner Grundmann and Christos Mantziaris, "Fundamentalist Intolerance or Civil Disobedience? Strange Loops in Liberal Theory," *Political Theory* 19 (1991): 572–605.

17. Taylor argued this earlier in "The Diversity of Goods" and "The Nature and Scope of Distributive Justice."

a constitutive good in the way Taylor claims. Before turning to this investigation, however, we must get as firm a grip as possible on the problem Taylor raises.

The first point to note, then, is that the above dilemma points to an alternate model of rational conflict resolution. Surely a conflict between goods, one of which constituted discourse ethics, would call for a different form of rational conflict resolution than that provided by a discourse-ethical procedure inasmuch as one of the contested goods is whether one should adopt just such a procedure. This, I think, is precisely Taylor's point: that contemporary society is beset by conflicts at the level of such goods, conflicts in which impartial moral approaches are themselves caught—such that they cannot stand above them as they allege. One cannot begin to resolve such conflicts if one has not first of all simply understood their origins in the various traditions making up the conflicted modern identity—hence Taylor's lengthy investigation in *Sources of the Self*.[18] To carry through an actual conflict resolution—if it is possible—one would presumably have to show either how one of the constitutive goods takes precedence in the conflict situation, or how the various conflicting goods can harmoniously coexist—which again would seem to require an account showing which good takes precedence in which situations and to what extent.

Second, the above kind of conflict resolution would reverse the relation between the moral and the ethical, for Taylor has more in mind than the kind of consideration of goods required by discourse ethics. Rather than enjoining on the participants in a conflict resolution a perspective taking aimed at locating those thin values and points of mutual understanding that would allow further cooperation, Taylor's model would apparently require participants to work out a shared *substantive* identity or framework within which conflicting goods are rightly ordered. Such a framework goes beyond the discussion of key terms and mutual empathetic understanding implied by (U). Rather, Taylor would seemingly have to insist that a rational conflict resolution presupposes a substantive framework able to command general assent. But how can such assent be gained if detached models of moral argumentation are inadequate in the way that thinkers such as Taylor and MacIntyre maintain? Since both still want to avoid an out-and-out relativism, they hold forth ethical-

18. For more concise statements, see Taylor, *Sources*, pp. 495–521; also his *Ethics of Authenticity* (Cambridge: Harvard University Press, 1992).

hermeneutical modes of reasoning about the good.[19] For Taylor, who has been strongly influenced by MacIntyre's theory of practical reasoning, one must reconstruct a genealogy of a certain identity and good that would include and surpass other competing genealogies, thereby revealing their partiality. Thus if disputes can only be resolved by adjudicating between conflicting constitutive goods, rational conflict resolution must involve considerably more than a discourse-ethical procedure; at best one could follow the latter only *after* the real work of an ethical-hermeneutical discourse was complete.

This link between morality and ethics may sound somewhat familiar. Did we not admit that a moral discourse might sometimes have to shift over to an ethical discourse, say when one party thought the other's self-deception so deep that it blocked a reasonable degree of cooperation? This suggests that moral discourse does, even for Habermas, depend to some extent on a prior ethical consensus. In fact—our third point—Taylor goes much farther than this, for he grounds moral discourse in ethical discourse *in principle*. Though recognizing widespread agreement on certain moral intuitions,[20] Taylor nonetheless maintains that founding a moral theory at the level of such agreement ultimately masks the real, deeper conflict potentials in contemporary Western society. Such conflicts not only exist between morality and other goods, such as self-fulfillment, but also surface even *within* morality itself in the competition between various conceptions of justice.[21] So even if procedural approaches might play a limited role in conflict resolution, they will be effective only in cases where the underlying goods *already* are such as to allow for overlapping intuitions on certain moral norms. A moral theory stopping at that point has not gone far enough to explicate the full rationality of just conflict resolution, and thus will be of little help when such convergence is not forthcoming, as it may not be *even for questions of justice*. The devastating corollary follows that discourse ethics has failed to reconstruct the objectivity or binding force of normative validity claims.

Fourth, Taylor's in-principle reversal of the moral-ethical relation in effect erases the distinction altogether, thereby redefining the moral domain itself. This emerges, on the one hand, in the kind of question at

19. Taylor, *Sources*, pp. 71–75; MacIntyre, *Whose Justice?*, chaps. 18–20.
20. Taylor, *Sources*, p. 495; see also "Comments and Replies," pp. 237–239.
21. See not only Taylor's *Sources*, pp. 498–499, but also his "The Diversity of Goods" and "The Nature and Scope of Distributive Justice."

stake in morality. For Taylor, "the center of moral life" involves the attempt to integrate in a consistent form of life the various values (or virtues) that cover *both* justice and self-realization issues.[22] On the other
hand, solving such problems of integration devolves primarily on the
expressive-disclosive power of language, i.e., its power to constitute evaluative domains: "We express our moral ends and our understanding of
ourselves as humans in such a way that we thereby at the same time understand and justify our ends. . . . Language plays a constitutive role
with regard to these ends, norms and customs: it is only through their
articulation in language that our norms and purposes can also be
changed."[23]

Fifth, if Taylor is correct then the prospects for rational conflict resolution would seem to grow considerably dimmer. The difficulty with his
proposal is that, on the face of it, it sets the requirements for rational
consensus all but out of reach, inasmuch as reaching consensus would
depend on bringing individuals or groups to change their concrete *identities*. This links consensus formation with processes of ethical character
formation that, depending on the individual or group, may require decades to undergo.[24] Not only that, the rational reconstruction of such
processes across a whole society would pose a Herculean task for the
theorist.[25] For such a reconstruction would have to produce and defend
against all comers a certain framework or vision of the human good
(within which a diversity of goods could coexist and be harmoniously
ordered) as emergent from the centuries of diverse traditions intertwin-
ing to form the modern identity. As Taylor insists, such an account does
not amount to a "basic reason" guaranteed to sway all rational agents;
rather it articulates a vision of the good that "may help further definitions
of what is basic."[26] In view of this and his emphasis on the disclosive function of language, it is not surprising when Taylor suggests that the real
task is less one of argumentation than of art and aesthetic criticism, for
ultimately it involves a "search for moral sources *outside* the subject

22. Taylor, "Language," p. 32.
23. Taylor, "Language," p. 34.
24. MacIntyre's model of epistemological crisis especially suggests this; see *Whose Justice?*, pp. 361f, 393ff.
25. In "Author Meets Critics: *Sources of the Self*," Central Division Meeting of the
American Philosophical Association, Chicago, 27 April 1991, MacIntyre leveled a charge
similar to this, arguing that Taylor's argument actually requires 1800 pages rather than
500; Taylor, for his part, admitted his hope that a unified conception of goods is possible,
though he remains an "agnostic" with regard to Aristotelian attempts to postulate such a
unity in advance.
26. Taylor, *Sources*, p. 77; I draw also on his APA comments.

through languages which resonate *within* him or her, the grasping of an order which is inseparably indexed to a personal vision."[27] In view of the scope of such a task and the quality—and complexity—of reasons it produces, it would seem unlikely to gain even that fragmented adherence that MacIntyre imputes to modern rationalist moralities and takes as an indication of the inadequacy of such theories.[28] It is not hard to see how taking this route could lead to an indefinite postponement of a generally convincing moral cognitivism.

Sixth, the above difficulties do not of themselves ground a rejection of Taylor's thesis. Habermas realizes that if Taylor's analysis holds, then—the aesthetic turn aside—grounding the force of moral validity claims requires a philosophically defensible sketch of a specific way of life as generally fulfilling. He also realizes that the prospects for successfully carrying through such a project are dim.[29] But if that is true, then Taylor must fail to account for the cognitive force of moral validity claims, and thus fail to account for the basis of a rational social consensus—this seems to be Habermas's ultimate concern. Unfortunately, pointing out these drawbacks does not go far enough to deal with the larger question. True, Taylor's attempt at moral cognitivism—if it could be called that—would fail. But this does not of itself erase the arguments aimed at showing that morality rests on a constitutive good. For those arguments may well be compelling independently of whether one can then go on to show that only one constitutive good should command universal assent. Thus there is need to show that the discourse ethics enterprise does not depend on such a constitutive good, or at least not on one particular good among others. This issue is complex enough, though, to warrant a preliminary excursion on more familiar terrain.

EXCURSUS. RAWLS ON JUSTICE AND THE GOOD

Before taking up Habermas's response to Taylor, it will help to turn first to another neo-Kantian who has squarely faced the issue, John Rawls. From the start Rawls acknowledged that his theory of justice required at least a "thin theory of the good." One must note, though, at exactly what stage this theory enters his conception of justice. Rawls brings in a thin conception of the good—a statement of the primary goods any rational

27. Taylor, *Sources*, p. 510; also pp. 490–493, 510–513; and his *Ethics of Authenticity*, pp. 81–91.
28. MacIntyre, *After Virtue*, p. 21.
29. EzD, pp. 177f; for his doubts about the aesthetic turn, see EzD, pp. 182–183.

agent desires, whatever else he or she desires—in order to get some purchase on how agents in the original position can, indeed must arrive at
consensus on the principles of justice.[30] As a purely formal procedure,
though, the original position itself can be characterized simply in terms
of the symmetry relations necessary to ensure a fair outcome.[31] To be
sure, in characterizing the original position Rawls brings in a number of
things beyond the procedure itself, such as the formal constraints on the
concept of right, the circumstances of justice and, in addition, minimal
features of the choosing parties, including the basic goods they want. In
what follows I will distinguish these latter items, which pertain to the
content of the choice, from the *formal* procedure as such.[32] From the perspective of this distinction, we can see that Rawls only needs to introduce
the theory of the good *subsequent* to his characterization of the formal
procedure so that he can monologically derive determinate results from
a fictive discourse. In discourse-ethical terms, this means the theory of
the good represents one theorist's supposition about the values real
agents hold. Precisely because he already knows what minimal, "primary
goods" motivate such agents, Rawls can work through his thought experiment and arrive at two fairly substantive norms of justice. Mean-
while, the right retains priority both in the sense that the principles of
justice so derived do not depend on comprehensive views about the good
of human life and in the sense that the formal procedure precedes the thin
theory of the good.

Since his *Theory of Justice* Rawls has expanded his use of the term
"good" to the extent that one might well say that his political conception
of justice is equivalent to a political theory of the good.[33] As Rawls puts
it, his theory of justice, while not presupposing any one comprehensive
theory of the good, "*must* draw upon various ideas of the good." Thus
the good and justice are "complementary," in that "justice draws the
limit, the good shows the point."[34] This later rendition still assumes a
thin theory of the good, according to which everyone in a democratic
society considers "human life and the fulfillment of basic needs and purposes as in general good, and endorse[s] rationality as a basic principle
of political and social organization." On the assumption that citizens are
free and equal, this allows one to specify certain primary goods in terms

30. See Rawls, *Theory*, pp. 395–398.
31. Rawls, *Theory*, pp. 136–142.
32. For Rawls's discussion of these items, see *Theory*, pp. 118–150; I am also indebted
to the useful summary in Kenneth Baynes, *Normative Grounds*, pp. 58–61.
33. This is Richardson's reading in "Problem of Liberalism," p. 13.
34. Rawls, "Priority of Right," pp. 251–253; for the quotations, see pp. 253, 252, resp.

of which one can work out the basic structure of a just, well-ordered society. Rawls then goes on to note how the resultant social structure not only delimits permissible comprehensive views of the good but also promotes certain political virtues as goods and requires citizens to affirm the intrinsic good of a well-ordered political society.[35] If I understand Rawls correctly, this amounts to little more than a terminological expansion of the use of "good." While he admits that at a certain level of abstraction one cannot separate a political theory of right from a theory of the good, he actually cedes little of substance regarding the priority of right, for the notion of good at issue must not depend on any particular comprehensive theory of the good any more than does the theory of justice it informs. Nor does it alter the priority of the procedure vis-à-vis the good.

The above indicates that one can both equate the right and the good at a very abstract level and make substantive moral norms depend on a thin consensus on goods without jeopardizing the priority of right. The real challenge Taylor raises concerns the question whether acceptance of the formal procedure itself requires a prior acceptance of a theory of the good. We phrased this earlier as the question, What grounds a rational acceptance of the discourse-ethical procedure? In Rawlsian terms, we are asking for a justification of the description of the original position. In *A Theory of Justice*, Rawls provided such justification with his notion of a "reflective equilibrium." The original position reflects, on the one hand, our widely shared intuitions about the conditions under which a deliberation over the principles of justice ought to proceed. Hence one must check it against something like our intuitions about the moral point of view or the abstract principles of fair contract. On the other hand, the description of such conditions must also be checked to see whether the principles arrived at in the original position "match our considered convictions of justice or extend them in an acceptable way."[36] One can take this a step further by checking the theory of justice for its coherence with the results of other disciplines such as developmental psychology.[37]

This first answer to our question says nothing about a possible relation between the formal procedure (the original position) and the good, for it only tells us *how* one can justify the description of the procedure.

---

35. Rawls, "Priority," pp. 254–271; the quote is on p. 254; for a summary see p. 274 n32.

36. Rawls, *Theory*, p. 19; see also pp. 18–21.

37. For a discussion of narrow and wide reflective equilibrium, which is only implicit in *A Theory of Justice*, see Baynes, *Normative Grounds*, pp. 69–70; Baynes draws on Rawls's "The Independence of Moral Theory," *Proceedings and Addresses of the American Philosophical Association* 48 (1975). 5–22.

Since his *Theory of Justice*, however, Rawls has said more about the substantive nature of what justifies the description of the original position. In his turn to "Kantian constructivism," Rawls associated the original position with Kantian ideals of autonomy and a well-ordered society. On this interpretation, the original position is a procedural representation of Kant's Categorical Imperative.[38] He has subsequently emphasized the notion of "overlapping consensus," arguing that such ideals represent "intuitive ideas . . . latent in the public political culture of a democratic society."[39] Hence individuals should be able to affirm his theory of justice "from within their own distinct views" about the more comprehensive good of human life, such that the conception of justice represents the outcome of an "overlapping consensus."[40]

Here Rawls assumes that there in fact exists in contemporary liberal-democratic societies a moral-political consensus sufficient to ground assent to a political conception of justice that would govern a stable constitutional regime. Although each individual agrees to this conception from within his or her own distinctive views about the good life, Rawls himself does not need to derive it from any such substantive doctrine. Hence if agreement to the original position is equivalent to the agreement to this political conception of justice in Rawls's more recent parlance, then such agreement does not presuppose the prior acceptance of some one *particular* conception of the good. Even if, for *each individual*, acceptance of the political conception is rational only in view of that individual's fuller self-understanding, this need not mean that the justificatory structure of Rawls's argument has made the ethical prior to the moral, as Taylor suggests. Rawls's overlapping consensus argument is not intended to "go all the way down," as it were, but rests rather on confi-

38. See, for example, Rawls, "Kantian Constructivism" and "Justice as Fairness." Rawls had already introduced the idea of a well-ordered society as one "designed to advance the good of its members and effectively regulated by a public conception of justice" in *Theory*, pp. 4–5, 453–462; quotation, p. 453; see Baynes, *Normative Grounds*, pp. 51–57; Baynes summarizes these Kantian ideals as containing the following features: (1) the conception of justice is based on noncontroversial beliefs, is known to be accepted by all citizens and to regulate the basic social institutions; (2) the citizens are and consider each other to be free and equal, and have a sense of justice and the ability to choose and revise their conceptions of the good life; (3) Humean circumstances of justice obtain; (4) the conception of justice is stable over time.

39. Rawls, "The Idea of an Overlapping Consensus," p. 6 (hereafter cited as "Overlapping Consensus").

40. Rawls, "Priority," p. 269, also 270f; also "Overlapping Consensus," pp. 9–11; these shifts in emphasis in Rawls's thought are pointed out by Doppelt, "Is Rawls's Kantian Liberalism Coherent and Defensible?"

dence in a certain moral convergence or overlap among different substantive views.[41]

At the same time, however, Rawls emphasizes that this overlap con-
verges on certain moral-political *values* and *ideals*, and these do seem to
bear a considerable burden of the justification itself.[42] This distinguishes
his approach from a Hobbesian social contract, which presupposes only
the individuals' enlightened self-interest.[43] As already noted above, these
values or ideals are given with the conception of society as a system of
cooperation and persons as free and equal.[44] Gerald Doppelt has thus
argued that the Kantian ideal Rawls employs does in fact presuppose a
theory of value and hence the intrinsic good of a society that allows all
individuals to be self-determining.[45] If this assessment is correct, then
how does Rawls maintain the priority of right? Doppelt argues that this
Kantian ideal does not represent a particular conception of the good with
which persons may reasonably disagree, but is rather a metavalue setting
down the preconditions for the pursuit of more substantive conceptions
of the good (which is not to say they would not rule out some choices
and life plans).[46] On this reading, then, one might think of Rawls's political conception of justice as articulating the conditions underlying individuals' various pursuits of the good in a democratic pluralist society. In
affirming the good of their more comprehensive life plans, they must
also affirm such conditions, thereby making an overlapping consensus
possible.

Doppelt goes on to object, however, that this Kantian ideal is only one
among several competing ideals latent in the liberal-democratic tradition.[47] Within that broad tradition, he argues, we can also find a bourgeois "competitive individualist," as well as patriarchal and altruistic
strands. Other theorists have found still further differences. Taylor, for
example, further divides bourgeois individualism (or atomism) according to whether social inequalities are justified on the basis of property or

41. Taylor, *Sources*, pp. 88–89; in his "The Domain of the Political and Overlapping
Consensus," *New York University Law Review* 64 (1989): 233–255, esp. pp. 245–248,
Rawls treats overlapping consensus not as justification but as evidence for the stability of
his conception of justice; since I am concerned with the latter's rational *acceptance*, however, such overlap remains relevant to the kind of justification that interests me here.
42. Rawls, "Domain of the Political," p. 241, for example.
43. Rawls makes this point in "Overlapping Consensus," pp. 2, 10–12.
44. Rawls, "Overlapping Consensus," pp. 7, 11, for example.
45. Doppelt, "Rawls's Kantian Liberalism," pp. 819–821.
46. Doppelt, "Rawls's Kantian Liberalism," pp. 822–824.
47. Doppelt, "Rawls's Kantian Liberalism," pp. 842–847.

talent.[48] As contrasted with such variations, Rawls's egalitarianism must appear all too particular. In that case, Rawls's articulation of an overlapping consensus appears successful only because he masks tensions and conflicts within that tradition.

But Doppelt undermines his own—and others'—objection in an instructive way when he argues that proponents of these rival ideals could agree to enter the original position, i.e., the veil of ignorance would not exclude them. If this is true, then the tensions within the liberal-democratic tradition do not cut deep enough to call the formal procedure into question; at most they affect the specification of primary goods. It is true that Rawls then has the problem of showing how the original position could issue in an agreement on substantive justice principles. But the fact that each of these ideals could be entertained in the original position implies that Rawls's formal procedure itself does not rest on an exclusionary conception of the good.[49] At least to some extent, one could make the same argument against Taylor as well, maintaining that the alternative conceptions of distributive justice arise only subsequent to the original position as a formal procedure.[50] Thus our opening distinction between the formal procedure and its content (what the procedure must deal with) allows us to locate a level at which Rawls's ideal, even if inspired by Kant—and even if it involves a metavalue or metagood—does not yet imply the more comprehensive Kantianism that would exclude other strands in the liberal-democratic tradition.[51]

In fact, in emphasizing the notion of "overlapping consensus," Rawls himself has explicitly rejected the Kantian moral ideal as a suitable basis for a political conception of justice, precisely because of its overly comprehensive nature. He apparently recognizes, as have others, that such an ideal is not shared by all those endorsing a liberal-democratic society.[52] What Doppelt's penetrating analysis inadvertently reveals, however, is that a number of liberal-democratic traditions besides Kantianism can agree on the original position as a fair procedure; disagreement concerns

48. Taylor, "Distributive Justice," pp. 305–309; cf. also Robert N. Bellah et al., *Habits of the Heart: Individualism and Commitment in American Life* (Berkeley: University of California Press, 1985).

49. Doppelt, "Rawls's Kantian Liberalism," pp. 844–847.

50. I have in mind here Taylor's "Distributive Justice."

51. Baynes, *Normative Grounds*, pp. 59–60, notes how the original position, even as involving merely symmetry conditions, involves the ideal of cooperation between free and equal persons; I take this as supporting Doppelt's point that Rawls does rely on a metavalue.

52. See Larmore's critique of Rawls's "Kantian expressivism," *Patterns*, pp. 118–126; also pp. 77–84.

rather the goods and values agents in the original position may reasonably endorse. In this sense, Rawls's original position, as a representation
of the moral point of view, remains prior to goods and does not embody
a particular conception of the good. It is far from clear that all those
endorsing a liberal-democratic regime would accept Rawls's list of primary goods. But this only shows that the lone theorist cannot guarantee
the acceptability of a political conception of justice simply on the basis
of a monologically conducted procedure. Rather, those adhering to rival
ideals would have to carry on a *real* debate in order to arrive at the principles of justice governing the basic social structures.

At the same time, one must admit that this overlapping consensus of
liberal-democratic *traditions* on the original position does not take in all
the viewpoints currently found in modern liberal-democratic *societies*.
Elaborating this will show how one must reply to Taylor—and perhaps
agree with him. Note to begin with that Rawls presents an argument for
why his political conception of justice "is appropriate given the historical
and social conditions of a modern democratic society."[53] It is this argument that most fully addresses the rational grounds for adopting his theory of justice (and the original position).[54] As presented in the 1987
"Overlapping Consensus" article, the argument took the following form:

(1) In contemporary (Western) liberal-democratic societies there exists a permanent plurality of conflicting comprehensive (ethical) views
about the meaning and good of human life.

(2) Only an "oppressive use of state power" would maintain agreement on a single comprehensive view of this good.

(3) But a stable liberal-democratic regime must be one that the majority of citizens freely endorse.

(4) Such a stable regime is possible on the basis of already existing
shared (noncomprehensive) moral-political values.[55]

These simply summarize what Rawls takes as contemporary "facts."
These facts become relevant, however, only in light of the basic "intuitive

53. Rawls, "Overlapping Consensus," p. 1.
54. Baynes, *Normative Grounds*, maintains that Rawls's justification of the theory of
justice, already committed to avoid both "the Scylla of foundationalism and the Charybdis
of a comprehensive moral doctrine" (p. 72), can only steer clear of relativism by heading
towards discourse ethics (pp. 68–76). The argument I am about to reconstruct, however,
indicates yet another route, similar to that taken by communitarians such as Taylor and
MacIntyre, which at least presents itself as nonrelativistic.
55. Rawls, "Overlapping Consensus," pp. 4f; see also his "Domain of the Political,"
pp. 243–244.

idea" from which Rawls takes his point of departure: "the overarching fundamental intuitive idea, within which other basic intuitive ideas are systematically connected, is that of society as a fair system of cooperation between free and equal persons."[56] This already familiar ideal going back to *A Theory of Justice* now casts a different light, however, for it allows us to see the above list of facts as something like a reconstruction of the problem for which Rawls's political conception of justice will provide the most "appropriate" answer. This intuitive idea both frames and *motivates* Rawls's entire argument, for it sets the goal or task of his political philosophy as that of finding a stable basis for social-political consensus. The conception of society both allows the problem or task to emerge as such and broadly specifies a desirable—hence "good"—solution as one that best realizes just such a system of cooperation between free and equal persons.

My point is that the above facts can motivate the acceptance of Rawls's political conception of justice only if his concept of social cooperation is assumed to be *desirable*, i.e., a good. Thus, having listed the above factual features, Rawls must add:

(5) "Since we are concerned with securing the stability of a constitutional regime, and wish to achieve free and willing agreement on a political conception of justice . . ."

These facts, in other words, do not amount to an argument unless one adds an assumption about the *general desirability or good of a stable cooperative social system*—the focus of our concern or what we "wish to achieve." Only after the addition of this assumption can Rawls go on:

(6) Therefore, "we must find another basis of agreement than that of a general and comprehensive doctrine," i.e., we must find the basis of agreement in a noncomprehensive theory of justice that articulates an overlapping consensus.[57]

In this context the original position becomes the procedure that all would find acceptable for arriving at terms of cooperation commensurate with Rawls's intuitive conception of society.[58]

56. Rawls, "Justice as Fairness," p. 231.
57. Rawls, "Overlapping Consensus," pp. 4–5; cf. "Justice as Fairness," pp. 234–235; he speaks of the task of political philosophy in ibid., p. 226.
58. Rawls, "Justice as Fairness," pp. 234–239.

The above considerations make it reasonable to refer to this conception of social cooperation as Rawls's "constitutive good." For we can view the above six-step argument as something like a "sociohistorical reconstruction" of the point of the political conception of justice—what problem it addresses. Indeed, Rawls suggests just this when he introduces the argument as intended to show the appropriateness of his justice theory. That being granted, however, it is not quite fair to accuse Rawls of "inarticulacy" about this moral source. In delineating the appropriateness of his solution, he at least points to a certain historical experience—the Wars of Religion—and he argues, in addition, for the ability of his conception to overcome a long-standing "impasse in our political culture," that between Locke and Rousseau.[59] While I cannot here enter into a lengthy discussion of Rawls's strategy, it would appear that he has made at least some effort at precisely the kind of "articulation of moral sources" Taylor envisions. For Rawls directs our attention to a certain historical development that has given rise to both a problem and a background of shared values. The political conception of justice then culls from this background those elements able to ground cooperation in our historical situation, and so solve the problem.

But is the admission of such a constitutive good really so interesting in any case? After all, at this level of abstraction talk of a "constitutive good" seems rather empty insofar as it simply coincides with what has been traditionally identified as the domain of justice problems. That is, justice traditionally has to do with the regulation of social cooperation. In taking this as some kind of constitutive good, one has done little more, it would seem, than point to the importance of social justice in general. We would thus have another terminological concession that really cedes nothing about the priority of justice over particular conceptions of the good.[60]

Yet Taylor's challenge is not dismissed so easily. We asked what justifies the description of the original position, and we saw that this description depends on a reconstruction of justice as a contemporary task. The conception of justice implicit in Rawls's reconstruction of the modern (liberal-democratic) problematic, however, excludes certain premodern conceptions of justice from the start. One might also question it from

59. The quote is from Rawls, "Kantian Constructivism," p. 519; Rawls refers to the Wars of Religion in "Overlapping Consensus," p. 4; cf. also "Justice as Fairness," esp. pp. 225–230, where the sociohistorical approach is quite pronounced.
60. Taylor, too, acknowledges the possibility of such a move in his "Cross-Purposes," p. 172.

a "postmodern" point of view. In fact, we do not even have to look beyond contemporary Western societies to find such views. However noncontroversial it appears, it is quite conceivable that some persons could reject it—such as a Nietzschean for whom social stability represents a stagnation of the will to power, or a rabid traditionalist for whom a government based on anything short of a fully enforced substantive conception of the human good merits only righteous resistance. Here I name only two possibilities, which we can take as representative of the issues at stake. It is alternatives such as these, rather than those Doppelt points to, that constitute the real challenge to Rawls, for they call the formal procedure itself into question. If these alternatives, or ones similar to them, actually exist within contemporary Western culture, then the claim that Rawls's conception of justice depends at most on metavalues—values that constitute the condition for the pursuit of more comprehensive goods—begins to weaken, and with it the priority of right. For if viable alternatives exist, then Rawls's account of the moral point of view begins to take on the appearance of one particular point of view among others, one possible constitutive good among several. Theoretically, such alternatives would challenge Rawls to provide an argument as to why their proponents should accept the original position at all.

One may pose such alternatives, however, only with a certain caution. It is true that Nietzschean and traditionalistic strains of thought do exist in our culture and have continually called rationalist moral-political programs into question. The question they raise, however, has a certain peculiarity to it. In raising the question, Why enter the original position to begin with?, such challengers might simply be asking a narrower version of the question, Why be moral? In that case Rawls might object that answering this question lies outside the scope of his enterprise. After all, one can hardly be expected to develop a moral theory for individuals lacking a moral sense (or sense of justice) altogether. If certain individuals and groups are not interested in social cooperation with strangers and other groups, or simply do not *see* the problem, there is little his reconstruction can do. He could thus simply concede that actually bringing individuals to see the reasonableness of adopting the moral point of view involves a style of discourse beyond the considerations he has in mind.

Hence I view these alternatives as skeptical demands for the *theoretical* grounds of the original position.[61] Nonetheless, even skeptical chal-

61. Cf. EzD, p. 208, for a similar challenge.

lenges such as these have a way of expanding into alternative research programs of their own, with their own definitions of society, identity, and so on.[62] In order to avoid full-scale theoretical battles, I define these challenges rather modestly, simply to fix a theoretical difficulty immanent to Rawls's project: does accepting the original position, even as mere procedure, not rule out from the start an adequate recognition of certain other goods the pursuit of which may not be unreasonable? Although rather extreme, such counterexamples point out how Rawls's argument indeed relies on the prior acceptance of a certain way of framing the justice problematic—the acceptance of a constitutive good, if you will—which seems to admit of alternatives, at least conceptually. To that extent, proponents of the alternatives might object that the original position already frames the issue in such a way that their very entry into that position decides specific conflict resolutions against them. Unless Rawls can show such alternatives to be illusory, his argument would seem to retain a decisionistic moment at its basis.

At stake here is the suitability of liberal-democratic metavalues for providing the overarching perspective for rational consensus formation—whether such metavalues do not exclude *viable* goods from the start. By raising this possibility, such skeptical challenges undermine our liberal-democratic confidence that, if the original position does depend on a constitutive good, it is a metagood or metavalue without viable alternatives. That these radical alternatives seem to exist today in a practical sense and enter into actual conflicts weakens such confidence, raising the question of how rational a procedure the original position can be if it would rule out some participants' self-understandings from the start.

Precisely at this point Rawls's sociohistorical argument, as I have been calling it, *must* be taken a step further. For if this argument moves entirely *within* a certain set of traditions and recalls *particular* historical experiences, then it would ultimately assume an ethical-hermeneutical character. Rawls's reconstruction of the justice problematic would then have a distinctly ethical ground. In fact, some have taken this to be the basic thrust of his position since *A Theory of Justice*, and the foregoing reconstruction shows that such a reading was not implausible.[63] But then how can he respond to the above challengers, who in some sense question the values underlying liberal-democratic traditions? Insofar as Western

62. An example from the Nietzschean perspective would be Foucault; for an expanded traditionalist argument one might look to Joseph de Maistre.

63. See, for example, Onora O'Neill, "Ethical Reasoning and Ideological Pluralism," *Ethics* 98 (1988): 705–722.

societies shelter more than such traditions, some response to this challenge is desirable. To respond, Rawls might have expanded his sociohistorical argument into the kind of genealogy or articulation of moral
sources Taylor envisions—in which case, Rawls and Taylor would not
have been very far apart on their views about practical reason, if Rawls's
reconstruction is a kind of rudimentary liberal-democratic genealogy.
That this undermines the priority of right is not so serious as the threat
it poses to Rawls's claim to have found a basis for rational social consensus. For then all the difficulties inhering in Taylor's approach would
devolve on his own.

It is not surprising, then, that Rawls took pains in his 1989 "Domain
of the Political" article to reassert the universalist dimensions of his conception of justice by insisting that the basic "facts" making up his argument "are not . . . historical contingencies. Rather, they are rooted in
the difficulties of exercising our reason under the normal conditions of
human life."[64] While Rawls's account of these difficulties or "burdens of
reason" adds an intriguing extension to the above sociohistorical reconstruction, it is not clear whether it provides him with the alternative he
needs to meet the challenges noted above.[65] For his argument still simply
assumes the widespread acceptance of liberal-democratic values. To
ground these values without taking the route mapped out by Taylor, yet
a further alternative recommends itself, as I hope to show in the next
section.

III. A CONSTITUTIVE GOOD FOR DISCOURSE ETHICS?

We took the detour through Rawls's theory of justice as a kind of training
exercise for answering the question, What grounds the rational acceptance of a discourse-ethical procedure? In Rawls, the parallel question
concerns the grounds for accepting the original position or, more generally, for accepting the ideal motivating Rawls's enterprise, that of social
cooperation among free and equal persons. We raised this question in
order to approach Taylor's charge that the acceptance of procedural conceptions of morality depends on a prior constitutive good that remains
unarticulated. The upshot of the excursus was to show that the kind of
argument Rawls uses to prepare the ground for his theory of justice—
what I call his sociohistorical argument or reconstruction—does indeed

64. Rawls, "Domain of the Political," p. 239.
65. Cf. Baynes, *Normative Grounds*, pp. 68–76.

point to something like a constitutive good, for that argument reconstructs the sociohistorical problematic that motivates an acceptance of
the original position. Moreover, insofar as this reconstruction calls on a
limited set of historical experiences it appears to ground the moral-
political theory in ethical considerations, however much the recon-
structed ethos remains a very diffuse one. Does discourse ethics depend
on a similar underlying ideal or constitutive good? After reviewing evidence for an affirmative response to this question (subsection 1), I shall
clarify the burden of argument involved in the claim that discourse ethics
depends on a metagood (subsection 2); I shall then close with a brief
comparative assessment of Habermas's project (subsection 3).

I.

Evidence that discourse ethics relies on a constitutive good lies ready to
hand, even aside from Habermas's famous statement, "Reaching understanding is the inherent telos of human speech."[66] Consider first the derivation of (U) in Chapter 3. For the derivation to work it was necessary
to delimit a specific plausibility context, that of rational conflict resolution. In fact, we had to enter this context in the derivation as the definite
assumption that "a pluralistic group decides to resolve their conflicts of
interest cooperatively by reaching argued agreement" (Chapter 3, section
III, premise [1]). But (U) constitutes the procedural core of discourse ethics, and so it would seem that the acceptance of that procedure rests on
the acceptance of argued agreement as a good.

Consider, second, that in Chapter 4 the priority of justice in discourse
ethics depended on a big "if": "If we want to decide normative questions
having to do with the elements of living together not by the direct or
masked resort to force, . . . but rather by a nonviolent conviction based
on a rationally motivated agreement . . . ," then questions of justice must
be given priority.[67] As in Rawls, this argument depended on a characterization of the context as pluralistic, such that justice questions alone
could issue in general assent, at least in principle. In this context morality
is seen as an alternative to violence in situations where religious and
metaphysical worldviews can no longer command general assent. Thus
one seeks the basis of cooperation not in decisions to pursue the same
goods but in relation to the generally binding value orientations that reg-

66. TCA 1:287.
67. NR, p. 118.

ulate *inter*action.[68] In any case, this simply repeats the premise entered
in the derivation, only now with explicit reference to the relation between
moral and ethical discourses. By introducing this "if," however, discourse ethics seemingly subordinates moral conflict resolution to a prudential consideration of whether it is good to resolve conflicts discursively for the sake of cooperation with persons not sharing one's own
conception of the good life. Inasmuch as such resolution might often constrain an individual's or group's pursuit of the good life, it may appear
as a cowardly compromise, especially for more traditionalistic conceptions of the human good. This apparent prudential element would not
only weaken the force of moral obligation—a consideration that led
Kant to sever morality from happiness—it would confront discourse ethics with the problem that its assumption of a will to discursively achieved
cooperation simply singled out one possible good among several.

Third, one should note how Habermas ties morality to solidarity.
Here I refer to the anthropological links we briefly noted in Chapter 4:
"Since moralities are tailored to suit the fragility of human beings individuated through socialization, they must always solve *two* tasks at
once."[69] More specifically, moral norms "aim [*zielen*] directly at the inviolable character of the person as a symbolic structure that forms and
reproduces itself in relations of reciprocal recognition. They also aim indirectly at the preservation and development of the physical existence of
the person to whom respect is due."[70] While this link is not, in fact, part
of the argument for a discourse-ethical procedure, its connection with a
teleological language of "tasks" and "aim" does indicate a "point" or
"purpose" of moral norms and, more generally, of morality as a whole.
This suggests in turn that the thin common goods we loosely associated
with norms are not just goods arrived at through discourse but, in some
sense, the goods that motivate the acceptance of a discourse-ethical procedure to begin with. Perhaps it would be more accurate to say that the
norms and values endorsed in real discourses have their sense in relation
to the metagood of respect for personal integrity and well-being. Insofar
as this metagood allows us to see the point of the entire moral procedure,
one will have difficulty avoiding Taylor's attribution of a constitutive
good.

Fourth, one should not overlook how Habermas's notion of cooperation amounts to an almost concrete ideal that functions as a moral

68. EzD, pp. 177–178.
69. ME, p. 200.
70. EzD, p. 174.

source for discourse ethics. This is quite clear in the following text, which I quote at length:

> I have a conceptual motive and a fundamental intuition. . . . The motivating thought concerns the reconciliation of a modernity which has fallen apart, the idea that without surrendering the differentiation that modernity has made possible in the cultural, the social and economic spheres, one can find forms of living together in which autonomy and dependency can truly enter into a non-antagonistic relation, that one can walk tall in a collectivity that does not have the dubious quality of backward-looking substantial forms of community.
>
> The intuition springs from the sphere of relations with others; it aims at experiences of undisturbed intersubjectivity. . . . Wherever these ideas appear, . . . they are always ideas of felicitous interaction, of reciprocity and distance, of separation and of successful, unspoiled nearness, of vulnerability and complementary caution. All of these images of protection, openness and compassion, of submission and resistance, rise out of a horizon of experience, of what Brecht would have termed 'friendly living together'. *This* kind of friendliness does not exclude conflict, rather it implies those human forms through which one can survive conflicts.[71]

The connection between the theoretical concept of solidarity and the above quoted images are unmistakable. Once again, one can hardly avoid applying Taylor's notion of "moral source" or constitutive good to these images. They form that deeper background that gives point and purpose, a definite aim, to Habermas's entire project. That is, discourse ethics aims to elaborate or reconstruct the rationality that would have to inform and govern the "undisturbed intersubjectivity" pictured above. This picture describes a good "prior" to or constituting discourse ethics in some sense, for if one were not attracted by the vision of such a life— if one were attracted instead by the image of a closely knit clan, or by that of an ancient honor-shame society—one would most likely not accept the discourse-ethical procedure, either.

In my opinion, Habermas need not deny that discourse ethics draws its motivating power from a constitutive good like that depicted above. Although I initially posed the issue theoretically, as that of the rational grounds for entering a discourse-ethical procedure for conflict resolution—or as a premise in an argument for (U)—as we moved through the above points the issue gradually shifted to a different level. In the quoted text we see how the theoretician himself is motivated by certain images and particular historical experiences that, precisely as particular and concrete, always partly escape full theoretical absorption. Such images

---

71. From an interview with Habermas in *Autonomy*, pp. 125–126.

and experiences always belong to a particular historical ethos, beyond which their theoretical power becomes problematic. An admission of just such particularity is what communitarians like Taylor ask of neo-Kantians and other liberal theoreticians. I have tried to indicate in the excursus that Rawls is not completely silent on this score; and in various interviews Habermas acknowledges such sources even more explicitly— recall, for example, his confession of postwar disillusionment with German traditionalism.[72] Less clear is whether such a good occupies, or ought to occupy, a role in a theoretical argument for the rational acceptability of discourse ethics.

At a theoretical level, the key question is whether or how such sources function in the argument for the basic principles of discourse ethics, (U) and (D). One has in effect accepted (D) once one accepts the idea of basing social cooperation on discourse. And this idea, or something very much like it, constitutes a key premise in the argument for (U) and in the argument for the priority of justice questions. The above indicates that something like a constitutive good, a vision of cooperation among autonomous individuals, stands behind this idea. I shall refer to this as the good of rational or autonomous cooperation. If one did not value such cooperation and the rational agreement upon which it rests, one would probably reject discourse ethics altogether. Does this mean that, in the final analysis, the good is *theoretically* prior to justice in discourse ethics?

2.

Now at this point Habermas could—and in fact does—reply that anyone who failed to appreciate the value of rational cooperation, i.e., social cooperation based on mutual understanding, simply does not feel the force of the moral 'ought'. If discourse ethics attempts to reconstruct just such force, however, it can hardly be expected, as moral theory, to *produce* or create that force for persons who lack a feel for it. In this sense, answering the question, Why be moral?, cannot be part of the reconstruction of the force of moral claims, for this reconstruction must presuppose that force as given.[73] I shall elaborate on this point a bit further in Chapter 6; here it is important to note that, in calling for the articulation of motivational moral sources, Taylor's project apparently aims at produc-

72. See, for example, Habermas, *Autonomy*, pp. 191ff; also "Ethics, Politics and History: An Interview with Jürgen Habermas," conducted by Jean-Marc Ferry, *Philosophy and Social Criticism* 14 (1988): 433–439 (hereafter Interview on Ethics).
73. See EzD, pp. 184–189.

ing just such force.[74] In Habermas's view, however, this alters the very meaning of the philosophical enterprise in an unacceptable way, and it is first and foremost for this reason that he rejects it.

The basic difficulty lies in the aesthetic redefinition of philosophical argument that Taylor's project requires. As already indicated above, Taylor would seemingly require philosophers (and others) to develop generally convincing accounts defending a particular integration of a given culture's diverse goods. If this means disclosing motivational sources of morality, however, then such accounts would depend as much (or more) on aesthetic and artistic languages and forms of expression as on philosophical argumentation. In Habermas's view, philosophical argumentation reconstructs intuitions that competent actors already have; such arguments essentially differ from the "world-disclosive arguments that lead us to see things in a radically new light."[75] Thus Taylor's project would seemingly overreach the bounds of philosophy. But even if this endeavor could be viewed as a philosophical one, say as a kind of reconstruction of the various goods underlying the modern project,[76] the chances are slim in today's society that this route will lead to a convincing reconstruction of the force of normative validity claims able to ground rational conflict resolution. In fact, one might well doubt the prospects for achieving such a reconstruction even *within* a cultural milieu as pluralistic as ours; all the more must one doubt its ability to supply grounds for rational cooperation *across* cultures. If we add to this Habermas's desire to account for the normative force of the critique of tradition, it is not surprising that he would question Taylor's approach on these negative grounds alone.

If we put aside the aesthetic aspect of Taylor's proposal, then Habermas's objection is not unlike Kant's argument against grounding moral obligation on a theory of happiness.[77] If one assumes that such obligation is unconditionally binding and that reconstructing this unconditional binding force constitutes the task of moral theory, then one does well to hesitate before setting out on the path Taylor has taken, given the likely

74. This is how Habermas reads him; EzD, p. 184; cf. Taylor, *Sources*, pp. 510–513.
75. EzD, p. 189.
76. Taylor could also reply that he has an interdisciplinary project in view, i.e., one involving both philosophy and the other humanities and arts; this seems to me the more likely reading of his project, in view of his stress on artistic "epiphanies," in *Sources*, chaps. 23 and 24.
77. See Immanuel Kant, *Critique of Practical Reason*, trans. with an Introduction by Lewis White Beck (Indianapolis: Bobbs-Merrill, 1956), pp. 59–67; also his "On the Proverb: That May Be True in Theory, But It Is of No Practical Use," in *Perpetual Peace and Other Essays*, trans. Ted Humphrey (Indianapolis: Hackett, 1983), pp. 65–67, 78–81.

variation in conceptions of happiness. As I have already indicated, however, this does not suffice as an argument against Taylor. The foregoing evidence that discourse ethics does indeed draw on a constitutive good, together with Taylor's perceptive analyses of the goods so deeply laid within our culture, place a certain burden of response on Habermas. At the very least, one might expect an account of how discourse ethics avoids smuggling in a particular ethnocentric conception of the good. Only in this way can one avoid the problems we saw threatening Rawls's theory of justice.

The necessary argument would have to defuse Taylor's objection by showing that, if discourse ethics amounts to a theory of the good, it is a good with such unique status vis-à-vis other goods that its priority simply *is* the priority of right over these other goods. In fact, Habermas has an argument of just this sort, made in response to Agnes Heller. Here I postpone to Chapter 6 a direct response to Taylor (made prior to *Sources of the Self*), in which Habermas draws on an interpretation of Humboldt;[78] in my opinion, this "Humboldtian argument" is best understood in light of the earlier argument against Heller, which is both clearer and more complete. It gives us a good sense of the sweep of Habermas's claims and the burden of proof that the rebuttal of Taylor ultimately involves. Although a full defense of this rather ambitious argument lies outside the scope of this study, we must at least examine the kind of claims it makes if we are to determine the theoretical relation between discourse ethics and the good. Hence the remainder of this chapter will focus on the argument against Heller. I shall first summarize the argument and then address each step in turn.

In a different context, Heller argued in a way very similar to Taylor. Like him, she raised the question concerning the grounds for adopting communicative rationality as a value.[79] In reply, Habermas argued against the attempt to "stylize communicative rationality into a *particular* value, for or against which we can take sides."[80] His reply notes, first, that once actors decide to settle disputes on the basis of argument they have no alternative but to accept "the rationality inherent in linguistic understanding," i.e., a discourse-ethical procedure. Second, the decision not to argue at all is not a *viable* alternative. From the perspective of the communicative relations that make up the lifeworld, the pro-

78. "Reply," pp. 215–222.
79. Agnes Heller, "Habermas and Marxism," in *Habermas: Critical Debates*, ed. John B. Thompson and David Held (Cambridge: MIT Press, 1982), pp. 21–41, esp. pp. 28f.
80. "Critics," p. 226.

cesses that reproduce such relations can only take place through the communicative action that commits one to raising and redeeming validity claims. In other words, a society can sustain itself only if, on the whole, its members take each other seriously at the communicative level, i.e., respond to the illocutionary force of one another's claims. Of course, it is always possible for individual actors to adopt a strategic attitude according to which individual success, rather than mutual agreement, takes precedence. But even the individual cannot maintain such an attitude over the long haul without pathological or self-destructive consequences to his or her sense of identity. Third, Habermas argues that these unavoidable structures remain formal, and thus do "not extend to the concrete shape of an exemplary life-form or a paradigmatic life-history."[81] This third point distinguishes Habermas's project from Taylor's attempt to spell out a concrete way of life that would integrate the multiple moral sources of Western culture. In what follows I want to break the above argumentative points into two theses and make a few remarks on each, showing their relevance to an understanding of how discourse ethics does and does not involve a constitutive good.

The "No Alternatives" Thesis. The first two of the three points in the reply to Heller comprise a series of moves that, taken together, claim that the metavalue of autonomous cooperation is without viable alternatives. In fact, I think this claim involves three steps, which one might diagram as follows:

The Central Claim	Corollary
(i) All individuals/societies depend on processes of communicative action;	(i′) No alternative forms of social coordination (such as strategic action) can fully replace linguistically mediated cooperation.
(ii) but one is involved in such processes *only if* one is committed to redeeming validity claims in arguments;	(ii′) No alternative form of conflict resolution can fully replace that of argumentation.
(iii) but one is so committed *only if* one is willing to adopt discourse-ethical procedures such as (U) as idealized representations of rational argumentation.	(iii′) No alternative form of argument can fully replace that of impartial moral discourse.

81. "Critics," pp. 227–228; the quote is from p. 228.

Establishing the above "no alternatives" claims would involve an enormous burden of argument, even when one restricts their applicability to contemporary societies. In fact, each step entails its own theoretical demands: (i) would involve one in a theory of society, (ii) in a theory of communicative action, and (iii) in argumentation theory. In order to rebut Taylor's thesis, at each of the above steps one would have to argue that the acceptance of the given step (or theory) did not presuppose or surreptitiously smuggle in a predecision for a particular conception of the good over which reasonable persons could disagree. This is the point of the corollaries. However, one should note the manner in which the overall line of argument attenuates the claim for a discourse ethics: in order to show that discourse ethics does not smuggle in a particular conception of the good it is enough to argue for its unavoidability in at least *some* domains of action from which no one can *fully* withdraw.

Naturally, this still leaves problems with each step. We do not need to hash these all out here; nor is it necessary to establish whether discourse ethics must rest on an "ultimate" justification or not.[82] I can, however, illustrate the kind of questions a thesis such as Taylor's could raise at each step. With respect to the move to (iii), for example, one could ask whether a particular constitutive good does not somehow lie *between* the decision to argue and the acceptance of a discourse-ethical procedure, such that by adopting such a procedure other possible goods have been *eo ipso* excluded. With respect to (ii), one could ask whether a commitment to argument does not elevate a particular kind of rational autonomy to the status of a constitutive good such that the good of alternate forms of cooperation, such as those based on authority or trust, cannot emerge as such. To get around this, Habermas would apparently have to show that, in the last instance, authority and trust also have a basis in reasons. This would allow him to move from the claim that personal and social reproduction require communicative action (i) to the claim that individuals in any society are committed to argumentation in virtue of their involvement in communicative action (ii).

Taylor would probably not disagree with the opening step (i), that social reproduction depends on communicative action.[83] Yet even if he

82. On this issue, see Habermas, DE, pp. 82–99; EzD, pp. 185–199; Karl-Otto Apel, "Normatively Grounding 'Critical Theory' through Recourse to the Lifeworld? A Transcendental-Pragmatic Attempt to Think with Habermas against Habermas," in *Philosophical Interventions*, ed. Honneth et al., pp. 125–170.

83. See Taylor, "Language," pp. 23–29; note that Taylor does disagree with Habermas's division of communicative action into three validity dimensions (ibid., pp. 32–35);

grants this *and* the cognitive basis of communicative action (ii), instructive problems remain. To get a sense of these consider Habermas's argument against radical skepticism; here we find (i) and (ii) combined. In his reply to skeptics who would avoid the pragmatic presuppositions of argument (and thus [U] in practical questions) by refusing to argue altogether, Habermas, as well as others such as Karl-Otto Apel, have argued at length for the artificiality of such avoidance.[84] For such skeptics must still interact with others in a sociocultural form of life, which means they must orient themselves to normative validity claims. But precisely this commits such skeptics to argumentation, for "there is no form of sociocultural life that is not at least implicitly geared to maintaining communicative action by means of argument."[85] Habermas concludes:

> That is why the radical skeptic's refusal to argue is an empty gesture. No matter how consistent a dropout he may be, he cannot drop out of the communicative practice of everyday life, to the presuppositions of which he remains bound. And these in turn are at least partly identical with the presuppositions of argumentation as such.[86]

If the skeptic attempts to dodge this by acting only strategically—thus not on the basis of reaching agreement on validity claims—then the cognitivist must show that there is no substitute for contexts of communicative action as a whole. The claim is that the skeptic could not achieve his or her identity outside of such contexts: one withdraws to a purely strategic style of interaction only at the risk of one's sanity.[87] Precisely this explains why rational mutual understanding occupies "a special position," to answer Taylor's question.[88] Nonetheless, the claim does not quite go far enough, for it remains *within* a particular form of life—the skeptic can still ask why he or she should argue with outsiders or persons with a different cultural heritage.

In fact, this problem infects the entire sequence (i)–(iii), unless Habermas can extend the notion of society involved in (i). How does Habermas show that the imperative toward rational cooperation extends without alternatives not only to all those sharing in a form of life but

this implies a doubt about whether a specifically discourse-ethical mode of conflict resolution (iii) can be connected with (i) and (ii).

84. See DE, pp. 100–102.
85. DE, p. 100.
86. DE, pp. 100f.
87. DE, p. 102.
88. Taylor, "Language," p. 31.

also across different cultures and language groups? He has, it is true, made allusion to various historical experiences that lead to a growing awareness of the unavoidability of rational cooperation across cultures and language groups;[89] he has also referred to the fact that there are no more self-contained traditional forms of life.[90] The former references in particular remind one of Rawls's sociohistorical argument insofar as they refer to actual learning processes. Precisely this, however, should alert us to a problem. For, as we saw, Rawls had difficulty motivating certain "unmodern" skeptics even to enter his original position. In appealing to the Wars of Religion and the liberal-democratic tradition his argument took on a strongly ethical character, which rendered his grounding of the moral point of view problematic—the metavalue to which Rawls appealed turned out to inhere, after all, in a particular ethos. If Habermas too were to stop with particular historical allusions, we might expect similar difficulties to attend his grounding of morality. If rational cooperation is a constitutive good for discourse ethics, and if the grounds for

---

89. For example, Habermas, Interview on Ethics, p. 436, refers to the cross-cultural learning processes taking place within the West:

> These countries are . . . on the way to post-national societies. One can mention European integration, supra-national military alliances, worldwide economic interdependencies, economically motivated waves of immigration, the growing ethnic variety of the population. Beyond these there is the thickening of the network of communication that has sharpened the perception of, and sensitivity for, abridgements of human rights, for exploitation, hunger, misery, for the concerns of national liberation movements and so forth.

The latter references show that the relevant developments are not simply political but moral in orientation. Habermas concludes that "a consciousness also spreads that there is no other alternative to universalistic value orientations." He goes on to describe this orientation as follows:

> Relativizing one's own form of existence to the legitimate claims of other forms of life, according equal rights to aliens and others with all their idiosyncracies and unintelligibility, not sticking doggedly to the universalization of own's own identity, not marginalizing that which deviates from one's own identity, allowing the sphere of tolerance to become ceaselessly larger than it is today—all this is what moral universalism means today (ibid.).

For a further development of these points in the legal-political arena, see Jürgen Habermas, *Staatsbürgerschaft und nationale Identität: Überlegungen zur europäischen Zukunft* (St. Gallen: Ekker, n.d.); for a translation of the latter, see "Citizenship and National Identity: Some Reflections on the Future of Europe," *Praxis International* 12 (1992): 1–19; the translation will also appear as an appendix to Habermas's *Between Facts and Norms* (forthcoming, MIT Press).

90. Habermas, *Autonomy*, p. 209; also EzD, pp. 206f; for an illustration of the pathologies that can develop from a group's attempt to isolate itself, see the critique of terrorism by Albrecht Wellmer, "Terrorism and the Critique of Society," in *Observations on "The Spiritual Situation of the Age,"* ed. Jürgen Habermas, trans. Andrew Buchwalter (Cambridge: MIT Press, 1985), pp. 283–307.

accepting such a good to the extent Habermas requires reside in a particular historical experience, then discourse ethics begins to look as though it ultimately rests on a style of argument more akin to Taylor's genealogical "articulation of moral sources," which aims to reconstruct the deeper, thicker considerations that lead one to adopt the good of morality to begin with. To get beyond this impression, we must turn to Habermas's argument for moral formalism.

The Formalism Thesis. In the third and last point in the reply to Heller, Habermas maintains that discourse ethics and the notion of autonomous cooperation it requires do not amount to substantive ideals or proposals about the good of human life. Therefore, if such cooperation functions as the constitutive good of discourse ethics, then this good specifies no more than formal, universal structures from which one cannot derive a substantive doctrine of the good life. If this claim holds up, then the constitutive good of discourse ethics should be acceptable *apart* from the concrete historical experiences that led *our culture* to conclude to its lack of alternatives. In other words, that such cooperation appears to have no alternatives for us is not just a contingency of Western history, but rather actualizes a possibility set down in universal structures of communication, a possibility open in principle to every culture. This also means that rational cooperation is not simply something we must endure or put up with given our circumstances—as though our real identity were that of, say, fanatical warriors who nonetheless realized that nuclear weaponry precluded the exercise of their real potentials for glory. In such a case, the warriors would presumably strive to do away with such weapons— or limit them to tactical usability—so they could get on with the real business of producing heroes in war. If Habermas's argument works, this scenario must be judged irrational, for the historical developments leading up to the lack of rational alternatives to cooperation would themselves be rationally reconstructible, i.e., one could show that they led, not to the frustration of the "good" of war making, but rather to a *rationalization* of the lifeworld, such that a *better* or rationally preferable state of affairs had been achieved.

The kind of arguments one has to make to establish the above point number among the most ambitious and difficult of Habermas's projects, and any assessment of their chances for success lies beyond the scope of this study. We can, at most, take up an adaptation specifically designed to answer Taylor (Chapter 6). Here the important point is that Habermas does indeed make arguments of this sort, and that this very attempt has certain implications for how discourse ethics does or does not involve a theory of the good. Put simply, such arguments attempt to bring the theory of communicative action to bear on a theory of modernity in order to show that social evolution displays structural homologies with individual ontogenesis.[91] The idea has a long history, going back beyond Hegel. Nor is it wholly unreasonable: precisely the intersubjective, linguistic character of individual insight and learning encourages one to expect that such learning and insight will in some fashion both depend on and produce collective learning processes.[92] If individual learning, in both the cognitive and moral spheres, moves through a series of developmental stages, why then should we not at least look for such development on a broader social scale? Habermas does not, however, construe such development along the lines of a Hegelian-style philosophy of history pretending to proclaim what must "necessarily" happen: insight into the metavalue of rational cooperation does not emerge from a necessary movement of history. Rather, if I understand him correctly, Habermas's argument need only show that once *contingent* historical dynamics create a situation—such as one dominated by internecine warfare, or by the threat of nuclear holocaust—where rational cooperation becomes an attractive alternative to other forms of conflict resolution, one can argue on the basis of the developmental logic and theory of communicative action that the move to rational cooperation represents an "epistemic gain," to use Taylor's phraseology. That is, one can argue that the move to cooperation represents an *insight*, which in turn has implications for the stability of this solution inasmuch as genuine insights cannot be forgotten at will.[93] One argues not that certain historical developments *had* to happen but how, given the prior level of learning, no *rational alternatives* existed within certain limits.[94]

91. See Jürgen Habermas, "Historical Materialism and the Development of Normative Structures," in CES, pp. 95–129.

92. Habermas's attempts to pursue this idea have taken a variety of forms: for his reception of Weber's version of the project, see TCA 1:143–271; TCA 2:43–92 examines Durkheim's explanation for the development of moral universalism, while 2:153–197 reconstructs the process in terms of the uncoupling of system and lifeworld. A direct systematic discussion of this issue can be found in Klaus Eder's *Geschichte als Lernprozeß? Zur Pathogenese politischer Modernität in Deutschland* (Frankfurt: Suhrkamp, 1985), esp. parts one and two; see also Max Miller, *Kollektive Lernprozesse: Studien zur Grundlegung einer soziologischen Lerntheorie* (Frankfurt: Suhrkamp, 1986).

93. DE, p. 105; *Discourse*, p. 84: "One feature of this enlightenment is the irreversibility of learning processes, which is based on the fact that insights cannot be forgotten at will; they can only be repressed or corrected by better insights."

94. As he writes in CES, p. 98: "This logic says nothing about the *mechanisms* of development; it says something only about the range of variations within which cultural values, moral representations, norms, and the like—at a given level of social organization—can be changed and can find different historical expression."

This last point should mute the specifically ethical overtones to Habermas's argument. Unlike Rawls, he need not rely solely on a *particular* historical experience. The historical allusions adduced above recall the *Western* road to cooperation; they do not map out how other cultures will arrive at this good. Rather, for each culture the "same universalistic content must be appropriated out of the particular life context and be anchored in the particular cultural form of life."[95] If Habermas is correct, at some point each culture should be able to reconstruct for itself the considerations leading up to its own insight into the unavoidability of the rational cooperation underlying discourse ethics. This, at least, is the claim.

3.

The above argument attempts to address Taylor's claim that moral theories such as discourse ethics depend on a constitutive good. My strategy aimed at showing that, if discourse ethics does involve such a good, it at least proposes it as a unique sort of metavalue that one cannot rationally reject except in an abstract fashion. And if that proposal carries, then the proponent of discourse ethics can easily concede the language of "good" to communitarians such as Taylor.

The argument, if it succeeds, would suggest certain gains over Rawls. We saw how Rawls had difficulty responding to at least two skeptical challenges to the original position (as bare procedure). Although the foregoing analysis of Habermas's argument would have to be considerably supplemented, it does indicate possible starting points for a response. Insofar as the Nietzchean dismisses the importance of consensual cooperation *within* a lifeworld, one could adduce communication-theoretic arguments showing how much the Nietzschean's very ability to pursue ends at all depends on the deep-seated background consensus underlying such cooperation.[96] Insofar as the traditionalist dismisses the importance of cooperation with other groups, one could adduce a theory of modern rationalization processes showing how today's world leaves no viable alternatives to such cross-cultural understanding. Versus the claim that such arguments must ultimately run along ethical-hermeneutical lines, one could grant that within any form of life this is

95. Habermas, Interview on Ethics, p. 437.
96. Naturally, an adequate response to Nietzschean critiques, which call the very notion of personal identity into question, would take one into areas far beyond those explored in this chapter.

indeed the case; but cutting across such arguments, with their references to the concrete dynamics of each group's insight into the value of cooperation, there exist universal formal structures that allow all to agree on the rationality of their variously routed trips to the telos of rational cooperation. In this way, then, a theory of communicative action-become-theory of modernity could at least begin to address the difficulties Rawls encountered in justifying his program to "unmodern" or antimodern persons outside the liberal-democratic tradition, without having to fall back solely on the forms of argument advocated by Taylor and MacIntyre.[97]

Of course, the above argument would have to shoulder a large burden of proof—but then this is no less the case with Taylor's approach. The issue turns, finally, on the relative success of two entire research programs. In this sense, the question about whether the good or right is prior admits of no middle ground and no ready answers. One must choose a research program and go with it. But this is not to say that these two programs cannot usefully inform each other. In fact, Habermas's argument depends to some extent on Taylor's. That is, if each culture can only arrive at an insight into the metavalue of rational cooperation by appropriating the lessons of its particular historical experiences, then the genealogical account employed by Taylor need not simply oppose the more formalistic approach of Habermas. Habermas would no doubt have to reconstruct the Western genealogy differently than Taylor if it is to issue in a moral universalism that is more than just one value or good among others. But he could, I think, usefully draw on Taylor's insights, and he would seemingly have to employ the same *kind* of ethical-hermeneutical argument as Taylor.

In a second sense, too, Habermas can make room for Taylor's analyses, for discourse ethics does not need to claim to solve *all* conflicts in modern society. Insisting on the necessity of discourse ethics does not rule out the importance of attempts, such as Taylor's, to work out attractive visions of the good life. I have already noted how discourse ethics attenuates the scope of the moral claim: it suffices if there are at least *some* conflict domains from which one cannot *fully* withdraw. Although I have delimited these domains as involving issues in which ongoing social cooperation is at stake, this hardly tells us much about the concrete nature of the moral domain. Here it remains unclear to what extent so-

---

97. In Chapter 6 I shall attempt to make this quick summary a bit more plausible by indicating the key to all these responses.

cieties can relieve members of the burden of consensual modes of cooperation through recourse to nonlinguistic media such as money and
power. Chapter 4, too, remained somewhat obscure on this point, noting
finally that the concrete delimitation of the moral domain must depend
on actual attempts at discourse. Only through the attempt to reach consensus can one determine whether a dispute admits of consensual resolution, or whether only compromises are possible.

The upshot is that the real work in the Taylor-Habermas debate remains to be done. The present chapter amounts to no more than a
lengthy preparation spelling out the theoretical perspective from which
the proponent of discourse ethics must set to work. While it was important to situate discourse ethics at the abstract level at which the debate
between liberals and communitarians began, in my opinion the real issues lie elsewhere, in the analysis of the actual sorts of conflicts afflicting
contemporary industrial and postindustrial pluralist society. Here one
must inquire after the real relevance and limits of discourse ethics for
specific kinds of conflicts.

Before moving on to such issues in Part Three, one further clarification
of the scope of the moral claim over against the above delimitations—as
of the claim of discourse ethics over against an ethics of the good—must
be noted. In Chapter 6 I will attempt to strengthen the plausibility of
Habermas's approach in comparison with Taylor's by showing how, despite the ways in which discourse ethics can make room for the ethical
hermeneutics of Taylor, it must nevertheless insist on the priority of justice or, if you will, the constitutive good of rational cooperation.

The Solidaristic Basis
of Moral Insight

Chapter 5 construed the Taylor-Habermas debate in the broadest possible terms, as a confrontation of research programs. At that rarified level
no single study—let alone a single argument—can decide the issue.
Nonetheless, after such lengthy investigations as those that occupied that
chapter, to conclude simply that the issue must await the relative success
of two research programs may seem rather unsatisfactory. This makes it
tempting to provide a definite argument that would at least increase the
relative plausibility of Habermas's approach in comparison with Taylor's. And in fact, such an argument can be found. In an earlier exchange
with Taylor, Habermas adapted the ambitious project outlined above in
order to counter Taylor on the latter's own ground, Wilhelm von Humboldt's theory of language. To summarize, Habermas argued that Taylor's reading of Humboldt remained too much in the thrall of the latter's
still not fully discarded Hegelianism; if Taylor were to follow more consistently the intersubjectivistic thrust of Humboldt's analysis of language,
he would have to abandon the attempt to ground morality in a substantive vision of the good life, i.e., in what amounts to a Hegelian concrete
totality.[1]

To be sure, we should not deceive ourselves that this argument is less
ambitious than that in Chapter 5; the contested reading of Humboldt

---

1. See Taylor, "Language and Society," in *Communicative Action*, ed. Honneth and
Joas, pp. 23–35; Habermas's reply is found in the same volume: "A Reply," pp. 215–222.

turns on Habermas's attempt to carry through the paradigm shift away from the philosophy of consciousness, so that the Humboldtian argument points to a confrontation of research programs no less than the reply to Heller. Moreover, in addressing the issue in terms of the Humboldt-Hegel relation and the notion of totality, Habermas moves on historical and conceptual terrain somewhat removed from the present study. Nonetheless, the basic thrust of Habermas's argument can be distilled for our purposes, without too much strain. As I shall reconstruct it, the argument turns on the intuition that, given the communicative structure of human reason, it eventually becomes *cognitively* problematic for reflective actors to make a considered choice affecting others (in potential conflict situations) without at least considering what these others have to say about the matter. To be sure, the argument depends on contingent empirical factors, as the term "eventually" indicates; here I simply assume that objective social developments both within and between societies—developments in material production, trade, communications, and so on—have already brought us to a point where this eventuality is more retrospective than prospective. If that is indeed the case, and if the communicative structure of reason has the cognitive implications I claim it does, then the metavalue of rational cooperation must increasingly constitute the overarching perspective appropriate for potential conflict situations.

If the cognitive implications to which I refer reside primarily in an intersubjective notion of insight, then one can recast Habermas's Humboldtian argument within the scope of the present study. To begin I shall present the key features of this argument and reformulate them in terms of my previous analysis of moral insight; this will bring out the central objection to Taylor's approach (section I). To clarify this objection as well as render it a bit more plausible, it helps to consider two alternative approaches that would deny any unique status to the good of cooperation (section II). This latter consideration, while not a knock-down response, does serve to clarify the basis of discourse ethics; in particular it introduces us to a deeper understanding of the relation between moral insight and solidarity (section III).

I. MORAL FORMALISM: CLUES FROM A READING OF HUMBOLDT

Humboldt's intersubjectivistic concept of language supplies the way into the relevant argument. By way of preliminaries, Habermas takes pains to show that Humboldt predates Mead by a century in conceiving language as the medium in which individuation and socialization occur concomitantly in processes of reaching understanding. As Habermas presents it, Humboldt's basic idea goes something like this: the very thing that separates nations and cultures—the diversity of languages—also unites them in making communication among them possible via translation. If language thus "individuates" peoples, it does so "in such a wonderful manner that precisely by virtue of this division it awakens a feeling of unity; indeed, it appears as a means of at least creating an idea [of such unity]."[2] What is more, the mutual understanding that language makes possible between different cultures *preserves* their differences, i.e., it does not obliterate the uniqueness of each culture's language.[3]

From the above Habermas draws the kernel of a reply to Taylor's thesis:

> The idea [of unity] to which Humboldt is alluding here lends expression to the rational potential of speech—that is, the telos inherent in the very process of reaching understanding through language. This goal of reaching universal understanding has to make itself felt as a tendency permeating society as a whole, because and in so far as the latter makes use of the mechanism of reaching understanding for its own coordinating purposes.[4]

I want to focus here not on the interpretation of Humboldt but on the way in which the cited text summarizes the reply to Heller analyzed in Chapter 5. In the above text Habermas forthrightly applies the language of "good"—i.e., goal and telos—to that "unity" for which processes of mutual understanding strive. If this "unity" corresponds to the rational cooperation I have been tentatively calling the "constitutive good" of discourse ethics, then Habermas claims here that the goal of rational cooperation is (a) universal, (b) built into language itself, indeed (c) in such a way that it "has to make itself felt." In the context of Humboldt's internationalistic theory of language, these three points accomplish the essential steps in the reply to Heller, for they claim that the metavalue driving processes of mutual understanding is not simply one good among others, nor a good with which one could dispense if one so desired. Nor can one conceive it as a substantive conception of the good life, for it is

2. Wilhelm von Humboldt, *Ueber die Verschiedenheiten des menschlichen Sprachbaues*, in Humboldt, *Werke in Fünf Bänden* III: *Schriften zur Sprachphilosophie*, p. 160, cited by Habermas, "Reply," p. 219 (I have slightly altered the translation).
3. "Reply," pp. 218–219.
4. "Reply," p. 219.

built into language itself—that is, built into processes constitutive of *any* language and not just of this or that particular language.

The interesting point here lies in the way in which this argument links the moral formalism thesis with the "no alternatives" thesis (both spelled out in Chapter 5): precisely because cooperation inheres in universal structures of communication, it should eventually increase its hold on society as a whole—i.e., it should appear more and more as the epistemic gain or process of rationalization in relation to which no viable alternatives exist. By linking this from the start with structures of language as such, Habermas/Humboldt takes any claim for the good of rational cooperation beyond the concrete confines of this or that ethos and into a formal-pragmatic realm.

This last move, however, assumes the paradigm shift away from the philosophy of consciousness. Rather than argue this in terms of a concept of totality, our previous argumentation-theoretic account of moral insight (or rational conviction) allows a more congenial way of posing Habermas's argument. By way of transition, it helps if we first identify the "rational potential" of language by which it exerts its universal "unifying" force. We note, therefore, that Habermas picks up on Humboldt's notion of the unifying power of language as follows:

> National languages not only constitute the delineating borders of a form of life, they serve simultaneously as a medium that crosses these borders, a medium in which the different totalities—each of which is the spirit of a people (*Volksgeist*)—meet the others and, each from its respective standpoint, come to an agreement on the world of all that is knowable "lying between them." In other words, languages, as the form-giving principles guiding the shape taken by the individual totality of each respectively particular worldview and way of life, only have an effect to the extent that, by virtue of their universalistic core, they enable translations to be made from each language into every other language and determine the point of convergence towards which all cultural developments are aimed.[5]

Here Habermas begins to turn Humboldt's earlier-cited remarks towards his own purposes. The key point is that the unifying power of languages lies in their convergence on a common world "lying between" the various perspectives represented in the diverse languages. This means that a language only discloses or constitutes certain objects in a medium of validity claims open to a testing beyond the boundaries of the language itself.

5. "Reply," p. 220 (trans. altered); the quotation is from Humboldt, "Ueber das vergleichende Sprachstudium in Beziehung auf die verschiedenen Epochen der Sprachentwicklung," in *Werke* III, p. 20.

In other words, competent speakers are not simply concerned about what the descriptive resources of a particular language allow them to say; they are also concerned that what they can say holds up in practice. Even within a particular form of life, the viability of a language game depends not only on its world-disclosive powers but "on the successes within the world of the practice that it makes possible."[6] Hence there is no need to conceive language games as self-contained prisons; on the contrary, their validity dimension makes learning processes possible, and not simply in relation to external nature. Once speakers of different languages encounter each other, the orientation to validity that both sides share simply in virtue of their linguistic competence provides an impetus to reaching understanding. Learning is thus possible *between peoples* as well. This seems to be the idea behind Habermas's claim that "by virtue of their universalistic core" languages both enable translations and determine convergence on the knowable world "lying between them."

Admittedly, an impressionistic account such as this cannot replace a more detailed theory of communicative action working in conjunction with the empirical study of actual linguistic practices. Important for our purposes is how the Humboldtian analysis of language just sketched bears on moral formalism. Should the analysis hold up, it would imply that the demand to test claims for their intersubjective validity represents a universal pragmatic structure inherent in language as such. This suggests at least the possibility of a formal-procedural moral theory grounded not in a particular worldview, nor recommending this or that concrete conception of the good life, but rather taking its point of departure from the pragmatics of redeeming moral validity claims. Such a theory would be a formal one insofar as it presumably could abstract from the particular disclosive powers of this or that language and find its basis in a telos shared by all languages. A telos of this sort would satisfy Habermas's formalism thesis, i.e., his claim that the good of discursively achieved cooperation, or mutual understanding, does not amount to a substantive conception of the good life. Substantive goods must be disclosed by particular languages; their realization generally involves one in a concrete form of life. But the good of mutual understanding resides in the validity orientation of language as such. At least in principle, it should display a certain independence of the particular worldview disclosed by this or that language.

6. "Reply," pp. 221–222; see also *Discourse*, pp. 318–321, 330–335, for the same argument turned against Castoriadis.

Habermas's argument against Taylor, however, does more than merely suggest a possibility: he maintains that a workable moral theory *must* be procedural. In what follows I want to reformulate his argument in terms of the concept of moral insight developed in Part One. Here I assume that Taylor would not seriously dispute a cognitivist approach to morality, if we take "moral cognitivism" in a broad sense, as the view that questions such as What ought I/we do? or, How ought I/we live? admit of intersubjectively binding answers, i.e., criticizable validity claims the production of which requires corresponding insights. Rather, the issue turns on where one locates practical insight and the rational conviction it produces.

Taylor represents one approach to this issue. In grounding moral theory in the constitutive power of background languages, Taylor links practical insight to the power of *particular semantic systems*. The insights through which one answers morally relevant questions are made possible precisely in virtue of the particular meanings that constitute the relevant values and goods. There is no need to deny here that understanding a language, or semantic system, depends on involvement in the practices of a given community. I am not reducing language to its structure at the cost of its practical dimension.[7] That is, by using the term "semantics" I do not mean to imply that the meanings constituted by a language exist in abstraction from what people using such a language actually *do*, in what action situations they utter one thing and not another. Taylor does not fall behind this basically Wittgensteinian point.

All the same, his semanticist account does fall short of a fully intersubjective notion of practical insight. For Taylor tends to have language constitute both meaning *and* justification: "Language plays an indispensable role as an expressive medium in the overall domain of practical reason. We express our moral ends and our understanding of ourselves as humans in such a way that we thereby at the same time understand and justify our ends."[8] This suggests that answering moral questions depends on appropriating the right language. It follows that the task of moral theory, insofar as it deals with the answering of moral questions, is to articulate this language. In Hegelian terms, the moral theorist must articulate a concrete totality: a substantive vision of the good life.[9] The moral theorist must provide an attractive account of how the substantive

7. Taylor brings out this distinction in "Language," pp. 24–25.
8. Taylor, "Language," p. 34; translation amended; for the original German, see Taylor, "Sprache und Gesellschaft," p. 51.
9. Cf. "Reply," pp. 218f.

strands tying together cultural traditions, individual identities, and social-institutional forms of life can be so integrated as to allow a rational resolution of the tensions and conflicts that beset such totalities.

Taylor does not deny that languages and forms of life emerge today— even within a given society—in the plural. However, his focus on the constitutive semantic power of language does not do justice to the fact that such languages, in constituting answers to moral questions, thereby raise validity claims the illocutionary force of which goes beyond the boundaries of the language in which the answer was first formulated.[10] Because the practices of forms of life impinge on one another, and because the claims associated with those practices admit of mutual translation, there arises both a pressure towards, and the possibility of, reaching an understanding.[11] If a group's claims are associated only with practices that do not disturb other groups, there is no pressure; if the practices and claims are so opaque to other groups that they must remain incomprehensible, then mutual understanding fails and social coordination must recur to effect either compromise or the domination of one group over the others, or of the others over the one. But if the practices both impinge on one another and raise competing claims admitting of translation, then—on an intersubjective notion of insight—neither side can rest content, in a cognitive sense, with the constitutive power of *its* language, but must enter into a dialogical reflection with the others so as to reach a consensus settling both the cognitive uncertainty and the practical conflict.[12]

The linchpin to this form of moral cognitivism lies in the notion of insight or rational conviction upon which confidence in a claim's validity rests. If the claim represents a normative expectation impinging on other groups, then those holding the claim cannot base their rational conviction solely on the constitutive powers of a particular language. On the contrary, the notion of conviction contained in (U) implies that one can

10. "Reply," pp. 221f.
11. This does not mean that translatability is wholly prior to mutual understanding; on the contrary, the orientation to validity shared by all viable languages also generates the pressure to *bring about* those agreements that first make translations available between different language groups.
12. One does not have to presuppose an implausible degree of translatability between languages in this scenario; in fact, the growing consensus on human rights and democracy puts the burden of proof on those who would deny such translatability; see EzD, p. 202; for more extensive arguments against exaggerated incommensurability theses, see Stout, *Ethics after Babel*, pp. 205–218; Manfred Frank, "Gibt es rational unentscheidbare Konflikte im Verständigungshandeln?" *Das Sagbare und das Unsagbare: Studien zur deutsch-französischen Hermeneutik und Texttheorie*, expanded ed. (Frankfurt: Suhrkamp, 1990), pp. 590–607.

confidently maintain a normative claim vis-à-vis others only insofar as one has confidence that the others could be equally rationally convinced, hence convinced within the constitutive structures of their *own* language *after* they have tested their conviction against one's own.

At this point in the argument Taylor might attempt to pull the notion of rational conviction back onto the substantive ground of a particular totality, arguing that conviction between different groups or persons can only obtain insofar as both groups succeed in creating a *third* constitutive language. On Taylor's account, such a language would have to have all the "thick" motivational features associated with each group's initial language. Hence there follows the Herculean task imposed on aesthetically sensitized theorists of pulling together into a harmonious substantive totality the variety of traditions and cultures at stake in a given conflict, in order once again to ground cognitively redeemable validity claims about how to resolve such conflicts. By locating moral theory at the level of a substantive vision of the good life, moral cognitivism cannot get off the ground until theorists have resolved the concrete conflict potentials inherent in diverse traditions. Precisely the enormity of Taylor's task induces Habermas to shift moral theory away from this substantive level and ground it in the idealizations informing the *performance* or *pragmatics* of the mutual search for rational conviction.

Once again we see that the issue between Habermas and Taylor turns on the relative chances of two research programs. Here I am less interested in this fact than in exactly how these two different approaches rest on different conceptions of moral insight. In the postscript to Part One I distinguished two levels at which one might apply the term "insight." Direct insights organize experience, thereby rendering it humanly meaningful; reflective insights ask the further question, Is this way of organizing experience in fact correct? In Taylor's terms, direct insights constitute or disclose objects of experience, and to that extent constitute goods and values as well. In the context of a particular social coordination problem, we can further distinguish between the manner in which the participants' language forms a background that first constitutes the problem as such, on the one hand, and the manner in which the participants' creative exercise of their linguistic competences draws on background resources to fashion new ways of looking at the problem situation, such that the problem can be resolved, on the other hand. Of course, for many conflicts it will be enough to draw upon already available background norms and values, and creative exercise will be minimal. In acknowledging that language involves both "structure" and "practice,"

Taylor's analysis takes in both this background dimension of language, by which conflicts and their solution are structured, as well as the fact that participants can go beyond their pregiven background and creatively redefine their situations along with the language by which they structure situations.[13]

It is precisely at this point that Habermas takes a further step, maintaining that the use of language not only involves constitutive and creative accomplishments but a *reflective* or critical moment as well: in fact, creative accomplishments are called forth by practical questions and problems, and as such head toward the further question, Is this solution right? or Is it appropriate? A moral theory that takes its point of departure from the practice of not simply proposing but also *redeeming* validity claims cannot rest content with the constitutive power of particular languages. It must look to the further practices by which achievements in semantic creativity are tested against other languages and points of view. And if these practices are to achieve their goal of mutual understanding, they must consist in formal structures of language use, i.e., structures available in principle to language users of any form of life.[14]

Demonstrating the existence of such structures would take us into a theory of communicative action and perhaps eventually into comparative linguistics. Short of such studies, I can at least propose the following consideration: as soon as one links the validity of a particular conception of morality with its acceptability to *other* groups, one has committed oneself at some level to a formal-procedural moral theory. For in that case the substantive disclosure of moral sources within a given language no longer suffices to establish the corresponding moral claims as valid. One need not deny the importance of world disclosure for morality. Rather, my point concerns the decisive status accorded to the intersubjective character of moral insight: what my language "discloses" to me (or my group) no longer *suffices* for moral conviction, but depends on our ability to convince speakers of other languages that our moral norms hold for them as well. In the next section I will adduce further support for this argument by turning it around. We shall then see that if such a

---

13. As Taylor puts it: "Social tradition can continue to exert an influence through individuals only to the extent that it is continually renewed by them—like all structures, it continues to exist by virtue of practice. And in the course of this it necessarily undergoes changes, be it as the result of creative achievements and deliberate innovations or owing to the pressure of ecological, economic or political conditions, or even, ultimately, owing to some unclassified event [*Geschehen*]." See Taylor, "Language," p. 25.
14. Cf. *Discourse*, pp. 299–300.

formal account involves a constitutive good, it is a good exerting a unique claim on our attention.

II. THE "NO ALTERNATIVES" THESIS: THE LATENT POWER OF THE OTHER

In the previous section I attempted to trace back the difference between Habermas and Taylor to diverging views on the nature of rational conviction about legitimate norms. It is the intersubjective notion of insight, I contend, that ultimately lends the Habermasian research program its plausibility: if practical insight in fact rests on a pragmatically structured intersubjective basis, then there is some plausibility to the idea that discourse ethics lays claim to a metavalue enjoying a unique status vis-à-vis other values and goods. Now if one construes this metavalue as the constitutive good of rational cooperation (or cooperation based on mutual understanding), then establishing its unique status involves two theses, as we saw in Habermas's reply to Heller: a moral formalism thesis and a "no alternatives" thesis. My strategy in this chapter, then, is to ground the plausibility of both theses in the intersubjective notion of insight. Section I dealt with the formalism thesis: inasmuch as the disposition towards rational cooperation inheres in formal structures of insightful will-formation, the metavalue or good of such cooperation resists assimilation to a substantive vision of the good life. In the present section I want to take this a step further, suggesting how the intersubjectively structured basis of conviction allows us to make sense of Habermas's "no alternatives" thesis. "Proving" a thesis of this scope, of course, is out of the question. It will satisfy me simply to make the following claim plausible: if rational will-formation rests on an intersubjective basis, then there exists an immanent practical disposition toward rational cooperation *against which* alternative forms of will-formation can maintain themselves only precariously in today's world, where the need for social coordination extends ever more intensely beyond local boundaries. In this sense, then, the good of rational cooperation has, for certain domains and on the whole, no viable alternatives—at least for reflective agents.

Now this way of understanding the "no alternatives" thesis involves a number of qualifications, which must first be clarified (subsection 1). In order to render the thesis itself plausible, it helps to entertain its opposite: that an agent could always dispense with the goal of rational cooperation (subsection 2). What such alternatives deny, of course, is the link between insight and solidarity noted in (U); in section III, I will argue that the deepest "good" informing discourse ethics lies in this notion of solidarity.

I.

I take Habermas's "no alternatives" thesis as carefully qualified; one cannot identify it with a philosophy of history in the Hegelian sense. The claim, as I understand it, amounts to this: the immanent structures of communicative action generate a certain pressure for rationalization processes to develop in a specific direction, in contrast to which alternative paths must appear irrational or repressive. As a sheer matter of fact, individuals and groups can and have taken these alternative paths. However, inasmuch as communicative action directs practical insight along specific lines, alternatives must constantly work against possibilities for learning built into communication itself. This renders such alternatives metastable at best, and unstable in the long run and on the whole. But what kind of qualifications does one make with a phrase such as "on the whole"?

One qualification, which already appeared in section I, defines the domain of rational cooperation as that where the practices and claims of at least two individuals or groups conflict. This corresponds to the standard posttraditional definition of morality. By approaching the issue in terms of a notion of practical insight, however, one can see how this definition, rather than appealing to an individualistic—or worse, arbitrary—domain criterion, actually marks off an area subject to a peculiar *cognitive* burden: that area of social life where one's rational conviction of the rightness of a practice encounters opposed convictions and practices, and thus can no longer stabilize itself simply *within* a form of life or tradition.

To begin with, then, opponents of the "no alternatives" claim must tailor their counterclaim to just this area of conflict if they are to oppose Habermas on his own ground. At least two further qualifications follow. Habermas does not deny that, for any *particular* conflict situation, cooperation based on moral norms may appear to those involved as one of several goods among which they can, in fact, choose.[15] To hold the contrary, one would either have to deny the possibility of immoral action or conceive the good of cooperation as so abstract and all-inclusive as to be uninteresting. Nor does discourse ethics depend on the claim that actors

15. EzD, p. 188; cf. also pp. 135f.

always *ought* to coordinate their plans on the basis of mutual under-standing. Habermas recognizes that such a demand would quickly over-burden the communicative capacities of actors; hence it is quite rational to hand over a good deal of this coordinating power to strategic action steered by "nonlinguistic media" such as monetary instruments, or the exercise of power, etc. The economic sphere, for example, relies more or less on individuals' strategic reactions to anonymous market effects to ensure (supposedly) an efficiently coordinated distribution of goods and services. A society thereby spares itself the overwhelming tasks required for a planned economy in which economic decisions are made on the basis of a discourse directly assessing the relative needs and productive capacities of various spheres. Beyond some rather abstract considera-tions, determining the exact degree to which nonlinguistic media can al-leviate the need for explicitly consensual communicative action remains an empirical question.[16]

In sum, discourse ethics makes a rather modest claim for its allegedly unavoidable good. It allows one to acknowledge fully the value of self-interest, or of goods and values besides that of rational cooperation, in their respective domains. In addition, it does not deny the possibility of choosing not to pursue the good of cooperation in any given situation; neither does it assume that all social action must be explicitly coopera-tive. Rather, it claims that in today's world rational actors cannot *in general* forego the good of cooperation in contexts marked by conflict po-tentials. This is far from inflating such cooperation into a kind of categorical imperative for every particular situation. At the same time, it has enough strength to subordinate contexts of strategic and teleolog-ical action to communicative action in principle—right retains an over-arching priority over the goods informing strategic/teleological action, as I shall suggest later.

Therefore, denying the privileged status of the constitutive good of discourse ethics implicates one in a rather strong counterclaim to the ef-fect that agents can act rationally without *ever* basing their choice on the good of rational cooperation. One might mitigate this, of course, by ar-guing that rational cooperation is itself a derivative good—say the result of deeper strategic considerations—and thus appears as a particular

---

16. See TCA 2:153–197 for Habermas's developmental analysis of the emergence of nonlinguistic modes of social coordination; 2:199–299, esp. 261–282, where he criticizes Parson's attempt to cast *all* social action in these terms: this sets abstract limits to a non-pathological recourse to nonlinguistic media of coordination; cf. also *Discourse*, pp. 349–367.

good in comparison with other possibilities flowing from this deeper source. Rational choice theories represent just such an attempt; in order to make themselves plausible they must, like Habermas's theory of communicative action, develop into entire research programs. To the extent that such alternatives manage to do this, we have to do with a debate not unlike that between Taylor and Habermas—a debate, that is, far exceeding the scope of this study. Hence the present argument has the quite modest aim of indicating the burden of argument set for such alternatives by the results reached thus far in this study. To specify the counterclaim yet more precisely, I will approach it from the perspective of the single actor deliberating about what she ought to do in the face of several possible goals or actions. Although some might question this starting point itself, I adopt it here for the sake of argument. In any case, imagine an actor having certain desires and interests interpreted within a cultural heritage, and standing before a set of possible actions that would bring about different states of affairs. On what basis—on the basis of what kind of practical insight—does she decide to act?

2.

Rather than develop an entire theory of action, let us consider two possible principles of decision, each of which implies a certain notion of practical insight different from that given in (U). By framing the issue this way we can quickly compare discourse ethics with two alternatives that agents in fact adopt often enough. Since each of these alternatives will claim that following (U) is merely one option a rational actor may adopt, we can ask what it would mean to follow the given alternative *exclusively*. Thus I take the counterclaim to be that a rational actor may dispense with (U) *generally* in favor of the alternative principle.

Both alternatives represent extremes. One is the principle, 'That action/norm is right by which one furthers one's own self-interest (or happiness, or good)'. I shall call this (SI) for short. The other states: 'That action/norm is right by which one follows/enforces the dictates of the group's worldview'. This rather traditionalistic principle prioritizes what we might call "group value," so let us call it (GV).[17] Whereas the first elevates the individual's good above all else, the second makes the group's

17. These two orientations roughly correspond to the two dominant social-psychological models of the person; see, for example, E. Allan Lind and Tom R. Tyler, *The Social Psychology of Procedural Justice* (New York: Plenum, 1988), pp. 221–242. Note also that one should not limit these decision principles to situations where the action in

good "constitutive." In a manner parallel to (U), choosers can employ these principles to "justify" substantive norms or maxims of action. For example, (SI) would presumably validate the norm 'One ought to lie if this will advance one's own interests', while (GV) might validate 'Nonbelievers are to be excluded from political office'. Despite their rather crude character, I trust the reader has had sufficient experience of their practical force in actual decision making.

Now one should note that two actors, one following (SI) and the other (GV), would be able to apply the relevant principle to many situations without conflicts of principle. Thus, in situations where self-interest or group value is taken by other involved persons as the appropriate standard, the conflicts that arise concern the agents' competing concrete goals and not the principles by which the agents choose these goals. Eventually, however, situations will arise in which acting on either of these principles will lead to conflicts, i.e., situations where not everyone agrees beforehand that self-interest or group value should determine action. Now what would it mean to say that in such conflict situations one still has, in general, the option to adopt (U) or not? Suppose our actors decide to exercise their freedom to reject (U) and stick with (SI) and (GV), respectively. This leads them to validate and then pursue certain actions, say X_{si} and X_{gv}, respectively. Suppose further that those affected adversely by their decisions were to appeal to their reason by claiming "You ought not to do X_{gv}" or "You ought to moderate your pursuit of X_{si} to take account of its impact on us." Discourse ethics is predicated on the illocutionary force of such appeals, such that they demand argued responses from those to whom they are made. But if making such a response presupposes a particular good of rational cooperation, then our followers of (SI) and (GV) would presumably have the option of disregarding the cognitive force of such appeals as a *general* way of proceeding, i.e., in *all* cases.[18] The following will test the consequent in this conditional statement. If this consequent should appear problematic, then by *modus tollens* discourse ethics does not presuppose a particularistic conception of the good.

Naturally, one can generally disregard the other's appeal in the sense

---

question has a merely instrumental relation to the good of self-interest or group value. It also includes cases where the action is seen as intrinsically good, hence cases in which the individual's self-interest simply coincides with the performance of the validated action, or where the group's worldview holds that a certain action is a good in itself.

18. Naturally, when those making the appeals have the power of sanction, actors following our alternatives have their own strategic reasons for considering the appeal externally, i.e., as a possible predictor of the other's resort to force.

that one can, as a matter of fact, disregard it in any situation. The discourse ethics I have been concerned to elaborate presupposes that one would in any case *feel* the force of the other's appeal, at least to some extent. This suggests that a reflective person, at least, could disregard the other's appeal only with a certain feeling of guilt or unease, or she would have to dismiss it on the grounds of some reason she at least gave to herself. The reason is that the other's claim *objectively* alters the choice situation confronting the person reflecting on what she ought to do, thereby changing the conditions for an insight into an acceptable response to the situation.[19] Thus the value or good of mutual understanding exercises a pull intrinsic to the situation, one that exists even if our actor chose to disregard it. Now if such a value really is merely one optional value, then (U) can always be rejected without cognitive difficulties in favor of alternatives such as (SI) and (GV). Such an option, I want to suggest, requires that one always be able to take a *different kind of attitude* towards others' appeals. One must disregard the other's appeal *as* an appeal with cognitive force. This disregard may take at least one of two forms depending on the principle one follows and the notion of insight underlying it.

Someone following (SI) examines a situation in terms of furthering her own goals and interests. This implies the strategic-teleological model of action, whose paradigm is that of the lone actor over against an environment populated with factors either furthering or hindering the actor's success. These factors can include other persons and relationships which the actor finds satisfying; nonetheless, the common denominator in their evaluation remains the actor's personal happiness or success. In this environment the others' appeals can never appear in their own right, but only as vectors in a force field within which the actor must learn to maneuver if she hopes to realize her plans. These appeals can only signal possible obstacles the actor must either take into account or somehow "get around" if she is to succeed. In this situation a certain "surface argumentation" may develop, but the intrinsic seriousness of the others' claims for the actor's own opinions and normative expectations will not be heard. The self-interested strategist thus assimilates practical insight to the purposive-rational capacity for a thorough strategic calculation of situational possibilities.

A traditionalist actor following (GV) takes a somewhat different attitude, but with the same results. For her the group's worldview poses a

19. Cf. PV, pp. 115, 116, 118.

claim so absolute that any appeals not congruent with that worldview fall on deaf ears. To be sure, the follower of (GV) may also be willing to argue; the difficulty lies in the unassailableness of the background assumptions supporting her worldview.[20] As soon as the other's appeal challenges those assumptions, it falls off the traditional globe and ceases to have any weight. Even here, however, the traditionalist may be able to give reasons to the other: "Naturally you cannot appreciate my position, for you have not had the (privileged) experiences (or background or upbringing) that I have had." Now the affected other will find this difficult, for the traditionalist would impose certain normative expectations on others who have not shared in precisely those experiences grounding insight into the norm. The traditionalist, then, assimilates practical insight to the dictates of a privileged access to a particular tradition and experience.

These two examples raise the general question, What do I/we do in the face of conflicting claims regarding behavior I/we have come to view as legitimate from the standpoint of self-interest or a group's worldview? To maintain consistently an attitudinal alternative to (U) such as (SI) or (GV) in *this* context would require a kind of imperviousness, a cognitive impermeability, to further questions about the validity of goods and values constituted within a particular point of view. One would have to be impervious to the other as a source of questions and reasons, and this in turn implies a certain monological notion of practical reasoning, for both (SI) and (GV) reduce the source of insight to a *single* voice: either the monologue of self-advancement (or even individual authenticity) or the monolith of a single tradition.[21]

I do not mean to deny the fact that people can and do quite easily manage to close their ears to one another. That is not the issue at stake in the Habermas-Taylor debate. Rather, the issue is whether and to what extent they can ignore affected others when they approach the moral situation in a *reflective attitude*. Moral theory, it seems to me, must at least assume such an attitude. In that case, the alternatives, taken to the level of overarching principles for reflectively deciding moral questions, claim no less than this: that in conflict situations giving rise to the question, How am I/we to act? one need not consider the cognitive force of the

20. Cf. TCA 2:188–190.
21. In fact, traditions almost never speak with a single voice. The intolerant kind of traditionalism depicted here, then, must conceive itself in fundamentalistic terms that reduce traditional complexity to clear and simple answers. For those aware of the diversity in their own tradition, there is generally a greater willingness and ability to seek points of contact and agreement with those outside the tradition.

questions, arguments, and counterarguments of other involved persons who will be affected by how one decides. The scenario, in other words, is one in which an agent's actions will affect others, the agent strives to act on the basis of her "considered judgment" and, all that notwithstanding, she finds no intrinsic necessity to take the others' point of view into consideration. But this, it seems, must pose a problem. For a considered judgment is a judgment based on insight and hence a judgment presenting itself as rational. Agents following (SI) or (GV) must therefore deal with the fact that other persons, to all appearances just as rational, object to their chosen course of action. There thus exists a contradiction between the reflective attitude demanded by moral questions and an attitude consistently oriented by (SI) or (GV). One would have to ask whether such agents have actually perceived the choice situation as a moral one at all.

How can agents following (SI) or (GV) deal with the rationality of others? How do we explain the obvious fact that even reflective agents can and have managed ·vith not a little consistency to act on such principles? In fact, such phenomena can be explained, for precisely the cognitive uncertainty of modern pluralism generates mechanisms for avoiding others' challenges. In this way, the practice of these alternatives actually witnesses to the power of a latent intersubjectivity that asserts itself by its absence, as it were. I already noted above how each principle deals with others' reasons. One might extend the point by noting that the alternative can either *neutralize* the other's reasons or *invoke a higher normative context*. The self-interested actor will typically attempt to dismiss the force of moral reasons altogether as illusory. For example, she may rationalize her dismissal of the other's appeals by claiming that the other too is—behind the mask of reason giving—interested in the exercise of power just as much as herself, and would react the same way if positions were reversed.[22] For the traditionalist these options often coincide: precisely her access to a reason inaccessible to others negates the force of their counterarguments. I do not want to tarry over the details of such strategies. Rather, I want to focus on how they reveal what they deny—would they be at all necessary except as preventive measures against the threat posed by the intrinsic, individual- and group-transcending power of another's questions and claims? Both mechanisms absolve one of engaging the other's claim as a validity claim. One is

---

22. This might be equivalent to invoking a higher norm if it implies that the other would recognize a higher-level norm defining the situation as a strategic one in which ordinary moral claims do not obtain.

thereby spared a measure of cognitive uncertainty—but only at a cost. In section III, I will inquire further into this high-priced absence in order to uncover the real heart of discourse ethics.

III. INSIGHT AND SOLIDARITY

I considered the alternative principles of will-formation (SI) and (GV) in order to lend some prima facie plausibility to the claim that the meta-value of rational cooperation cannot easily be ignored on the whole—one does so today only by incurring certain rationality costs that work to destabilize alternatives to (U)-governed cooperation. Again, I am not denying such alternative principles their due; we must not lose sight of the fact that the material of moral discourse consists precisely in individual interests and group values. At stake is only whether the principles based on such interests and values can provide stable *overarching* perspectives for arriving at rational practical conviction. In this section I want to clarify further the positive grounds for this thesis in a cognitive notion of solidarity.

If we connect the foregoing with the analysis of (U) in Part One, we can say that the primary cost of such alternatives is that incurred by their consistent need to suppress the solidaristic moment of practical insight. As we saw in Chapter 3, the discourse-ethical account of practical insight enjoins each participant to submit proposed action norms to assessment by all those affected; the individual's rational conviction is possible only in view of the others' rational acceptance. The core notion of justice tacit in each individual's right to his or her *own* rational consideration of proposed norms is thus indissolubly linked with a solidaristic duty to submit one's own rational consideration to that of everyone else. Individual autonomy thus goes hand in hand with a universal solidarity. It is above all this solidarity at the heart of rational conviction that the two alternatives either deny or foreshorten.

To be sure, the (GV) principle recognizes those substantive lifeworld solidarities consolidated by a particular worldview. Here we must keep in mind the distinction drawn in Chapter 4 between these prereflective lifeworld solidarities and the notion of solidarity inhering in (U). By locating the source of rational conviction in adherence to a particular worldview, (GV) collapses the validity dimension of a particular ethical-moral language to a semantic, constitutive level. This means that for (GV) the validity character of normative claims rests not on their inter-subjective redeemability but directly on the particular substantive content of the claim. Solidarity is achieved directly at the level of content, in other words: individuals support one another precisely because they follow *these* norms and *not* those.

Certainly this level of concrete solidarity plays an indispensable role in human life. Our interpersonal relationships deepen and take on a greater richness to the extent that we share commitments to specific traditions that make a claim on us. Nor is there any point in denying Gadamer's contention that individuals must "always already" largely presuppose the unproblematic character of their traditions. The difficulty lies in taking (GV) as a general attitude towards practical issues that *have become* problematic. In that case, (GV)'s fixation on semantic solidarity, as it were, denies the pragmatic level of solidarity: for (GV), we are not united by our ability, as autonomous and rational agents, to take positions on validity claims on the basis of insights into the legitimacy of moral values, but only by our prudent adherence to particular pregiven values. In so collapsing solidarity to the substantive-semantic level, (GV) also negates the individual's autonomous role in the evaluation of normative validity. At most, individual insight resides in the prudential capacity to apply group standards, or, conversely, to identify (and thus avoid) departures from these standards.

(SI) allows for a certain solidarity as well, but again a solidarity reduced to the level of content. After all, even thieves will maintain a certain loyalty to one another so long as interests coincide. Thus a self-interested actor will support others, and seek the support of others, on the grounds that they pursue *this* goal and not *that* one. As with concrete group solidarities, here too we need not deny the importance of such self-interested associations for human living. The difficulty, again, lies in elevating (SI) to a general attitude toward practical issues. Although the individual indeed retains a power of autonomous insight here, it is an insight that remains at the level of a strategic means-end calculation. Thus individual autonomy does not depend on the normative claims of others. If (GV) heads toward a (group) solidarity without autonomy, then (SI) defines (individual) autonomy apart from solidarity.

I do not mean to identify these rather crude characterizations of the two alternative notions of solidarity with any developed theoretical positions. The description of these alternative models of will-formation can at most indicate prima facie burdens of proof that theories such as Taylor's or rational choice theory face in relation to discourse ethics; or perhaps they are only shadow images such theories must dispel in order to get going. Rather, the problematic character of these alternatives is designed to lend at least a prima facie plausibility to Habermas's "no alternatives" thesis. According to that thesis, if discourse ethics presupposes the constitutive good of rational cooperation, this good is one that cannot be fully replaced in certain domains of action. If, on the contrary, rational cooperation is merely one particular good among several alternatives, then it should be plausible to conceive reflective actors as exclusively choosing such alternatives over the good of rational cooperation. For example, it must be possible to imagine agents following principles such as (SI) or (GV) precisely in those contexts for which discourse ethics outfits itself. But if following such principles appears somehow inappropriate or problematic—if it appears to miss something we take as important to being human—then there is reason to believe that adopting discourse-ethical procedures does not exclude such attractive alternatives after all. Thus these supposed alternatives cannot amount to plausible "other goods" *eo ipso* excluded by the discourse-ethical option for the good of rational cooperation. This is not, to be sure, a knock-down argument; and one may still reasonably ask whether discourse ethics can do justice to legitimate forms of self-interest and group value. But my aim has been a rather modest one: to suggest that reflective actors cannot readily dispense with the cognitive intersubjectivity given with (U) as an overarching perspective in certain domains of action—and thus cannot dispense with the metavalue of rational cooperation.

The particular absence or gap that renders the alternatives problematic is felt most keenly, I think, in the way both imply a certain imperviousness to the other's appeal. They require me to engage only the reasons of others of *like* disposition: those who either can further my goals and happiness, or who accept my own worldview. The other who is different, who questions my choice, might receive a strategic consideration as one who might cross my plans; or perhaps I will grant this other the benefit of posing as a mere practice target for my dismissive "arguments." In both cases, the other's claim has been assimilated to my own point of view. But insofar as the other eludes such assimilation, insofar as the other potentially poses questions for my point of view, she remains opaque, mute.

By peering through this gap in the alternatives, we can glimpse the opposite intuition at the heart of discourse ethics: an openness to others who are different or of different minds. Apart from the consideration of the others' questions and arguments, one cannot rationally claim to be convinced of the rightness of a norm or action. This demanding idealization, of course, requires a suitable contextualization if it is to be at all practicable. I will address the difficulties presented by real contexts of discourse in Part Three. Here I want to differentiate the discourse-ethical notion of solidarity from that contained in the alternatives. In locating rational will-formation in (U), discourse ethics goes beyond both alternatives and lays claim to a deeper level of solidarity based on each individual's rational autonomy. Solidarity and autonomy are not separated, nor is solidarity restricted to the substantive level of like interests and worldviews.

In Chapter 4 I distinguished two elements in the discourse-ethical concept of moral solidarity. On the one hand, solidarity implies a concern for the individual's welfare; on the other hand, this welfare becomes a matter of concern in connection with moral values shaping the structure of cooperation in a lifeworld. Such moral values constitute what I have termed "specific moral solidarities" issuing from the discursive processing of prereflective lifeworld solidarities. Since individuals bring their concrete identities and needs into discourse—their particular worldviews and cultural values—the resulting points of agreement reflect more abstract, mediated endorsements of such values, or perhaps even their direct endorsement. In this fashion the particular values around which concrete lifeworld solidarities have already coalesced are transformed, or perhaps screened and selected for their universalizable moral potential. Insofar as discourse yields consensus on substantive moral norms incorporating a thin common good, one can identify the structures of cooperation given with that good as specifically moral solidarities. For example, the right to freedom of religious expression goes beyond the concrete solidarities existing within religious groups to a broader, more abstract moral level, where each group can recognize and endorse the others' equal right to such expression.

Modes of moral cooperation such as that described above, however, ultimately issue from (U)'s demand that each submit his or her proposals to the consideration of all. Precisely this demand, which contains the intersubjective notion of insight, distinguishes the discourse-ethical enterprise from projects such as Taylor's. The concept of insight or rational will-formation, then, already involves a solidaristic moment that *undergirds* the specific moral solidarities and concern for individual welfare distinguished above. What ultimately generates one's concern for the welfare of the other, what requires participants to undertake a cooperative search for moral values around which a rational cooperation among autonomous persons can develop, are the cognitive pressures that issue from the validity character of language itself: the discourse-ethical "fact of reason" that my rational conviction depends on yours and vice versa.

This fundamental connection with others has been expressed in various ways. Larmore speaks of the "equal respect" underlying liberal neutrality; Hegel's notion of mutual recognition is not far removed.[23] David M. Levin has recently drawn on phenomenological insights (primarily Merleau-Ponty's) to uncover the ground of this cognitive intersubjectivity in "corporeal reversibilities."[24] Although I do not consider these other formulations wholly antithetical to the approach taken here, in the present context I want to designate this intersubjectivity at the heart of practical insight a "rational human solidarity." I choose this term for the following reasons: (a) as "rational," it makes itself felt first of all in a *cognitive* manner, as the requirement that the individual's autonomous rational conviction depends on that of others; (b) as "solidarity," it includes the *other* in one's own rational will-formation; (c) as "human," it does not rest content with concrete coincidences of worldview or interests, but extends to *all persons* capable of questioning and arguing.

The plausibility of the "no alternatives" thesis, then, ultimately depends on whether practical insight has such a solidaristic moment, which agents confronting growing coordination problems can resist only in part and in the short run. My argument, in sum, is this: If rational cooperation represents the constitutive good of discourse ethics, and if such cooperation turns on the rational conviction of those involved, then this good enjoys a privileged status: the intersubjectivity of rational conviction represents a dynamic that cuts across particular cultures and destabilizes modes of coordination that deny the solidaristic basis of will-formation. The solidarity existing at the heart of practical insight constitutes an immanent disposition, as it were—inhering in language use itself—to subject social coordination to processes of mutual understanding. Alternatives must therefore rely on mechanisms that counteract this disposition, mechanisms that become increasingly costly. Naturally, a full defense of this thesis would take us into empirical analyses of the problems facing modern social coordination. How far this disposition extends and the relative force it exerts against countervailing ten-

23. Larmore, *Patterns*, pp. 61–67; cf. also Hegel's *Phenomenology of Spirit* on the struggle for recognition—here too one catches sight of the individual's need for the other's uncoerced assent. Cf. also Stephen Darwall, *Impartial Reason* (Ithaca, N.Y.: Cornell University Press, 1983). Darwall links impersonal reasons and values with intersubjectivity in a way that captures some of the points I make here.

24. Levin, *The Listening Self: Personal Growth, Social Change and the Closure of Metaphysics* (New York: Routledge, 1989), chap. 5; the quoted phrase is found on p. 172.

dencies—what kind of systemic barriers it would confront—remain unclear. One would have to assess the thesis, too, by comparing its relative explanatory and interpretive success against alternatives such as systems theory, rational choice theory, or Gadamerian hermeneutics.

The latter admissions bring us once again to the limits of the present study. There are other limits as well to what we can accomplish here. As Habermas has emphasized, one cannot expect moral theory to *create* a solidaristic disposition in individuals. For those too cynical to bother with the other's appeal, moral theory proves too weak to convince them to take that appeal seriously. For those who simply fail to perceive that appeal in the first place, moral theory arrives on the scene "too late." In these two senses, then, moral theory cannot "answer" the question, Why be moral?[25] What it can do, as I have tried to show, is indicate on communication-theoretic grounds why those who are neither pathologically asocial nor terminally cynical are responding to demands of reason when they take the moral point of view—and are not simply blinding themselves to other values of equal importance. In *this* sense the question, Why be moral (as opposed to aesthetically creative, or efficient, etc.)? does have an answer.

IV. CONCLUDING SUMMARY

The foregoing analysis suggests some further refinements to our earlier discussion on the priority of right (subsection 1). I shall then close Part Three with a backward glance at the course of this rather involved reply to Taylor (subsection 2).

1.

Tracing discourse ethics back to an intersubjective notion of insight has a number of implications. Given limitations of space, I present these simply as a list of tentative conclusions.

First, if my conviction about a choice of action or lifestyle is intrinsically susceptible to others' questions, reasons, and claims, then one can define the moral domain in less contentious terms than a simple identification of cognitivism with universality. Such a straightforward identification tends to denigrate other domains and values (such as happiness,

25. EzD, pp. 184–185.

self-interest, one's particular tradition), as feminist objections indicate. If on the contrary one starts with an emphasis on the intersubjective quality of practical insight, then Habermas's definition of the moral domain follows simply from the fact that practices and associated claims impinge on one another. In that case the priority of moral universality in these contexts need not imply any derogatory judgment about other domains and values—for example, that the latter are merely subjective, personal, or noncognitive.

Second, if one *does* take the other's appeal on its own cognitive terms, then the moral perspective in principle sets the limits to the other domains, be they strategic or ethical. With regard to the ethical pursuit of substantive visions of the good life, one becomes aware of the limits of that pursuit the moment it impinges on others for whom one's own values remain opaque. If one cannot clarify those values before others so as to convince them that the same values make a claim on them, then compromise remains the only cooperative solution. Hence the moral perspective pinpoints not only definite norms but also the areas in need of compromise.

Third, the moral perspective renders domains of strategic action permeable with respect to a larger cooperative context, at least in principle, inasmuch as affected parties can bring to discourse the adverse effects or unequal burdens of a given form of "system integration," i.e., an anonymous form of social coordination through nonlinguistic media. This is not to deny that such systems form a "second nature" with their own "independent logic." Nor does it imply that one should replace them with wholly consensual action.[26] There are empirical limitations on what can be accomplished communicatively, and these cannot be changed at will. Moreover, forms of system integration serve the positive function of unburdening actors of the risky and time-consuming task of consensus. But insofar as basing social action on the anonymous direction of nonlinguistic media can have an adverse impact on some individuals, and insofar as these individuals can become aware of such impacts, they have prima facie grounds for questioning whether and how far the action in question must be delegated to nonlinguistic media. In concrete terms, workers can go on strike and theoreticians can argue about the moral suitability of capitalism. This suggests that some of Habermas's formulations of subsystems as areas of "norm-free sociality" must be inter-

26. *Discourse*, p. 352; also pp. 349–351.

preted with some caution.[27] If the acceptability of social action based on the anonymous coordinating effect of nonlinguistic media can be opened to question, then—even if there exist objective constraints on the ability to replace systems with consensual cooperation—systemic functioning must be open in principle to the power of those involved to legitimate it as a structure of (indirect) *cooperation* as well.[28]

Fourth, the above-elaborated senses of the discourse-ethical "priority of right" are not incompatible with calling rational cooperation the "constitutive good of discourse ethics," so long as one does not forget the unique status of this good. For, as rooted precisely in the validity dimension of language, its contours are at once formal and cross-cultural. Simply in virtue of the fact that human beings are language users, they find themselves subject to the intersubjective rationality operative in communication as such. It is, finally, in this sense that the good of mutual understanding has, on the one hand, no privileged association with a particular culture and, on the other, no viable alternatives in the world of today's international interdependencies. Because of these empirical interdependencies, conflict situations whose communicative structure intrinsically calls for a moral perspective force themselves upon us ever more frequently, and avoidance mechanisms become ever more costly.

Fifth, the priority of right in its discourse-ethical sense allows goods of self-interest and group value to receive their due within moral discourse. If, as Taylor contends, we find ourselves torn today between various hypergoods, then a perspective that does not boil down to simply one good among others should offer precisely the means for taking these various goods into account. Taylor suggests that the modern rejection of the good represents an overreaction to past situations in which one good (e.g., the nation) was overemphasized to the detriment of others.[29] If har-

27. See TCA 2:171, also 172–173, 196, for example; these must be balanced against other passages where he notes the reciprocal influences existing between system and lifeworld, such as 2:185. For criticisms of Habermas's ambiguity on this relation, see Thomas McCarthy, "Complexity and Democracy: The Seducements of Systems Theory," *Ideals*, pp. 152–180; James Bohman, "'System' and 'Lifeworld': Habermas and the Problem of Holism," *Philosophy and Social Criticism* 15 (1989): 381–401; and Axel Honneth, *Kritik der Macht: Reflexionsstufen einer kritischen Gesellschaftstheorie* (Frankfurt: Suhrkamp, 1985), pp. 277–279 (now available in English under the title *Critique of Power*, trans. Kenneth Baynes [Cambridge: MIT Press, 1991]).

28. Habermas has tended to formulate this point in terms of "the model of boundary conflicts" between communicative contexts and systems, as opposed to the Marxist-Hegelian "model of society influencing itself." *Discourse*, p. 365; in any case, "impulses from the lifeworld must be able to enter into the self-steering of functional systems." Ibid., p. 364.

29. Taylor, *Sources*, p. 503.

monizing goods is the issue, however, then precisely a proceduralism that encourages participants to bring their notions of the good to dialogue promises to preserve the full range of goods at stake in social action. An even greater moral sensitivity to goods can be secured in discourses of application, as the next chapter will indicate.

Sixth, we can now cure the unconditionality of the moral 'ought' of the hypothetical tendencies infecting it in Chapter 4. There it appeared that moral norms obligated one only on the assumption of a commitment to cooperation. Now, if the good of such cooperation were simply one conception of human happiness among others, over which reasonable persons could disagree, this would be tantamount to reducing morality to "counsels of prudence," in Kant's terms. If the good of cooperation enjoys a privileged status, however, then there is a sense in which human rationality itself requires this good. It is a good given with the rational potential of speech itself, in particular, with the power of validity claims to transcend local boundaries and submit themselves to a potentially universal testing.

In Chapter 4 I raised a question concerning the strategically motivated free rider in a moral discourse: could one not participate in discourse simply for strategic benefits in a given situation? We can now explain why this strategic participant has not really engaged in moral discourse at all. For one enters a moral discourse because one's prior confidence has been shaken by the questions and objections raised by affected others or, if one's confidence is not exactly shaken, because one at least believes that the other's questions and objections deserve a hearing and a genuine, reasoned response. The free rider, on the contrary, is concerned not with conviction but success, and feigns discourse only to guarantee such success. Thus insight into the 'ought', conviction about the rightness of a course of action, presupposes that one has first heard and engaged the *intrinsic* force of the other's appeal, the call to dialogue in a potential conflict situation. By grounding moral obligation in a discourse predicated on a search for an intersubjective rational will-formation—which takes the other's appeal as its unconditional point of departure—discourse ethics preserves at least some measure of the categorical quality of moral obligation, even if not in the strong sense Kant took as self-evident.

2.

In closing I want to recall the overall argument against Taylor, and then, by way of transition to Part Three, point out a dimension of the debate that presses for further consideration. The broader issue, recall, concerns whether discourse ethics depends on a constitutive good that, as existing alongside other possible goods, one is free to adopt or forego. If adopting a discourse-ethical procedure presupposes a will to cooperation based on mutually acceptable reasons, then this issue comes down to the question whether one can construe the good of such cooperation as open to the agent's personal disposition. If one can, then the ethical domain takes priority over the moral, and rational consensus in contemporary pluralist societies is accordingly undermined.

A rather straightforward response, which we first explored on Rawlsian territory, simply notes that if a procedural ethics presupposes a good, then this good occupies a special position—that of the metavalue presupposed in the choice of other goods, for example. The Rawlsian form of this move, however, stays within the (admittedly broad) confines of a Western liberal-democratic ethos. Habermas, who does employ images and language suggestive of such a constitutive good, has made a similar move, only without the restriction to a particular culture. In his reply to Heller, he notes that the good of mutual understanding is without alternatives, on the one hand, and falls short of a substantive vision of the good life, on the other. As we saw, this puts an entire research program on the line, and can hardly be settled by any particular argument.

In Chapter 6 I sought a way of rendering this program at least initially plausible by returning to the communicative rationality at the heart of discourse ethics: the intersubjective notion of insight. This makes the same points as the reply to Heller, only within a more confined space. To summarize, I argued first that attention to the validity dimension of language precludes conceiving the good of cooperation as a substantive good disclosed through a particular language; rather, cooperation depends on intersubjective structures of insightful will-formation that cut across the borders of particular languages. But could such a good be without alternatives? In order to test this I entertained two ways an agent might forego the good of discursively achieved cooperation and exclusively adopt either a strategic or a group-value attitude. This thought experiment suggested how attempts to reject such a good expose themselves to a kind of immanent contradiction, at least for the reflective agent: she must consider her choice rational, or insightful, even while other rational agents raise objections to precisely that choice. To maintain her attitude, then, she must find some way of either neutralizing or denigrating the rationality of others—in short, some way of rendering herself impervious to others' appeal. The need for neutralization mechanisms already witnesses to a pressure towards cooperation exerted from within language itself. Habermas's "no alternatives" thesis essentially maintains that in today's world such mechanisms cannot secure a stable basis for social action in spheres characterized by conflict potentials. If this is so, then we should expect that the alternatives make, in some fashion, a counterintuitive demand on their subjects—a demand whose hold must therefore weaken in the long run. More specifically, one might expect that they deny a constitutive element in practical deliberation. I then attempted to thematize this element in terms of a cognitive, "rational human" solidarity.

This closes my attempt to clarify the theoretical position of the general notion of the good in discourse ethics. The structure of the liberal-communitarian debate has made it necessary to clarify this rather abstract issue, even if the real issues of the debate lie at a more concrete level. In fact, despite the foregoing argumentation one might still reasonably ask whether and how the admittedly quite strong, indeed counterfactual discourse-ethical idealizations could possibly inform real conflict resolutions. The viability question can be raised all over again, this time with a view toward the real constraints of actual, concrete disputes and interaction.[30]

In Part Three I shall address these more concrete issues. Basically, there are two broad *topoi*: the question of particularity (or particular goods) and the question of situating discourse-ethical idealizations in a real social context. To prepare for the move to this more concrete level, it helps to acknowledge a sense in which Taylor's project has relevance for discourse ethics. Here I refer to the presuppositions for the actual practice of discourse ethics. Thus far I have set these aside in order to clarify the theoretical issue. But the latter, I suspect, is not Taylor's primary point. In delving into the motivational sources able to sustain the practice of morality, Taylor has more than theories in mind. Certainly the articulation of these sources involves a theoretical dimension one may classify as an ethical or even aesthetic exercise. How else would Taylor's book be possible? Moreover, one may well disagree with the intentions of such an exercise insofar as it concerns the theoretical grounding of morality. That being said, Taylor's argument can be set at a different level, one where disagreement is hardly plausible. For ultimately the "moral

---

30. For one formulation of this question, see Charles Taylor, "Cross-Purposes," pp. 159–182; esp. p. 176; also his *Sources*, pp. 515–518.

sources" that Taylor seeks operate inside the life commitments of actual persons, or else both these sources and morality itself do not operate at all. In the terms of this study, readiness to take the moral point of view must be anchored in the historical experiences and need interpretations of those expected to obey moral norms.

Habermas has acknowledged this point as follows:

> To become effective in practice, every universalist morality has to make up for this loss of concrete ethical substance, which is initially accepted because of the cognitive advantages attending it. Universalist moralities are dependent on forms of life that are rationalized in that they make possible the prudent application of universal moral insights and support motivations for translating insights into moral action. Only those forms of life that meet universalist moralities halfway in this sense fulfill the conditions necessary to reverse the abstractive achievements of decontextualization and demotivation.[31]

In Chapter 8 I will suggest a strong reading of this admission: it is not the individual's grasp of formal structures as such that motivates moral action, for such formal structures do not exist "as such," but only as embedded in lifeworld practices and institutions, and in individual psychological competences acquired through concrete experiences. More precisely, such formal structures only take on empirical appearance as *substantive* aspects of *specific* traditions and institutions. Only if one can point to these can one ever hope to situate a feasible practice of real moral discourse. The third and final part of this study attempts to situate the practice of discourse ethics.

31. DE, p. 109.

Discourse and Particularity

Introduction to Part III

One might encapsulate the basic charge against Kantian moral theories in a single word: abstraction. As Paul Stern summarizes the original Hegelian objections:

> In his justification of moral principles Kant must abstract from the entire domain of material purposes, empirical desires and teleological considerations concerning the true end of human nature; but . . . the consequence of such an abstraction is that the derived principles are so far removed from the actual context of human action that they do not meet the requirements of any plausible theory of moral volition.[1]

I have already noted how discourse ethics, even at an idealized level, addresses this charge. Specifically, I have tried to show that participants in a discourse-ethical procedure need abstract neither from empirical needs and goods nor from foreseeable consequences for the participants' "material purposes." The reflections in Chapter 6, moreover, indicate that— if one may allow the rather metaphysical form of expression—discourse ethics does not wholly sever itself from a conception of the "true end of human nature."

But the above moves still fall short of fully meeting the Hegelian and communitarian objections on at least two counts. First, insofar as the norms issuing from a moral discourse incorporate empirical goods and

1. Paul Stern, "On the Relation between Rational Autonomy and Ethical Community: Hegel's Critique of Kantian Morality," *Praxis International* 9 (1989): 234–248; here p. 237.

interests only under the umbrella of generalizable moral values, one can accuse discourse ethics of abstracting from those *particular* goods and consequences that emerge with empirical clarity only in concrete situations and interrelationships. Must not discourse ethics level out differences among participants, i.e., grasp the needs of the other only insofar as these can be assimilated to an—ultimately oppressive—public identity? This objection, which has recently been vigorously pursued by the proponents of an ethics of care, harkens back to the critique of Kant's rigoristic insensitivity for the concrete context and actual consequences of action guided by categorically binding moral laws.

As I shall attempt to show in Chapter 7, the charge of rigorism can be addressed by a discourse-ethical notion of context-sensitive application. Because this notion still operates at an idealized level, however, it remains vulnerable to charges of a second kind of abstraction, one that applies to the entire study.[2] For the analysis thus far depends on certain idealizations that real discourses can at best approximate. These pertain to both the participants and the conditions of discourse. On the one hand, discourse ethics must assume that individuals are willing and able to set aside narrow self-interest and open up their particular worldviews to questioning for the sake of mutual understanding. On the other hand, it makes idealizing assumptions about the conditions of discourse—that discussion can be freed from the pressures of action and pursued indefinitely. True, one should not expect a moral theory simply to describe the world as it exists; at the same time, the demands that a moral theory places on real human beings should be such that persons of good will can, at least for the most part, comply. In view of the strong character of discourse-ethical idealizations, one may rightly ask whether discourse ethics does not abstract too much from the empirical limitations of real actors and their conflicts, for instance, limitations in their ability to carry through the demanding tasks of mutual perspective taking.

Habermas too has acknowledged certain abstractive deficits incurred by discourse ethics. In separating moral issues from issues of the good life, discourse ethics distances moral norms from both specific traditions and forms of life; it also removes them from concrete contexts of action and from the motivating power built into the thicker conceptions of the

2. Onora O'Neill has insisted on the difference between abstractions and idealizations in her *Constructions of Reason: Explorations of Kant's Practical Philosophy* (Cambridge: Cambridge University Press, 1989), pp. 208–210. I use the term "abstraction" here in both cases simply to indicate the gap between the theoretical construction and reality.

good that form one's identity.[3] To address the problems raised by the latter two abstractions—i.e., from context and motivation—Habermas calls for two corresponding forms of compensation: abstract norms must be applied to concrete situations and they must be motivationally "anchored" in the individual's "internal behavior controls."[4] Whereas the problem of application is directly relevant to our focus on practical reasoning, the problem of motivation would take us somewhat afield insofar as it looks to the demands an abstract morality places on *actors*. The idealizing abstraction I mentioned in the previous paragraph, however, concerns not so much real actors (who may lack the motivation to comply with moral norms) as real *discourse participants* (who may lack the willingness and ability to properly carry out moral discourses). While Habermas acknowledges this latter issue under the rubric of institutionalization, we shall see that it involves much more than this.[5]

Of these various forms of abstraction, then, Part Three will address two: the abstraction from concrete situations and the idealizing abstraction from the limitations of real discourse. Chapter 7 will spell out the discourse-ethical notion of application as a response to concerns raised by proponents of an ethics of care. Here my aim is to show how discourse-ethical idealizations make room for situational particularities. In Chapter 8 I will attempt to locate the *real* sites where the practice of discourse ethics occurs. Of course, a full analysis of the discursive-moral features of these sites would require a number of additional volumes involving interdisciplinary research; within the scope of this study it suffices simply to point out these sites so that the reader has some sense that discourse ethics is feasible in the real world, despite its strong idealizations. To this extent we can respond to communitarian worries (especially Taylor's) about the viability of procedural moralities.

3. Jürgen Habermas, "Lawrence Kohlberg und der Neoaristotelismus," in *Erläuterungen zur Diskursethik*, pp. 83–87.
4. MC, pp. 178–184; also DE, pp. 102–109.
5. See DE, p. 92.

CHAPTER SEVEN

Care and Discourses
of Application

Impartialist moral theories, and neo-Kantian ones especially, have long grown accustomed to accusations of an undue abstraction from situational variations, feelings, and concrete relationships. That such criticisms issue from neo-Aristotelian and neo-Hegelian quarters is no surprise in view of their heritages, which include Aristotle's critique of Plato's Good on the one hand and Hegel's objections to Kant's notion of duty on the other. More recently, however, dissatisfaction with impartialism has become a general phenomenon, touching thinkers less easily classified in their allegiances.[1] Even in mainstream moral theory, attention to the difficulties posed by the concrete situation and potential conflicts between duties has been growing.[2] In my opinion, the family of difficulties at work here has been most clearly identified by feminist advocates of an "ethics of care."[3] In what follows, then, I shall turn to

1. Michael Walzer's *Spheres of Justice*, for example, argues for a pluralist conception of moral domains, while Bernard Williams, *Ethics and the Limits of Philosophy*, expresses skepticism about moral reflection in general; see also Williams's "Persons, Character and Morality," in *Moral Luck*, pp. 1–19.
2. R. M. Hare attempted to tackle the issue from a utilitarian standpoint in *Moral Thinking*; theorists more dubious about unitary, universalist solutions to moral conflicts include Stuart Hampshire, *Morality and Conflict* (Cambridge: Harvard University Press, 1983) and James D. Wallace, *Moral Relevance and Moral Conflict* (Ithaca, N.Y.: Cornell University Press, 1988). For an interesting recent proposal, see Henry S. Richardson, "Specifying Norms as a Way to Resolve Concrete Ethical Problems," *Philosophy and Public Affairs* 19 (1990): 279–310.
3. The key text is Carol Gilligan, *In a Different Voice*; another early criticism along the same lines was Norma Haan's "Two Moralities in Action Contexts"; the extent of the

this approach for an articulation of the potential problems for discourse ethics posed by particularity. Although a feminist critique of impartialism involves much more than the problems associated with contextualization, this constitutes one of the primary theoretical challenges for a discourse-ethical account of practical reasoning. My primary goal is to make room for certain feminist concerns, at least to some extent, within an impartialist account of morality. I shall proceed in three steps. The first will sketch the basic challenge, as the ethics of care has formulated it (section I). A second step will outline the basic discourse-ethical response in terms of a notion of application (section II). Lastly, I shall assess how far discourse ethics can go in addressing the issues raised by an ethics of care (section III).

I. THE ETHICS-OF-CARE CRITIQUE OF IMPARTIALISM

The basic feminist charge holds that by formulating morality in terms of the impartial adjudication of conflicting rights claims, neo-Kantians such as Rawls and Kohlberg reduce morality to an abstract, even monological, universalism.[4] In particular, impartialist reasoning of this sort must abstract (1) from the *particular features of concrete situations*— especially concrete interpersonal ties calling for precisely *non*universalizable moral judgments;[5] (2) hence from the concrete *needs* of, and *consequences* of an action for, particular individuals;[6] and along with this, (3) from the *emotional and affective features* of morality.[7] In each of these charges one may hear the echoes of philosophical debates going back at

---

issue is evident in Kittay and Meyers, eds., *Women and Moral Theory*; for a systematic philosophical treatment, see Noddings, *Caring*.

4. The monological reading of Kohlberg is suggested by Haan, "Two Moralities"; Andrea Maihofer applies this reading more generally to the Kantian moral tradition preceding Habermas; see her "Ansätze zur Kritik des moralischen Universalismus: Zur moraltheoretischen Diskussion um Gilligans Thesen zu einer 'weiblichen' Moralauffassung," *Feministische Studien*, 6, no. 1 (November 1988): 32–52, here p. 42.

5. Cf., for example, Haan, "Two Moralities," p. 303; Young, "Impartiality and the Civic Public," p. 61; also Lawrence Blum, "Gilligan and Kohlberg"; and Owen Flanagan and Kathryn Jackson, "Justice, Care and Gender: The Kohlberg-Gilligan Debate Revisited," *Ethics* 97 (1987): 632.

6. Seyla Benhabib, "The Generalized and the Concrete Other: The Kohlberg-Gilligan Controversy and Feminist Theory," in *Feminism as Critique*, ed. Benhabib and Cornell, pp. 88–90 (a revised version of this article is also found in Benhabib, *Situating the Self*, pp. 148–177); also Owen Flanagan and Jonathan Adler, "Impartiality and Particularity," *Social Research* 50 (1983): 585–586.

7. This line has been pursued in particular by Lawrence Blum; see esp. his *Friendship, Altruism and Morality*. For an overview of debates around this issue, see William C. Spohn, "Principles and Passions."

least to various criticisms of Kant: the problem of applying universal moral principles, the tension between principles of justice and conceptions of the good life, and the complicated relationships between moral principles and feelings.[8] Proponents of an ethics of care argue that neo-Kantians such as Rawls and Kohlberg have systematically favored just one side of the moral life. Hence, they maintain, a complete picture must account not only for the impartialist "justice perspective" but also for a more contextualist and interpersonal "care perspective."[9]

For Gilligan, however, these two perspectives, while both necessary for human life, cannot be integrated but only counterposed. They constitute something like the two figures found in gestalt images: for a given moral situation one simply has to take one perspective or the other, but one cannot simultaneously entertain both, or bring both together in a single moral perspective. This non-integrationist view has left a number of philosophers dissatisfied, including those sympathetic to the ethics of care. The search for a mediation is once again under way.[10]

Discourse ethics becomes attractive in this context, at least to some, because of the intersubjective twist it gives to Kant.[11] If one focuses on this intersubjective aspect, then moral theory appears capable of bringing in precisely those elements of morality that feminists missed in earlier forms of neo-Kantianism, yet in such a way that morality does not dissolve into an irreducible plurality of perspectives. We have already investigated at length how discourse ethics does not abstract from the participants' actual needs and desires. Nonetheless, Habermas's understanding of moral discourse remains problematic in light of the care perspective, and for a number of reasons. The basic problem, as I want to

8. Hegel confronted Kantian morality with the issue of application and the conflict between moral law and happiness; see G. W. F. Hegel, *Phenomenology of Spirit* §§ 582–631; regarding the conflict between justice and the good in this debate, see Lawrence Kohlberg, "A Reply to Owen Flanagan and Some Comments on the Puka-Goodpaster Exchange," p. 516; also Flanagan and Adler, "Impartiality," pp. 589f; the affective dimension of morality was highlighted by Hume and Schopenhauer.

9. I take these terms from Carol Gilligan, "Moral Orientation and Moral Development," p. 20.

10. In Gilligan, see "Moral Orientation"; for objections see Flanagan and Jackson, "Justice, Care and Gender," pp. 624–628; Flanagan and Adler, "Impartiality," pp. 591–593; Gertrud Nunner-Winkler, "Moral Relativism and Strict Universalism," in *The Moral Domain*, ed. Wren, pp. 115–118; George Sher, "Other Voices, Other Rooms? Women's Psychology and Moral Theory," in *Women and Moral Theory*, ed. Kittay and Meyers, pp. 178–189; finally, Carol C. Gould, "Philosophical Dichotomies and Feminist Thought: Towards a Critical Feminism," in *Feministische Philosophie*, ed. Herta Nagl-Docekal (Vienna: Oldenbourg, 1990), pp. 184–190.

11. See Benhabib, "The Generalized and the Concrete Other," pp. 92–94; also her *Critique, Norm and Utopia*, pp. 329–338; Young, "Impartiality," p. 69.

treat it here, is that he conceives morality in terms of *universalizability*, understood in a manner squarely located in the Kantian impartialist tradition. As his critics read him, this means that, quite simply put, everything particular falls from view: individual needs and feelings, particular conceptions of the good, all motives except that of finding the moral universal. Or, more accurately, *if* such items enter in, they do so only insofar as they can be universalized.[12] This is not to say that Habermas considers such items unimportant or irrelevant for human life. By distinguishing them from the moral realm Habermas does not intend to detract from their human significance.

II. THE DISCOURSE-ETHICAL RESPONSE: DISCOURSES OF APPLICATION

At least in its broad outlines, the discourse-ethical response to the above challenge is already familiar to the ethics of care. This response involves two moves: (1) an attempt to *defuse* the ethics-of-care critique by defining the object domain of morality in terms of universality, though without denying other domains of practical reasoning; (2) an attempt to *include* any remaining ethics-of-care issues under the cover of the contextualization of moral judgment.[13] We have already examined the first of these in connection with the liberal-communitarian debate. Before turning to the second move, let us restate the first move in relation to an ethics of care.

One of the strongest representatives of the ethics-of-care critique of impartialist definitions of morality is Lawrence Blum. In his *Friendship, Altruism and Morality*, Blum argues that friendship involves properly *moral* intuitions not captured by the notion of impartiality.[14] In response to this, the defenders of discourse ethics can claim that the issue is, at least in part, merely one of semantics. That is, they can grant that there exist particularistic domains of life whose practical significance, though not captured by impartiality, is often spoken of as "moral." Thus Habermas could grant Blum's point but then go on to distinguish—as he in fact does—two domains of morality (in a broad sense), to wit, the ethical and the moral (in a narrow, impartialist sense). Moreover, Habermas's distinction does not denigrate the ethical domain in the way other im-

---

12. See Young, "Impartiality," pp. 69, 72f; Benhabib, "In the Shadow of Aristotle and Hegel," pp. 20–22; see also Michael Walzer, "A Critique of Philosophical Conversation," *Philosophical Forum* 21 (1989–90): 86.

13. Benhabib identifies these two moves in Kohlberg; "The Generalized and the Concrete Other," p. 78.

14. See esp. pp. 43ff.

partialist theorists do when they label nonimpartialist domains as pertaining to "merely personal 'good'" or as "subjective."[15]

To this the proponents of ethics of care might respond by insisting that Habermas has denigrated nonimpartialist domains precisely by labeling them as "ethical," for they are thereby overridden by impartialist considerations in cases of conflict. If individual welfare does have any voice in moral discourse (in Habermas's sense), it is only *qua* universal. Precisely as particular it would seem to have a second-class status. Habermas has, it should be noted, granted that the ethical is probably the more important domain for human life.[16] The priority of an impartialist justice by no means pertains to the entire existential enterprise of living, but rather concerns a fairly restricted set of conditions for cooperation. Hence its "priority" should not be confused with its relative "importance" to the individual. But more than such protests are required to meet the ethics of care objection: at the level of a theory of practical reasoning, discourse ethics must make the second of the above-mentioned moves and in some way *include* the particular within the moral as narrowly construed—yet without once again dissolving the particular into impartially justified universal norms. For some of the least satisfying impartialist responses to an ethics of care are those which argue that care just *is* a further case of impartiality, i.e., that caring actions are instances of universal norms justified on impartialist grounds.[17] Discourse ethics attempts to meet this challenge with its account of application discourses.

Even aside from the ethics of care challenge, there are two internal motives for addressing the application problematic. The first lies in the desire to close a long-standing gap in Kantian moral theory. Kant's Categorical Imperative assumes one already has maxims of action which are appropriate for one's lifeworld but are in need of testing for moral validity. This is historically understandable when one views Kant's achievement as calling conventionalism into question: just because a norm "works" in a given social context does not make it morally valid from the standpoint of pure practical reason. Unfortunately, this starting point

15. These terms are found in Lawrence Blum, "Iris Murdoch and the Domain of the Moral," pp. 347f. Blum uses them to characterize the views of Bernard Williams, Samuel Scheffler, and Thomas Nagel.

16. In his address at Northwestern, "The Concept of Practical Reason Revisited," Northwestern University, Evanston, IL, 10 October 1988.

17. This type of response is described by Blum, "Gilligan and Kohlberg," p. 477. A more palatable variant of this approach is represented by George Sher, "Other Voices? Other Rooms?" Sher argues in effect that one can impartially justify "*principles* protecting the ability to satisfy demands of *personal relations*" (pp. 186f)—hence relational partiality can, as a whole domain, be impartially justified.

made it easy to collapse the difference between appropriateness and validity in the *other direction* and assume that valid norms are thereby also
appropriate for concrete situations—an assumption which lands one in
rigorism. To retain a postconventional stance which is not rigoristic,
then, one must differentiate validity and appropriateness, justification
and application.[18]

Among other things, this raises the problem of new situations. If all
one can do rationally is test norms, the construction of new norms for
new social situations would seemingly have to be relegated to an extrara-
tional context of discovery. In fact, the introduction of a notion of
context-sensitive application brings with it a further advance over Kant,
for it allows one to conceive of the impartial *construction* of norms for
new situations as rational.[19]

A second motive is internal to discourse ethics as a theory of moral
argumentation. This motive becomes clear if one attempts to interpret
the (U) principle in a strong sense, according to which the rightness of a
norm would depend on all those possibly affected being able to accept
the consequences of the norm's observance for every situation in which
the norm could possibly apply.[20] Strictly speaking, this would require the
participants in a moral discourse to possess an unlimited knowledge of
all the situations in which the norm could apply. This means that they
must have already determined, for complex situations in which several
norms might plausibly apply, which in fact ought to apply—hence they
must have settled issues of application in order to justify a single norm.
That in turn would demand that all norms be justified together, since
otherwise one would not know which norms would collide in complex
situations. In short, there would be only a single "super" discourse ar-
ranging the moral structure for the whole of foreseeable history—al-

18. Cf. Günther, *Sinn für Angemessenheit*, pp. 195, 207–208. Günther has presented
the most extensive discourse-ethical analysis of these distinctions to date; for a summary
of his conclusions, see his "Impartial Application of Moral and Legal Norms: A Contribution to Discourse Ethics," *Philosophy and Social Criticism* 14 (1988): 425–432; for
Habermas's summary, see EzD, pp. 137–142. For other attempts to elaborate a more palatable Kantianism, see Onora O'Neill, *Constructions of Reason*; Barbara Herman, "Integrity and Impartiality," *Monist* 66 (1983): 233–250 and "The Practice of Moral Judgment," *Journal of Philosophy* 82 (1985): 414–436.

19. Günther, *Sinn*, pp. 95, 132–146, develops this out of Mead; cf. George Herbert
Mead's "Fragments on Ethics," in *Mind, Self and Society*, pp. 379–389.

20. Albrecht Wellmer, "Ethics and Dialogue," in *The Persistence of Modernity*, pp.
145ff, bases a good deal of its criticism of discourse ethics on such a strong formulation;
for further discussion of the strong and weak formulation of (U) see Günther, *Sinn*, pp.
45–49; also his "Ein normativer Begriff der Kohärenz für eine Theorie der juristischen
Argumentation," *Rechtstheorie* 20 (1989): 167f (hereafter cited as "Begriff").

though this discourse would have to be redone each time an act of
noncompliance or other unforeseeable event changed the situational possibilities!

It is easy to see that such an idealization has outgrown the proportions
of a human morality. The most telling flaw in the account, perhaps, consists in the loss of the prima facie character of moral norms. That we
generally would consider it morally justifiable to lie in order to save the
life of an innocent person does not mean we accept lying as morally permissible in general. "Other things being equal," lying is morally prohibited; in a concrete situation, "all things considered," lying may be precisely the morally right course of action.

In order to preserve the above intuitions, Habermas's universalization
principle, as a definition of normative *validity*, must be given a weaker
reading. On this reading, what we seek to justify is simply prima facie
norms as summaries of legitimate expectations in typical, broadly defined situations. Discourses of justification operate thereby with a time
and knowledge index, i.e., the norm is valid only so far as it "incorporates a common interest at the present point in time and according to the
present state of knowledge."[21] "Knowledge" here is limited not only to
the empirical foreseeability of possible situational constellations in the
objective and social worlds, but also to the participants' current self-
understandings. We gain such knowledge from our experiences of ourselves and the world, and project on its basis imaginable typical
situations.[22]

With (U) thus limited, a space is opened up for a discourse-ethical
notion of application operative not all at once and once and for all in a
super discourse, but rather from situation to situation. In this notion of
situation-specific application discourses we find the central advance over
Kant's one-sided assignment of moral impartiality to justification alone.
The key unlocking the previously inaccessible realm of *Urteilskraft* to a
rational reconstruction lies in the kind of objections aimed at a problematic situational judgment: "the norm you followed is normally right, but
in this case there were special circumstances." The same kind of phenomenon can be observed in certain types of excuse giving, for instance,
when one excuses missing an appointment by saying, "I would have
come as I promised, but my daughter got sick at the last minute"—that
is to say, I agree I should keep promises, but in this case a more important

21. Günther, *Sinn*, p. 52.
22. Günther, *Sinn*, pp. 48–53; also EzD, pp. 138–142.

obligation arose.[23] Such examples display one of the central problematics of application discourses: collisions between norms taken as prima facie valid. In the ensuing discussion I want to focus on this problem, leaving aside that of the correct subsumption of particular cases under a single norm in the absence of competitors.[24]

What is the logic of an application discourse, then? To give an adequate answer to this we must avoid two extremes.[25] On the one hand, we should not imagine that norms come *already* packaged in a neat, lexically ordered system, so that conflicts between norms require us merely to compare their rankings. On this overly rationalistic view, we could hardly account for the difficulty and persistence of moral dilemmas. On the other hand, we should not give up on a rational concept of application and simply take shelter behind an intuitive "balancing" or "weighing" of colliding norms. This would simply lead us back into an unanalyzed notion of *Urteilskraft* or prudence. In fact, however, the kinds of accusation and excuse giving mentioned above indicate that concrete judgments can be criticized, and on rationally reconstructible grounds. If such criticism consists in the charge of overlooking, or insufficiently considering, mitigating factors or circumstances calling for a different norm than that actually followed, then it is precisely the *selection* of situation features that has to be defended. This in turn involves two kinds of consideration: first, taking account of all the normatively relevant situation features; second, justifying the singling out of those features that support the norm one actually applies.[26]

To understand the logic involved in the above considerations, let us start with a fairly simple scenario. Suppose that the participants in an application discourse already have a pretty good idea of what prima facie norms are justified according to (U). Since valid norms incorporate gen-

23. For an overview of research on excuse giving and the various types of excuses, see Monika Keller, "Rechtfertigungen," pp. 253–299, esp. 254–262; cf. also Scott and Lyman, "Accounts."

24. See Günther, *Sinn*, pp. 289–296, for a discussion of the subsumption problem, which involves meeting the potential criticism that the features of a given situation did not correspond to those presupposed in the applied norm (or did correspond to a norm that should have been applied); e.g., replying to a charge of promise breaking with, "You misinterpreted what I said: it was not meant as a promise." In fact, this problematic is not fully separate from that of selection: cf. Günther, "Begriff," p. 177.

25. See Richardson, "Specifying Norms," pp. 281–290.

26. One should recall here Toulmin's analysis of practical argumentation in *Uses of Argument*, pp. 94–145, according to which a deductive relation exists between a given situation description, a norm (the premises), and the moral judgment (the conclusion). Thus there is need for justifying not only the norm in general, but the given description of the situation as well.

eralizable interests, let us make the further strong assumption that each
participant can recognize which of his or her interests at stake in the situation are generalizable, and thus which interests can be connected with
a normative claim vis-à-vis the other participants. (Later I shall remove
this particular assumption.) Suppose further that all those affected by a
given application are able to enter the discourse. We might imagine that,
at first, each participant immediately latches on to a different norm and
different features of the situation, in accordance with the given general
interest that happens to stand out from his or her perspective on the situation. The process of discourse should then allow the participants to
compile a list of all the colliding norms and the relevant circumstances
picked out by those norms, assuming that each norm only specifies a few
relevant circumstances.[27] Having managed this much, their problem is
then to arrive at a mutually acceptable and coherent arrangement, ranking, or reconstruction of the colliding norms that would enable them to
settle on a definite, morally acceptable course of action.[28] But what does
such a coherent arrangement involve?

To avoid technicalities I shall remain at an intuitive level of analysis.
In such conflicts we typically *qualify* one of the conflicting norms so that
it harmonizes with the other norm in the given situation. For example,
we might hold that one ought not lie, unless lying is the only way to save
an innocent person from a malicious persecutor. Here the qualifier ("unless doing so, etc.") harmonizes the norm against lying with the duty to
protect innocent persons from harm. It does this by giving one norm
priority over the other for the conflict situation or by defining the scope
of the conflicting norms in such a way that they no longer conflict.
Whether we accept such a qualification will depend in part on its broader
implications, i.e., whether it would commit us to unacceptable norms
elsewhere. For example, a person might, on the basis of possible implications for euthanasia, argue against a proposal to remove life support
from a severely deformed newborn.[29] To deflect this argument, someone
else might look for relevant differences between deformed infants and the
aged infirm, differences that would permit the removal of life support in
the one case and not in the other. In other words, a qualification must
hang together in a reasonable fashion with other norms we consider

27. Again a very strong assumption, which seems to overlook the possibility of an indefinite extension of mitigating circumstances. I shall return to this problem later.
28. See Günther, *Sinn*, pp. 296–307; also his "Begriff"; although Günther often styl-
izes the first move as a complete description of the situation, this seems to be limited by the
quality of normative relevance; cf. *Sinn*, pp. 142, 144, 298, 304.
29. See Richardson, "Specifying Norms," pp. 303–305.

valid. Ultimately, the *coherence* of a system of norms and their specifications would probably have to recur to a moral theory able to demon-
strate the logical compatibility of the norms in the system and "explain
some of them in terms of others."[30]

Now if the meaning of any norm includes at least a tacit reference to
certain typical situations,[31] then such qualifications amount to further
specifications of the *meanings* of the colliding norms. We can also see
this in how the grounds for qualifying a norm refer to typical situations.
We can imagine the participants to an application discourse saying, in
effect, "Had we in our justification discourse considered this particular
eventuality as typical, we never would have agreed to such-and-such a
norm." For example, if truth telling *typically* resulted in the death of an
innocent person, one would not grant its prima facie validity. The norm
was never *meant* to overrule a general interest in life for the sake of a
general interest in honesty.[32]

Rather than go into the technicalities attending the semantics of application, I want to further develop its pragmatic and dialogical aspects.
Unless we bring in these aspects, the overly rationalistic image of application noted earlier is hard to avoid. For if application were simply a
matter of semantic specification, then it would seem that anyone who
understood the colliding norms should be competent to rank and apply
them. But—to continue this line of thought—anyone who participated
in the justification of the colliding norms should presumably understand
what he or she justified. It would follow that application discourses are
superfluous for justified norms: having agreed on their meaning at the
level of justification, each competent speaker would reach the same ranking in a question of application.

To get beyond the above image, recall the dialogical character of justification. Dialogicity involves much more than the insight that the individual needs the *material* input of others for reaching a judgment
about a norm's validity. While this is true enough, it rests on a merely
empirical limitation, and thus does not exclude the possibility, in prin-

---

30. Richardson, "Specifying Norms," p. 301; cf. Günther, "Begriff," pp. 178–183;
Günther points out that one's form of life will provide paradigms for coherently ranking
norms in typical situations.
31. See Chapter 2, sections II and III; Günther, *Sinn*, p. 28.
32. One could also speak of norm interpretation here, as Klaus Günther does in his
"Universalistische Normbegründung und Normanwendung in Recht und Moral," in *Generalisierung und Individualisierung im Rechtsdenken*, ed. M. Herberger et al., *Archiv für
Rechts- und Sozialphilosophie*, Beiheft 45 (Stuttgart: Steiner, 1992), pp. 49–51; see also
Günther, "Begriff," pp. 179, 182; EzD, p. 142; for one set of formal criteria for "specification," see Richardson, "Specifying Norms," pp. 295–296.

ciple, of arriving at valid norms monologically—one merely would have to be remarkably smart and well-informed. As the derivation of (U) in Chapter 3 indicates, the real grounds for dialogical procedures of justification lie rather in the nature of postconventional moral insight. As we saw, such insight depends in principle on alter's affirmative response. At the postconventional level of individual autonomy, normative legitimacy can only rest on the uncoerced assent of each person. This presupposes that no one can speak for another through recourse to a realm of a priori reason.[33]

Now there is no reason to expect this to change at the level of application. This becomes clear if we drop the strong starting assumption that participation in a justification discourse equips one with the competence to recognize the generalizable interests at stake in a concrete situation. On the contrary, at the level of justification the grasp of generalizable interests or moral values would most likely remain vague and somewhat indeterminate. In justification discourses, we may recall, participants must determine which affected interests make legitimate claims on all such that they can be incorporated in a norm as "generalizable." As we have seen, this determination is in turn mediated by values in terms of which interests can be communicated and the norm's consequences for such interests assessed. In concrete situations those same interests and consequences gain a further specificity—one can see much more clearly what impacts a norm's observance will have. When norms collide one can see that obeying one norm has negative consequences for the interests incorporated in another norm, and vice versa. This forces the parties to suggest ways by which the colliding interests can be preserved, which in turn forces them to spell out or further specify what they understand by those interests and the values they embody. (The abortion debate perhaps illustrates this sort of issue insofar as one can interpret it as a conflict between two generalizable interests or values, those of freedom of choice and innocent life. Whereas pro-life advocates interpret the value of innocent life in this context in a way that overrides free choice, pro-choice advocates do not. Both sides would agree, however, that innocent life and free choice both represent generalizable values able to undergird a number of other norms.)

This need for the further specification and ranking of colliding norms/values/interests pushes participants in an application discourse back to a position analogous to that occupied at the start of a justification dis-

33. Cf. Habermas, "Vorlesungen," pp. 124f.

course: for the purposes of the given application, each participant must
further specify those interests he or she accepted as generalizable for the
purposes of justification; but whether that specification is correct—
whether it amounts to a legitimate basis for mutual expectations—can
only be determined by a discursive intersubjective testing with all those
affected by the given specification. It follows that the formal criterion for
appropriate application has to be dialogical in nature. The norms must
therefore be qualified in such a way that the various generalizable interests of those involved interlock or harmonize—or are curtailed in a manner acceptable to all, if the case is especially dilemmatic. In other words,
each individual's proposed ranking of interests and norms must be submitted to examination by the others. If all agree to a proposed ranking,
then they effectively claim that the more detailed interpretation of the
meanings of the ranked norms preserves the acceptability those norms
enjoyed at the level of justification.

In this dialogical approach it is the participants' initial grasp of their
generalizable interests that becomes the heuristic for selecting the morally relevant situation features. Hence there is no reason to posit the
idealization of an "archangel" who fully describes a situation in all its
richness—one has to wonder whether this is even possible in principle.[34]
Rather we can consider the situation adequately described if all those
affected by the particular application not only agree that the colliding
norms are justified but convince each other that a certain application is
appropriate. The idea here is that each participant, given a sufficient
grasp of generalizable interests at the level of justification, can adequately
describe—at least by the end of the application discourse—how those
interests are further affected in the concrete situation. The sum of such
descriptions on the part of all affected parties should, therefore, adequately thematize all the relevant situation features. Of course, this itself
is an idealizing supposition. In real discourses of application, participants must work with norms whose justification remains fallible in principle; in addition, their own self-understandings are often subject to deception; finally, they have to rely largely on available cultural paradigms
for their situation descriptions and models of coherence.[35] Carrying out
a real discourse of application would no doubt pose a formidable challenge, but that is precisely my point in moving beyond the semantics of
specification. Application indeed follows a certain logic—it involves

34. The archangel image is from Hare, *Moral Thinking*, chap. 3.
35. Günther, *Sinn*, pp. 94, 304–306; "Begriff," pp. 181 183.

more than an intuitive weighing—but this by no means guarantees a quick resolution. Like (U) in discourses of justification, the above idealizations operate as regulative ideals that real discourses can at best approximate. To arrive at timely decisions in real cases, especially in more urgent issues, time-constrained institutional procedures are required, a matter I will take up in Chapter 8.

Even under the above idealizations, however, application discourses must normally be complemented by renewed justification discourses. For even if the prima facie norms have all been justified by (U), the application discourse, strictly speaking, only specifies that norm which is *appropriate* for the given situation. This appropriate norm is perforce more detailed inasmuch as it includes qualifications that note its priority in a more richly described situation. For example, in lying to protect an innocent person one has further specified the norm 'Protect the innocent' with the qualification, ' . . . even if it means lying'. Conversely, the norm against lying has been further specified, as already noted. Since these more detailed norms remain general, however, they are potentially universalizable norms in need of further testing for their *general validity*. Even if in real disputes these two moments of appropriateness and validity commingle, it is important to note their analytical distinctness if one is to avoid reducing application to justification or vice versa.[36]

III. RAPPROCHEMENT WITH THE ETHICS OF CARE?

We can now turn to an assessment of the discourse-ethical response to the challenge posed by an ethics of care. Let us begin by briefly noting the ways in which the above analysis at least partially responds to the relevant criticisms. The first point here is that so far as a discourse-ethical notion of application does take in care considerations, it does so without positing two moralities that are—at least in their underlying orientations—counterposed to each other. Rather, one has two independent but *supplementary* discourses, *both* of which express a single—admittedly impartialist—orientation: a justification discourse grounding prima facie normative validity in an impartial consideration of all the involved interests, and an application discourse grounding a norm's situational appropriateness in an impartial consideration of all the possible viewpoints on the situation.[37] This distinction is not fully clear in Kohlberg

36. Wellmer, "Ethics and Dialogue," for example, argues that justification boils down to application; see pp. 195–204.
37. See in Günther, *Sinn*, for example, pp. 93f, 97, 192ff.

and Rawls, which weakens their account of postconventional reasoning.[38] But it is precisely this distinction which—contra Haan and Gilligan—allows one to conceive a *postconventional* contextualism, i.e., a concrete morality that does not fall back to the conventional level of reasoning or to relativism.[39]

We shall have to return to the impartialism at work in application. For the moment it is important to note that such a concrete but impartialist morality of application gives questions of the good life and concrete consequences a positive role in moral reasoning, taken in the narrow sense. For precisely such factors make up the normatively relevant circumstances of an application, and thus bear on—help shape—the further specification of the meaning of a prima facie norm. In what follows I want to show this from an argumentation-theoretic point of view. My aim here is not to prove the plausibility of any particular case (or solution), such as the one that follows. For my purposes it suffices to show that *if* we can conceive of a case plausible enough to generate a dilemma (i.e., a conflict between our impartialist intuitions and our "care"-oriented intuitions), then the discourse-ethical account of impartialism does not forthwith lead to the conclusion that we must simply stifle our care for the particular relationships or goods and, keeping a stiff upper lip, obey the moral law. I want to explore the above account of application in order to show how it might allow the particular situation or features of a particular relationship—precisely *as particular*—to have a real impact on universalistic moral norms. In having such impact, moreover, the universal validity of such norms has not been negated as such. The norm remains valid, "other things being equal." Rather, one questions the norm in terms of its appropriateness—and here one could say, its *moral* appropriateness—for a given situation. The issue remains a moral one precisely because it turns on the claim that the justification of the norm did not intend—nor would have intended, had the issue been formulated—to override the particular good at stake in the given situation.

Suppose, then, a straightforward application of a norm—say, the norm that tenure-track positions in philosophy departments should be awarded on the basis of nationwide merit searches—would mean that a certain department, in making its hiring decision, would end up not hiring someone (call him John) who has been teaching in that department

38. Günther, *Sinn*, pp. 189–192.
39. Günther, *Sinn*, pp. 191–196, 198ff.

on yearly contracts for a number of years in hopes of eventually getting a tenure-track position there.[40] (Here I assume the department has not made any prior promise to John that he will eventually be eligible for a tenure-track position; I also assume that the department originally adopted the norm on the basis of fairness, and not simply in view of what is best for the department itself.) As a plausible objection to the straightforward application of this norm a member of the faculty might argue: "I would not have agreed to this norm for hiring procedures had I, at the time we justified the norm, foreseen the deleterious effects it would have on the good of this particular relationship."[41] The objection is that, under these concrete circumstances, the norm's observance is *not* "equally good for all"—hence not moral—in view of the disproportionate damage it would wreak on a particular person. Such a move in effect amends, or further specifies, the consideration of interests affected by a norm's general observance, only now in light of a closer consideration of exactly what interests are at stake in a concrete situation. Assuming this objection were to prove convincing to all involved, what positive solution might this discourse of application arrive at?

In fact, concerns about the exploitation of non-tenure-track (including part-time) faculty show that John's case may actually be part of a larger pattern that is becoming all too typical, and hence in need of general regulation. Yet even if our department addresses this case in the singular, and thus in a discourse of application, the considerations in section II suggest that it would arrive at a modified version of the original norm, for example, 'Tenure-track positions in philosophy departments should be awarded on the basis of nationwide merit searches, *unless* there is someone already in the department who has taught for X years on one-year contracts'. That is, even if we assume that John's problem is not typical, its solution seems to yield a general norm. If this is the result, one might question how much a particular good affects the norm itself. True, the good of a definite person (i.e., John) sparked the discussion that ended up modifying the original norm. But the specified norm N* can now be applied quite straightforwardly, seemingly without more than the

40. The example is inspired by Flanagan and Adler, "Impartiality and Particularity," pp. 594f; for a concrete proposal for the fair regulation of non-tenure-track faculty positions, see Kitty Berver, Don Kurtz, and Eliot Orton, "Off the Track, But in the Fold," *Academe* 78, no. 6 (November-December 1992): 27–29; see also the "Report on the Status of Non-Tenure-Track Faculty," pp. 39–48 of the same issue.

41. The structure of this counterfactual claim resembles the Aristotelian notion of *epikaia* as Martha Nussbaum explains it: in departing from a moral rule on the basis of *epikaia*, one does what one thinks moral lawgivers would have legislated had they known of the particular situation at issue; *Fragility of Goodness*, pp. 301f.

usual attention to situational particularities (barring the emergence of
yet a further special case). Moreover, if N* is not merely appropriate but
also valid, then all those possibly affected, including those who do not
know of John's particular situation, should be able to find it acceptable.

To do justice to particularity it would seem we must somehow get beyond general rules. This suggests the issue of exceptions to rules. What
could an "exceptional case" possibly mean in discourse ethics? More specifically, can the discourse-ethical account of practical reasoning draw a
distinction in principle between application as a unique singular judgment and application as the generation of a more complex or detailed,
but still general norm? For someone such as R. M. Hare, for example,
application boils down to the construction of very detailed norms tailored for specific situations. Such norms may well be less abstract, but
their moral character still lies in their universality, i.e., the fact that they
include no proper names or singular terms.[42] If, in the final analysis, application does no more than specify norms for more fully described situations, then one may well ask whether the discourse-ethical concept of
application can really serve an account of particular moral judgment. At
the very least, it would appear counterintuitive that actors consult highly
detailed moral norms in order to deal with the complications generated
by real situations.[43]

To see the force of this question it helps to recall the traditional account of moral judgment, according to which the correct application of
general moral rules depends on a virtuous individual's grasp of the
unique, concrete situation. This grasp requires an insight into the particular as such.[44] Thus in her analysis of the Aristotelian account of practical judgment, Martha Nussbaum argues that general rules, no matter
how "fine-tuned," cannot in principle ensure an appropriate application,
due to the mutability, indeterminacy, and particularity of practical contexts. By "mutability" she means that situations change over time and
harbor surprise; by "indeterminacy," the presence of contextual and personal variety; by "particularity," the nonrepeatable aspect of actual situations.[45] Although an understanding of general rules or norms is essential for picking out the relevant features of a situation, making judgment

---

42. Hare, *Moral Thinking*, pp. 40–43, 49–63; note that I do not follow Hare's terminology, which distinguishes between universality and generality. In my terminology, a
norm can be "general" (or universal)—i.e., it can lack proper names—while being more
or less "abstract," depending on how much situational detail it specifies.
43. See Blum, "Particularity and Responsiveness," pp. 327–328.
44. See, for example, Thomas Aquinas, *Summa Theologiae* II-II, q. 47, a. 3.
45. Nussbaum, *Fragility of Goodness*, pp. 301–304.

quicker and more stable in the face of passions, moral judgment ultimately requires, in addition to such rules, a "perception" of the concrete
particular. Since such perception involves "a complex response of the
whole personality," sound moral judgment depends on one's desires
being rightly ordered by the previous acquisition of virtue.[46] For this reason, prudent application has been traditionally viewed as inseparable
from those other moral virtues that order one's desires and passions, i.e.,
justice, courage, temperance and so forth.[47]

Now while the discourse-ethical account appears to make room for
mutability and contextual/personal variation, one may well ask whether
it can do justice to situational nonrepeatability. It is in this sense that I ask
whether it allows for truly exceptional cases. There are actually two difficulties here. First, can an application deal with a particular case without
issuing in a *semantically* general norm? Second, can it do so without a
pragmatic reference to what a (universal) justification discourse counter-
factually would or would not agree to? To address this let us return to the
example in which a faculty is faced with a need to decide whether to give
a tenure-track position to John, who has spent several years in the department on one-year contracts, or to conduct a broader search.

I.

Suppose, for the sake of argument, that all those affected by this decision
would accept superior merit as the *generally* valid norm for typical fair
hiring decisions. In other words, moral considerations lead the department to adopt a policy of conducting merit searches. Consequently, if the
"application" of this policy calls for a special discourse, the outcome
must be acceptable to all those involved, including the would-be finalists
in a search. Even if the finalists' participation in such a discourse must
be viewed as a counterfactual assumption, we can still ask what it might
take for them actually to agree that the case calls for an exception to the
merit norm. In order to make the conflict plausible, Flanagan and Adler
must adduce a number of particular circumstances, as it were a particular narrative describing John's special relationship to the department:
that he is competent, respected in the department, established at the institution and in the geographic area. Only in this way can John's investment in the institution and the attachment between him and his col-

46. Nussbaum, *Fragility*, pp. 304–309; the quote is from p. 309.
47. Again Aquinas, *Summa Theologiae* I-II, q. 58, a. 5; and qq. 59–61.

leagues begin to assume the status of a moral claim in some sense. But how could such a claim have any weight with other prospective applicants, such that they could agree to hiring John outright? John's ability to raise a moral claim on his behalf is crucial here; to see this, consider the following scenarios.

Scenario 1. Imagine first that John is competent and well liked but would probably not place among the finalists in a competitive hiring. In this situation the department members could inquire into the values incorporated in the merit norm and attempt to specify these for the particular situation. A host of concrete details would have to come into play here, particularities describing and assessing the unique situations of those concerned: for example, exactly how competent a teacher is John? Does the faculty find him a stimulating discussion partner and critic? One would also have to assess the situation of the possible finalists: are they likely to find jobs elsewhere if John is hired? Such questions as these attempt to specify the generalizable interests at stake in the situation: the students' interest in quality education, the faculty's interest in collegial contributions and attracting good students, the other applicants' interest in positions commensurate with their talents. Even if it seems farfetched to construct a discourse involving would-be applicants as discourse partners, the real participants—especially the graduating students—could put themselves in their place and ask whether, in view of the current job market, it is likely that hiring John would squeeze someone of superior talent out of a job.

One cannot predict the outcome of such an assessment. It is at least possible, though, that the department could specify "merit" in a way that justifies hiring John. After all, both faculty and students might agree his presence enhances the department, and a seller's job market might make it unlikely that other superior job-seekers will be left out in the cold. Thus the participants might be able to justify a decision to hire John on the grounds that the generalizable interests at stake in the original norm have been preserved. They have, in effect, preserved "the spirit" of the norm while violating its "letter." At least one can imagine scenarios in which each of those affected, given the right combination of circumstances, might agree to the department's not conducting a search.[48]

48. The plausibility of agreement in such cases can also be indicated by the fact that job applicants in many fields expect a certain number of the advertisements for positions to be perfunctory, set out to fulfill a general policy; in fact the company already has a definite person in mind. That the applicant's irritation at this need not amount to a generalized moral outrage reflects an awareness that there can be justified exceptions to the general requirement to conduct open searches.

This solution would indeed address the particular as such, for the decision to hire John depends on a host of accidental circumstances. Even if one could make an abstract list of "acceptability conditions" for hiring someone in such a conflict situation, the satisfaction of those conditions would require a very detailed investigation of the particular situation. No two situations involving such a conflict would be exactly the same, and much would depend on the situated assessments of those actually involved. But do we really have an exception to the norm in this case? One might argue, on the contrary, that this only represents a further, more detailed norm: 'Conduct nationwide merit searches unless someone already teaching on contract in the department can be hired without damage to the department's standing and without damage to the job chances of possible superior applicants'. (One could add still further qualifications, of course.) As stated, the norm does not seem too unwieldy to guide practice. I think a more plausible interpretation, however, would acknowledge this as a genuine case of *epikaia*, inasmuch as the decision to hire John departs from the original norm but arguably fulfills the "intention" behind it, i.e., preserves the values incorporated in it. Even in that case, though, one could argue that more abstract norms *have* been observed, for instance, norms such as 'A college department has a duty to preserve its academic quality in hiring' and 'Applicants deserve a chance at jobs commensurate with their talents, so far as the market permits'. In our scenario the participants could argue that they have preserved the former norm without violating the latter. If such norms are "imperfect" in the Kantian sense, then we should not be surprised that they require a close appraisal of particulars if one is to know how to apply them. In this way one might attempt to reconcile Nussbaum's point regarding particularity with Kantian rule-based morality.[49] But this still represents a thoroughly moral solution that does not get at the specific *kind* of conflict envisioned by proponents of an ethics of care, i.e., conflicts in which we find ourselves torn between ethical and moral considerations.

Scenario 2. Suppose, then, we sharpen the above conflict by assuming that the department's decision to hire John cannot be harmonized in the foregoing manner. Suppose, for example, that the job market is tight and hiring John means leaving Mary in the cold, without a position, even

---

49. In fact, Onora O'Neill maintains that both perfect and imperfect duties "underdetermine action." *Constructions of Reason*, p. 224; for an ethnomethodological formulation of this point, see Heritage, *Garfinkel and Ethnomethodology*, chap. 5.

though she is more qualified than John. Is it inconceivable that Mary could ever agree that such an outcome might be morally justified?

Even assuming an empathetic disposition on Mary's part, one would probably have to describe John's situation in rather desperate terms to make Mary's rational agreement plausible. Perhaps John is going through a particularly difficult period, and losing his job would create a hardship completely disproportionate to the hardship Mary would experience in not being hired. To obtain Mary's agreement, perhaps the damage done to John by compliance with the general norm would have to be such that he "would have to give up, in the name of the impartial good ordering of the world of moral agents, something which is a condition of his having any interest in being around in that world at all."[50] In any case, *particular narratives* would come into play, narratives featuring the situations of both John and Mary. Such narratives would, moreover, have to serve an assessment of how following the norm (or not) would affect each person's well-being. At least in principle, however, an agreement to hire John is possible, and not simply as a supererogatory act but precisely because the situation is such that Mary could say, "Had participants in a justification discourse foreseen this particular conflict, they would not have expected compliance with the merit norm on the part of those involved." That is, the impacts on John's well-being are such as to support a moral claim on his behalf. Does this imply that a general moral norm finally determines the outcome? Or have ethical considerations—considerations pertaining to the goods of particular individuals—actually taken on moral significance?[51]

To begin with the second question, note that the perspective governing the discourse is not an ethical one, for the participants do not ask, Who are we and who do we want to become? Ethical considerations do enter in, of course, inasmuch as who John and Mary are and want to become determines how the possible outcomes will affect them. Strictly speaking, though, the issue at stake is whether and how the identities and life goals of John and Mary pose moral claims on each other and the department.

Does this mean a moral norm is decisive? Apparently so, inasmuch as

50. This is how Bernard Williams describes a plausible conflict between an individual's character and moral obligation in his "Persons, Character and Morality," p. 14.

51. Citing Lutz Wingert, "Gemeinsinn und Moral," Habermas suggests yet a further interpretation that draws on the notion of *Zumutbarkeit*: even if the merit norm should prove to be the morally appropriate norm for the situation, its effects on John may be such that compliance cannot be reasonably expected (*zumutbar*) of John and the department; FzD, p. 198.

one could describe the situation as a conflict between two moral norms, the merit norm and some version of the norm against harming others. Although an outcome in John's favor would represent a true exception to the merit norm, the good or interest preserved by hiring John would be generalizable in the form of a norm against harming others. Nonetheless, the general rule (or more specified norm) applying in this case would have to remain even more open and vague than that in the first scenario. One might, for example, qualify the merit norm to the effect, 'Conduct merit searches unless someone already teaching on contract in the department would suffer a wholly insupportable loss and other possible applicants would not suffer such a loss'. But such a norm would do little more than explicate the fact that general norms must be sensitively applied. In particular, the assessment of "insupportable loss" would depend on a no doubt unique constellation of circumstances. The very fact that we often find it difficult to imagine (let alone predict) the outcomes of such conflicts when they are described to us indicates the nonrepeatable particularity at issue. That is, the outcome depends very much on a host of circumstances and particular relationships. Of course, such circumstances presumably make up a finite list of factors, and theoretically these could be spelled out in an extremely detailed norm. But this could hardly be useful as a *norm*, i.e., for guiding us in other sufficiently similar situations. Moreover, inasmuch as the relevance of the circumstances lies embedded in particular histories and narratives, even Hare's archangel could probably not apply such a "norm" beyond the actual case.

A further consideration buttresses the above point. Even if all those affected agreed to the exception on the basis of a finite number of situational features that seemingly could be made explicit in a new norm, in fact they need not consider themselves as specifying a new general, albeit more detailed, norm for hiring. True, they have at least set a precedent for the possibility of similar exceptions. But here it seems reasonable for the department to qualify their decision as follows: "In this case we deem an exception reasonable, but any future claims along similar lines must be assessed on a case-by-case basis." This brings out the intuition that there are morally relevant decisions one precisely does *not* consider amenable to semantically general norms, but only to case-by-case assessments. A general norm here could at most indicate *when* a special assessment is probably necessary. The example attempts to indicate how situational features constituted by particular relationships might plausibly lead a group to see their decision in such terms, i.e., as a decision calling for more than a straightforward subsumption of the particular under a universal norm.[52]

Thus I would hesitate to say that a general moral norm has been "decisive" for the case at hand. The general norm does little more than supply a cover or generally understandable reason for a decision to hire John. The truly decisive factors, however, lie at another level, i.e., in the host of considerations whose argumentative value for the participants can scarcely be separated from the stories they tell each other and, indeed, *how* they tell these stories. Complex considerations such as these do not lend themselves to a dry, decontextualized enumeration that could serve for settling future conflicts. To this extent, the notion that application requires perception or an intuitive weighing still retains some validity. Moreover, insofar as discourse ethics can allow for such particularistic assessments, notions such as care and empathy have a role in moral reasoning.[53] At the same time, discourses of application cannot be equated with friendship or forms of particular attachment, for friendship alone cannot justify John's being hired. At the very least, those who are not John's friends, namely the other possible applicants, could hardly find this a convincing reason for going against the merit norm. To further develop the possibilities for a rapprochement between the ethics of care and discourse ethics, let us turn to the pragmatics of application.

2.

Even if the semantics of application allows discourse ethics to meet the ethics of care halfway, one might question whether the *pragmatics* of application can accommodate particularist intuitions. According to the above analysis, an exception would only seem possible insofar as those in the application discourse can claim that a justification discourse would never have agreed to a merit norm that excluded the envisioned exception. Cast in this way, however, must not the exception be universalizable in some sense? That is, must not the participants to the application claim

52. A similar point seems to underlie Martha Nussbaum's proposal for viewing judicial procedure on the model of a reader's relation to the characters in a novel; she proposed this in her Julius Rosenthal Foundation Lectures, "The Literary Imagination in Public Life," Lecture III: "It Has Nothing to Do with the Law," Northwestern University School of Law, Chicago, 10 April 1991. Her point is that as a reader one has an intimate (and empathetic) yet distanced relation to each character in the novel, such that one can judge the conflicts between characters in a way that does justice to the richness of contextual detail. Such judgments are unique but informed by general principles and norms.

53. See Hoffman, "Contribution," pp. 64–67, 70–76.

that all those *possibly* affected by such a contingency would have agreed to its exceptional character, had they foreseen it in the justification discourse? Here the problem is not at the semantic level, but concerns rather a kind of pragmatic generality. The particularity of the situation is retained at the semantic level, but seemingly lost in a pragmatically abstract impartiality that assumes that everyone who accepts norm N would also accept the qualifier, 'except in this (unique) situation S'.

One must admit at this point that if those involved in the exceptional situation are to consider their decision rational, they must in some sense hold that any other rational person *would* accept this decision as a reasonable one, *were* he or she to occupy this situation in every respect. At the same time, however, one can point out that the actual application situation is *not* inhabited, *nor could have been* inhabited even potentially, by all those possibly affected by the abstract merit norm, i.e., all those who would be allowed in principle to participate in the justification of this norm. For other inhabitants of this situation would simply have made for a *different* situation. In the hiring situation at issue, it is precisely John and Mary (as well as affected members of the department, students, etc.) whose generalizable interests are being further specified. Hence it is precisely *they* who are allowed into this particular application discourse; precisely they have the privileged duty of further determining what exactly they agreed to when they accepted the merit norm in a justification discourse. Since none of the other possible participants in justification inhabits this exact hiring situation—nor is affected by its particular outcome, *ex hypothesi*—none of the others has anything to say, beyond rather general advice, about how the generalizable interests incorporated in the merit norm should look in that situation. Of course, the rather strong assumption here is that "those affected in this particular situation" can be delimited. As an application affects more individuals, or depends on fewer mitigating circumstances such that chances for its repeatability increases, the pressure grows to formulate departures from given norms as new, more detailed norms that would have to be justified in discourses open to all those possibly affected.

If the above considerations are at least plausible, then an ethics of care has something to offer discourse ethics. To be precise, discourse ethics can draw on the ethics of care for the articulation of the in-principle uniqueness of concrete situations. In addition, the importance of care and interpersonal responsiveness for moral reasoning in such situations would substantially fill out a discourse-ethical theory of practical reasoning.[54] If affectively charged attributes such as care, compassion and empathy play a significant role in the assessment of concrete cases, then the proponents of discourse ethics cannot ignore the relation between reason and emotion. Admittedly, these tasks are more easily described than carried out. But considerable progress has already been made, and a dialogical theory of practical reasoning can hardly afford to look the other way.[55] Here I can only suggest a possible place to begin.

As long as the reasons grounding exceptions to general norms are conceived solely in linguistic (i.e., semantic) terms as potential rules for acting in a certain *kind* of situation, it remains difficult to see how application discourses can deal with the particular as such. For the terms—rules and thematizable situation features—that work as reasons in situation S should in principle also work as reasons in any sufficiently similar situation S_i. Discourse ethics can meet the challenges posed by theorists such as Nussbaum and Blum only by expanding the notion of applicatory reason giving to take in the particular idiosyncrasies of the exchanges and interactions in which the real participants *actually* engaged in their quest for consensus. That is, the actual participants' expression of, and response to, the unique inflections, emotional expressions, gestures and other bodily aspects of the actual exchanges, as well as their shared histories, must be considered elements of a *rationally motivated* consensus in cases of application. Precisely because the consensus is local, the less thematizable elements of assessing arguments and reaching agreement can enter into the participants' sense of how each individual will be affected by various possible outcomes. Hence such elements will enter into the cogency of reasons.[56] Nor need this imply a conflation of rational consensus with de facto consensus, so long as the participants

54. See Levin, *Listening Self*, esp. chap. 5, and his *The Opening of Vision: Nihilism and the Postmodern Situation* (New York: Routledge, 1988), chap. 2; also Blum, "Particularity and Responsiveness," and his "Moral Perception and Particularity."

55. Habermas has recently acknowledged the moral relevance of emotions; see NR, pp. 142–143; for other work in this area see not only Blum, "Particularity and Responsiveness," but also Martin L. Hoffman, "The Contribution of Empathy to Justice and Moral Judgment," and Janet Strayer, "Affective and Cognitive Perspectives on Empathy," both in *Empathy and Its Development*, ed. Nancy Eisenberg and Janet Strayer (Cambridge: Cambridge University Press, 1987), pp. 47–80 and 218–244; also Sidney Callahan, *In Good Conscience*, pp. 95–113.

56. It is not clear how much this holds for discourses of justification, which presumably will include a much greater number of people. In principle, (U) would not exclude such elements inasmuch as it calls for an iteration of face-to-face exchanges. In reality, however, we should expect the mass media to play a greater role in justification, so that affective and prethematic elements will operate at a more generalized level.

can still make the idealizing suppositions that these prethematic, bodily, and historical elements of reaching consensus did not mislead or distort the discussion.

In short, at the level of application, discourse ethics is potentially open to the whole gamut of considerations raised in the ethics of care. This suggests yet a further extension of the discourse-ethical notion of solidarity: the discourse-ethical practice of application requires something like a concrete moral solidarity. Habermas has, in fact, maintained that solidarity already addresses the concerns of an ethics of care;[57] the foregoing analysis shows exactly how this occurs. Whereas from the standpoint of justification discourse ethics enjoins a solidaristic concern for each individual's welfare insofar as that welfare can be brought under generalizable moral values, at the level of application discourse-ethical solidarity turns the participants' gaze on the quite particular aspects of one another's welfare. It has the participants ask, "How do the moral values at stake in a norm play themselves out in this concrete situation, how do they intermesh with and make claims on these particular individuals and their life projects?" Where the situation is such that directly following generalized moral values would bring on consequences harmful to an individual, concrete moral solidarity calls on those involved to consider exceptions to the rule, or to innovate in their application of general norms, precisely so that the personal integrity that morality aims to protect does not fall victim to that very morality.[58]

Yet a problem remains. For does not the application remain impartial, as mentioned earlier? The challenge posed by Blum, however, is to understand the moral significance of particular relationships such as friendship without reducing such significance to what one can universalize, or even show to be permissible, from an impartial perspective.[59] The discourse-ethical account of application does allow us to conceive of a truly particularistic moral domain—in the narrow sense of "moral." Nonetheless, the perspective remains impartialist. In the hiring decision, for example, the participants strive for an impartial description of the

57. MC, pp. 181–182.
58. Nancy Fraser, "Towards a Discourse Ethic of Solidarity," *Praxis International* 5 (1986): 425–429, suggests one could extend this point about concrete moral solidarity to a consideration of the effects of general norms on particular groups (the "collective concrete other").
59. Note that Blum employs a very strong notion of impartiality (taken from Darwall, *Impartial Reason*) which he distinguishes from universality; see his "Particularity and Responsiveness," pp. 324–326. It is not clear to me that Blum would accept my use of "impartial."

situation, i.e., a description that does justice to *all* the relevant situation features as perceived by each affected person.

To some extent this brings us back to the valid distinction between the ethical and moral domains. In Habermas's terms, friendship would seem to fall in the domain of ethical considerations (though Habermas's analysis of ethical-existential discourse might have to be expanded to take it in), and one should therefore not expect it to fit into a concept of moral application. As Blum rightly points out, in caring for the good of one's friend one usually does not first ask whether a certain benevolent action is permissible on moral grounds—such permissibility is at most a background condition given with one's moral competence. As a competent moral agent, one already understands which types of situation call for impartialist considerations, and thus one already knows that certain situations involving friendship do not even call for the application of the Categorical Imperative.[60] In discourse-ethical terms, the ethically relevant aspects of friendship fall to a large extent outside the realm where application is necessary.

This does not deny that conflicts between impartialist morality and friendship can arise. Precisely these sorts of situations have been most troubling for moderate impartialists and ethics of care proponents alike. Such situations involve a conflict between the claims of a friend (or, more generally, some close relation) and the moral claims of other persons who will be affected by one's decision. Theorists often conclude, rather embarrassingly, that one must simply opt for one side or the other, albeit "with regret."[61] The discourse-ethical account of application thus promises to advance the discussion, for it at least offers a forum in which such conflicts can be rationally addressed. More specifically, it allows for the two-fold possibility that: (1) when impartialist moral norms conflict with individual interests as a rule, such norms could be modified in a way that mitigates such conflicts; (2) when such norms give rise to unusual conflicts, exceptions to the norm could be *rationally* entertained by those involved.

An example of the first case would be the delimitation of an impartialist norm in order to make room for the good of friendship in a certain type of situation. Here one has something like an impartialist justifica-

60. Blum, *Friendship*, pp. 52–55, 61–64.

61. Cf., for example, Bernard Williams, "Moral Luck," in *Moral Luck*, pp. 20–39; similar difficulties plague Thomas Nagel's *View from Nowhere*, and are not irrelevant to Susan Wolf's "Moral Saints."

tion for the claims of friendship. Blum has argued that such a justification is not possible, for it would have to be rule-utilitarian in form. Thus it must either appeal to "interests only contingently connected with friendship," in which case it is unlikely that friendship would be justified inasmuch as other forms of benevolence would better maximize utility. Or it must appeal to goods internal to friendship, in which case it cannot be an impartialist justification.[62] A discourse ethics of application, however, escapes this dilemma. For, in the first place, it would not presume to justify friendship as such, but only its priority for a certain type of situation in which one could expect frequent conflicts with a certain moral norm. Second, it has no need to fear an appreciation for the internal goods of friendship. As long as all those affected appreciate this good on the basis of their *ethical* authenticity, they may adduce such a good as grounds for delimiting or restructuring a moral norm. There is no reason to suppose, as Blum does, that impartialist norms must be based solely on "impersonal criteria."[63] For discourse ethics, impartiality attaches rather to the general acceptability of the reasons grounding a norm.

As far as the second case goes, it would hardly be reasonable to look to discourse ethics for permission to violate moral norms simply for the sake of friendship. But discourses of application do open the possibility of taking account of the impacts of norms on friendships. Insofar as the concrete good of those involved constitutes an important consideration in applying norms, the particular friendships at stake could at least enter into discussion as a possibly relevant factor. Admittedly, many such conflict situations will present genuine dilemmas in which consensus is not possible. Then one can perhaps compromise; perhaps, however, a regrettable hard choice is necessary. Nonetheless, discourse ethics makes an advance insofar as it shows how impartiality and the good of particular relationships need not involve such antithetical orientations.

62. Blum, *Friendship*, pp. 59–60.
63. Blum, *Friendship*, p. 60.

Situating Discourse Ethics

Toward the Analysis of Real Discourses

In Chapter 8 I hope to provide the reader with some sense that the foregoing analyses amount to more than finely spun cobwebs in a philosopher's attic, far removed from the everyday business of life. My aim is thus to situate discourse ethics in real processes of social interaction. Briefly, I shall proceed by formulating an initial obvious question, Where does one find discourse ethics actually being practiced (section I)? By way of reply, I shall turn to law and politics as illustrations of the real practice of discourse ethics (section II). The attempt to situate discourse ethics in legal and political procedures, however, engenders certain instructive aporias. Insofar as these aporias arise from a subject-centered notion of reason, the path beyond them points to a more thoroughgoing elaboration of an intersubjective rationality (section III). In closing I will return once more to the relation between solidarity and insight (section IV).

I. AN OBVIOUS QUESTION

We have traversed a considerable distance to achieve an overview of discourse ethics as an "idea," i.e., as a moral theory based on idealizations about reaching rational consensus in potential conflict situations. As an idea, it serves a regulative function; at the same time, Habermas has continued to insist that discourse-ethical idealizations are not merely regulative but also "constitutive" of discursive practices.[1] The demand-

1. See W, pp. 180–182; NR, pp. 131–133.

ing character of the idea sketched in the foregoing chapters thus leads
to the question, Constitutive of what (in the real world) and constitutive
how?

A quick answer to this question would first distinguish the strong
sense of world constitution from the constitution of normative validity
thematized in discourse ethics. I cannot understand what I am doing
when I raise a validity claim vis-à-vis a hearer without drawing on the
notion of something like an "ideal communication community": the
force of the validity claim posits the acceptability of that claim by any
rational person able to grasp the situation and possessing unimpeded
judgment. This does not mean that every competent speaker can give a
reconstructive account of the notion of validity; the "understanding"
here is at the level of "knowing how" rather than "knowing that." Habermas's point is that I would not know *how* to raise and challenge
normative validity claims without a practical prereflective grasp of
discourse-ethical idealizations. In this sense, then, *what* these idealizations constitute are certain communicative practices, to wit, those associated with the making and questioning of moral claims. *How* it constitutes such practices is by establishing certain idealized, generally
counterfactual suppositions about the conditions under which such
claims are warranted; if one spells out these conditions, one arrives at
something like (U), if the analysis so far is on track.

In this chapter I want to move beyond this rather abstract and perhaps
too quick reply. For if discourse-ethical idealizations are constitutive in
the sense just claimed, then their practical efficacy—the feasibility of discourse ethics—should display itself in the real world. As constitutive of
communication on morally relevant issues, we should not have to search
long or hard for such effectiveness, nor should we have to fall back on
programmatic, utopian pronouncements.

For this task it helps first to rephrase our question concerning the what
and the how of discourse-ethical constitution in a more straightforward
fashion: Where do we find discourse ethics actually being practiced? The
foregoing suggests we find it in everyday communicative practices, and
I have, in fact, continually alluded throughout this study to likely everyday scenarios in order to tease out the various intuitions that discourse
ethics strives to reconstruct. The intuitions to which I have adverted constitute practices of convincing reason giving. That is, I have tried to indicate the ways in which one person might legitimately challenge or criticize another's actions or norms of action from the moral point of view,
either before or after the fact. Just as instructive have been the ways in

which the other might respond to criticism in an effort to reach an understanding.

For Habermas, such everyday interactions represent the primary locus of discourse ethics.[2] However, it remains far from clear that references to ordinary reason giving suffice as a convincing basis for a discourse-ethical analysis of moral interaction. The difficulty lies in the fact that discourse-ethical idealizations extend so far beyond everyday interactions, and abstract from so many other interpersonal dynamics that always coexist in such interactions, that one might well grant the plausibility of my examples of reason giving but still question whether something like (U) functions as the constitutive element. For example, most everyday disputes end after one exchange of reasons (for example, you berate me for breaking a promise and I offer an excuse—end of story) or, if they prove more difficult, involve a host of further complications not mentioned in (U): the resort to subtle forms of pressure, a cooling of the relationship, the involvement of other emotional factors, and so forth. Often the cognitive question of whether a norm or action is justified simply drops from view and deeper interpersonal issues take over. To situate discourse ethics, then, we must go beyond simple everyday reason giving and locate something much rarer: real practices of *discourse*.

Recall that Habermas's notion of discourse carries some rather demanding criteria: those in a dispute must remove themselves from the pressures of action and gain a certain reflective detachment; they must then exchange arguments pro and con in an effort to arrive at a mutually convincing outcome; they may exclude neither any affected persons nor any relevant considerations from their deliberation, insofar as this is possible. Now as Benhabib has pointed out (and Habermas has acknowledged), reason giving is one thing, discourse in the strong sense required here is quite another.[3] If we are to have any confidence that the delicate and tenuous threads of everyday reason giving can supply the intuitive bases for the elaborate mechanisms of discourse outlined in this study, then we must be able to point to areas where such reason giving becomes strong enough to detach itself from the complications of everyday interaction and expand into something approaching a full-blown argumentative discourse. Otherwise it is all too likely that discourse ethics myopically overemphasizes just *one* aspect of reason giving to the exclusion

2. See, for example, FG, pp. 32–37; for the law-morality relation, see ibid., chaps. 3 and 4.

3. See Benhabib, *Critique*, pp. 318f; Habermas, "Critics," p. 253.

of muddy complications that might well prove *essential* in actual argumentation. Given the demanding character of argumentative discourse, however, the most likely place to search out its real practice would seem to be the forms of institutionalized discourse. Hence, in order to explore the possibilities for mitigating the suspicion of myopia, I turn first to the spheres of law and politics.

II. THE LEGAL-POLITICAL INSTITUTIONALIZATION OF DISCOURSE

In turning to law and politics I do not claim that it is only in these areas where institutionalized procedures display a moral, or fairness, dimension. One can, I suspect, find its traces in any number of institutional domains; in fact, some empirical studies of the social psychology of procedural justice suggest just this, as I shall indicate below (see note 34). Rather, I turn to this sphere because Habermas has already written on it, which makes it easier for us to determine how he conceives the relation between discourse ethics and legal institutions. I should add, however, that I am less concerned with the twists, turns, and intricate mediations by which Habermas situates moral discourse in legal-political processes than with the *fact that* moral discourse can and must situate itself in such processes. Hence I will go into the law-morality relationship only in enough detail to suggest that one *can* indeed locate an effective practice of discourse ethics in the real world. As we shall see, this does not mean that law can be reduced to an institutionalization of moral discourse. The more interesting theoretical question, though, bears on the fact that discourse ethics *must* embed itself in empirical procedures of some sort, if it is to affect real decision making. To anticipate, I will argue that one can adequately conceive this "must" only by carrying through the paradigm shift adumbrated in Part One. But first it is necessary to formulate the theoretical problematic underlying institutionalization (subsection 1). Then I shall briefly sketch Habermas's solution of this problematic in the legal sphere (subsection 2). We will then be in a position to appreciate certain aporias that lead one beyond a subject-centered notion of insight and instill notions of solidarity and trust at the heart of rational conviction.

I.

We can theoretically sharpen the question raised in section I by recalling the earlier analysis of the intersubjective notion of insight. Judging from

(U), it would appear that the kind of insight grounding the rational acceptance of a normative validity claim must be impossible in principle. As the analysis of (U) showed, I can be rationally convinced of the rightness of a norm only if I have grounds for considering you (and each affected person) to be just as rationally convinced. But you can be rationally convinced only if you likewise have grounds for considering my conviction a rational one. We have already seen this paradoxical formulation of reversibility, which points us beyond a subject-centered account of insight. Let us call this the "reversibility paradox." It can be dispelled, I suggest, if we remove the notions of insight and rational conviction from the individual subject's jurisdiction and instead conceive these as inhering in something *jointly* accessible to participants in a process of discourse. If rational conviction arises not as some interior mental event but *communicatively* in the public space created by a discourse, then such joint accessibility begins to appear less paradoxical.[4]

We can understand the turn to legal procedures as an attempt to deal with the reversibility paradox. One of the more readily apparent expressions of the paradox lies in what we might call "difficulties of material feasibility" suggested by (U). To begin with, it is almost always impossible to carry on a discourse with all those possibly affected by a decision, even in a restricted context of application. Justifying a general moral norm appears even less feasible. If nothing else, one cannot consult future affected generations. Nor can one be sure that past generations would agree, especially in cases involving the criticism and overturn of past norms. Here the paradox appears in the fact that the universalistic, transhistorical aspect of (U) would seem to exclude in principle the individual's formation of a rational conviction about a norm. And this is only the most obvious difficulty. The problem is reinforced when one inquires into the possibility of elaborating need interpretations, eliminating power differentials among the participants, and so on.

To solve the problem of material feasibility, we need only view the full-blown insight projected by (U) as a regulative idea that goes hand in hand with the *fallibilism* characterizing actual discourses. The rationally motivating force of a speaker's validity claim is grounded in the speaker's confidence that the claim rests on reasons that, though limited, lead one to believe the claim will hold up against future criticism. From this perspective, (U) formulates what it *would* be for a claim to hold up in this

4. I find Taylor's remarks on conversation quite suggestive in this regard; see "Cross-Purposes," pp. 167–170.

way. My conviction about the rational acceptability of a norm or action (or a group's conviction about the rationality of its consensus) falls short of that spelled out by (U) precisely to the extent that I have not carried out the universal perspective taking enjoined by (U). Thus my assertion of, or assent to, a normative claim must always include a degree of uncertainty, an awareness that it may fall to criticism at some point. Conversely, my assent gains strength to the extent that I have engaged in perspective taking with persons who are affected by the claim. It is precisely this limited perspective taking within a group that makes what I earlier called a "partial group insight" possible, i.e., the insight that occurs when the participants to a localized conflict resolution realize that all those present can rationally assent to a certain norm (see the Postscript to Part One).

Now this confidence in a consensus does not rest primarily on the substantive content of the supporting reasons, nor simply on the de facto extent of a consensus, but on the quality of the testing procedure leading to consensus. Later I will argue that within a discursive process, the quality of the substantive reasons or values underlying a consensus matters a great deal. From a formal-pragmatic perspective, however, the evaluation of substantive reasons simply lies at a different level of real discourse, the level at which a dispersed, society-wide reflection on substantive moral values, general interests, and norms takes place. But more on that later. The point here is that the participants' confidence in their consensus depends on the extent to which they have been able to broaden the processes of perspective taking that lead up to their partial group insight. This confidence in the validity of a claim or norm can then be expressed in a probable moral judgment.

The foregoing considerations already point to both the possibility and necessity of taking the step to institutionalized procedures. Given the unrealizability of (U) as such, the step to such procedures is necessary for real decision making; given that (U) can operate as a regulative idea, the procedural approximation of which can ground confidence in probable judgments, the step to such procedures is possible. This move to institutionalization may be necessary even in cases where consensus is forthcoming, given that real discourse can at best approximate the demands of (U). Institutionalization becomes even more pressing—but also more problematic—in more difficult conflict resolutions. To get a better sense of the issues involved, we must broach the possibility of failures to reach rational consensus.

Suppose, then, that although the best arguments in a moral discourse over a norm appear to support a given norm proposal N, the participants simply lack the time to consider adequately all the possible counterarguments and standpoints. Even if each participant de facto assents to N, the shortfalls in argumentation and perspective taking would weaken the group's conviction that N is right. Of course, it could also be the case that some participants still do not find it in themselves to assent. The important point here is that the participants are aware that they have not been able to process sufficiently all the relevant considerations and arguments, for the situation presses for a decision. For example, there may be gaps in their investigation of the likely impact of the norm on those affected. All the same, under such circumstances they can still suppose that the arguments *would* converge on a particular norm if they only had the time to pursue those arguments.

In such situations it is reasonable to turn to procedures that bring about a clear decision after engaging in a discourse structured to secure as broad a range of considerations and viewpoints as possible within the limited time frame. *Which* discursive procedure would best meet this requirement—whether an open debate followed by a vote, or an interview of experts followed by a committee's decision, or some other procedure—remains an empirical question that in all likelihood would receive different answers in different spheres of action. Beyond providing certain abstract criteria of fairness, then, discourse ethics cannot tell us how actually to reach a singular judgment in any particular domain. For that we must supplement discourse-ethical idealizations with empirical considerations regarding the domain in question. I will come back to the aporias lurking behind this conception. At this point I simply want to reinforce the necessity for taking the step to practicable procedures that specify how the idealized procedures of discourse ethics should be scaled down for limited spatiotemporal frameworks. Such institutionalized procedures would then allow participants to arrive at a *probable moral judgment*, i.e., a decision whose probability of being morally valid rests on how well the discourse-ethical criteria of normative validity have been linked with domain-specific constraints on decision making. To flesh this point out a bit, let us turn to Habermas's remarks on the relation between law and morality.

2.

At least three complications attend any attempt to locate discourse ethics, as understood by Habermas, in law and politics. The first is that I must approach matters from the opposite end as Habermas does. The question guiding Habermas's analysis of law is that posed earlier by Weber, How can modern law achieve legitimacy after the collapse of generally convincing religious and metaphysical worldviews?[5] Thus Habermas starts with law as his primary object of investigation and only turns to moral theory in order to explain (in part) the legitimacy basis of law. In the present study I am taking just the opposite approach: starting with discourse ethics as a moral theory and turning to law as a means of showing how discourse-ethical idealizations can have some purchase in the real world. In both cases, though, the solution is the same, assuming we can read "the legitimacy of legality" as "the institutional feasibility of morality" in the following:

> Legitimacy is possible on the basis of legality insofar as the procedures for the production and application of legal norms are also conducted reasonably, in the moral-practical sense of procedural rationality. The legitimacy of legality is due to the interlocking of two types of procedures, namely, of legal processes with processes of moral argumentation that obey a procedural rationality of their own.[6]

The idea that two types of procedures interlock or interpenetrate I shall call the "interpenetration thesis." Elsewhere Habermas uses other metaphors: morality is "ingrained in law," or "penetrates into the core of positive law," while legality is "made pervious" or "open to moral argumentation."[7] In any case, these metaphors suggest that one should be able to separate legal procedures into a moral component and a properly legal one. Just as the presence of the moral component lends legitimacy to the outcome produced by following definite institutionalized legal procedures, so these legal procedures instantiate moral idealizations in some sense.

The second complication lies in the fact that legal legitimacy involves much *more* than the approximation of moral idealizations, a point Habermas has come to emphasize more strongly in his latest work on law.[8]

5. For a critical overview of Habermas's treatment of law up to 1988, see Klaus Eder, "Critique of Habermas's Contribution to the Sociology of Law," *Law and Society Review* 22 (1988): 931–944; for Habermas's critique of Weber, see TCA 1:143–286.

6. LM, p. 230.

7. Habermas's favorite metaphor seems to be "interpenetration" (*Verschränkung*); the other quoted terms are found in LM, pp. 247, 244, and 246; they are loose translations of, resp.: "im Recht selber festgelegt"; "wandert ins positive Recht ein"; "für moralische Diskurse durchlässig"; and "zu moralischen Argumentationen hin geöffnet." These phrases are found on pp. 15 and 13 in Jürgen Habermas, "Wie ist Legitimität durth Legalität möglich?" *Kritische Justiz* 20 (1987): 1–16.

8. FG, esp. chaps. 3 and 4.

Strictly speaking, legal-political structures institutionalize, not (U), but the broader and more abstract discourse principle (D). One must measure the legitimacy of law, then, against a range of idealizations in addition to the moral, to wit, the various discursive logics informing the ethical evaluation of goals (or what is good for the polity), the technical-pragmatic assessment of efficient means and strategies, and, in addition, the nondiscursive ideals of fair compromise formation. The interpenetration of law and morality represents only part of the whole picture, then. It is thus more accurate to speak of the interpenetration of law and *discourse*.

The third complication arises from further differentiations within the legal sphere itself. A full explication of legal procedures would require a theory of legal argumentation that differentiated the many forms of such argumentation, from scholarly articles on law to highly structured court trials. Although we cannot undertake such a study here, we can gain some purchase on the topic if we begin with Robert Alexy's approach to the law-morality issue.[9] Alexy sufficiently demonstrated the fruitfulness of a discourse-ethical perspective on law to convince Habermas that court proceedings involved more than strategic action.[10] Specifically, Alexy advanced the thesis that legal reasoning is a special case of practical reasoning. He based this thesis on three claims: that legal reasoning has to do with practical questions; that it involves a claim to correctness; and that it proceeds under special constraints that preclude a simple identification between practical (or moral) and legal reasoning.[11] I take the first as unproblematic; the real issue, then, concerns the specific procedures by which the legal validity claim is arrived at.

To be sure, Habermas also criticizes Alexy's "special case thesis," maintaining that it inappropriately subordinates law to morality. In the context of judicial procedures Habermas writes:

> No doubt one can use moral discourses of application as a model for investigating legal discourses, for both have to do with the logic of applying norms. But the more complex validity dimension of legal norms prohibits one from assimilating the rightness of legal decisions to the validity of moral judgments. To this extent one may not conceive legal discourse as a special case of moral discourses (of application).[12]

9. See his *Legal Argumentation* and *Theorie der Grundrecht* (Frankfurt: Suhrkamp, 1986).

10. "I have . . . been persuaded by Robert Alexy that juridical argumentation in all its institutional varieties has to be conceived of as a special case of practical discourse," TCA 1:412 n49. To be sure, Habermas shares the critique of Alexy in Günther, *Sinn*, pp. 268–276, as we shall see.

11. Alexy, *Legal Argumentation*, pp. 211–220.

12. FG, p. 286; see also pp. 281–287.

This point is well taken, and it fits in with what I have already noted about the complexity of legal legitimacy. In what follows, then, I will use Alexy's analysis merely as a heuristic device for ordering material and introducing Habermas's interpenetration thesis. A full analysis of this thesis exceeds the scope of this study in any case. My aim here is neither to deny the complexity of legal legitimacy nor to reduce such legitimacy to moral idealizations. Rather, I merely want to indicate some ways in which legal procedures *do* capture the same or similar fairness intuitions as those explicated in (U) and thus foster the production of *just* decisions. To this end it helps to explicate the four ways in which legal and practical discourses are "inextricably" linked, according to Alexy. In what follows I will take these up one at a time, in each case indicating how Habermas either agrees with or further develops Alexy's point. More important, each point will suggest a way of locating the relevance of discourse ethics for real discourse.

(1) The first I have already discussed: to affect actual decision making, moral discourse has need of institutionalization. For Alexy this follows from the "weakness" of the idealized rules governing moral discourse, i.e., the fact that these rules do not of themselves guarantee a determinate outcome. We have already seen that the rules of discourse ethics are rarely if ever fulfilled by real discourses; Alexy also sees potential difficulties in the fact that these rules do not stipulate the normative premises to be taken as the starting point for discussion and do not fix all the steps in argumentation.[13] Habermas seems to have the same point in mind when he points out that the idealized procedure of discourse ethics is "incomplete." Whether or not the requirements of the idealized procedure have been sufficiently fulfilled by a real discourse to justify assent cannot be determined except from the participant level of those actually engaged in discourse. At this level, however, no consensus can insure itself against the possibility of new arguments that would destroy the earlier basis for consensus. Consequently, a certain and definitive closure to debate cannot be had.[14]

By contrast, legal procedures are definite enough to permit one to determine, "from the perspective of a nonparticipant, whether or not a decision has come about according to the rules."[15] For example, if a legally

13. *Legal Argumentation*, pp. 287f, also pp. 206–208. Note that Alexy has a much broader set of rules in mind than (U); he summarizes these in the Appendix to *Legal Argumentation*, pp. 297–300, and in his "Theory of Practical Discourse," pp. 151–190.

14. As Habermas puts it, a discourse-ethical procedure "guarantees neither the infallibility nor the unambiguity of the outcome, nor a result in due time." LM, p. 244; also FG, pp. 219f.

15. LM, p. 244.

binding decision on an issue is defined as the outcome of a simple majority vote taken after an hour of debate in the presence of at least two-thirds of those affected, then it is relatively unproblematic to determine whether or not a particular decision is legal. Thus the legal component fixes determinable limits to discourse such that a clear result can be reached following unambiguous procedures. While idealizations such as (D) or (U) imply that a given consensus, even a unanimous one, always remains open to revision on the grounds that participants were duped (to name just one possibility), legal procedures in the proper sense have relatively clear satisfaction criteria. To be sure, one must qualify this with "relatively," especially in view of the recent debates on the indeterminacy of law.[16] In any case, the foregoing suggests we can distinguish the properly legal component in institutionalized procedures by noting those criteria or procedural rules that place definite *limits* on a decision procedure that might otherwise be construed as directed towards discourse-ethical unanimity. Typically, such limits relax the requirements found in principles such as (D) and (U). For example, a rule specifying a two-thirds majority vote legally provides a clear and definite limit that relaxes the idealized requirement of reaching unanimous agreement. The process of debate preceding the vote, on the other hand, might be seen as instantiating the moral discourse proper insofar as it obeys the moral intuition that participants should strive to convince one another of the better argument and thereby win one another's votes in debate. Here we can see that the right to take part in or be represented in the debate, as well as the right to vote—in fact, any attempt to give all those affected a voice in the real discourse—constitute legal structures that create the space within which moral intuitions about justice can shape real discourse. At the same time, as specific forms, structures governing participation must also limit the open character of the corresponding moral intuitions. As Habermas summarizes this point: "While *the embeddedness of discourses in legal procedures* leaves the inner logic of such discourses intact, . . . procedurally configured institutionalization subjects them to specific temporal, social, and material limitations."[17]

(2) This brings us to Alexy's second link between moral and legal procedures. The two procedures interpenetrate insofar as both involve a

---

16. Alexy points out that uncertainty attaches even to legal procedures in *Legal Argumentation*, pp. 292–294; for specific illustrations of a more radical indeterminacy thesis, see Duncan Kennedy, "Freedom and Constraint in Adjudication: A Critical Phenomenology," *Journal of Legal Education* 36 (1986): 518–562; Jerry Frug, "Argument as Character," *Stanford Law Review* 40 (April 1988): 869–927.

17. FG, p. 219; cf. also LM, pp. 230, 241–242, 247.

"claim to correctness." In other words, a validity claim is at stake in both cases. By way of support, Alexy points to the fact that judges are required by law to justify their decisions and that legal procedures are structured as discursive searches for a correct decision.[18] In contrast to moral discourse in the broad sense, however, participants in a legal discourse strive to justify their claim only relative to a pre-existing legal order presumed as valid. Hence to analyze and legitimate fully the moral force of a legal claim one would have to connect it with a "theory of legislation and then a normative theory of society of which the theory of legal discourse would form a part."[19]

Rather than get tangled up in what Alexy might mean by this, I think it more helpful to view the rationally motivating force of a legal claim as involving a variety of validity dimensions, i.e., as open to potential criticism from several angles. If judicial decisions rest on interlocking legal and moral procedures, the participants might criticize a decision for failing to observe one or another legal procedural rule (resulting in a mistrial, for example), or they might criticize the judge's application of existing law. They would open a specifically moral discourse of application if they were to claim that the decision, whether legally permitted or not, somehow violated the intuitive demands of justice. This kind of issue arises, for example, in tort cases where one is legally permitted to press a suit for injuries due to another's negligence, even though the plaintiff is better off than the negligent party and not actually hurt. The problem here lies not in the general tort law but in its inability to make fine enough distinctions to account for all the morally relevant circumstances. Thus one could argue here that the application of a just law has led to an injustice in the concrete case. An issue of moral justification would arise if the participants contested the moral validity of the law applied in the decision; here discourse is more likely to gravitate toward possible legislative action that would correct the unjust law.[20]

As already noted, other forms of discourse also interpenetrate with legal procedures. Thus, legal-political decisions can also involve technical-pragmatic questions about effective means and strategies, ethical-

18. Alexy, *Legal Argumentation*, pp. 214–217.
19. Alexy, *Legal Argumentation*, p. 289.
20. In fact, it oversimplifies matters to assume in advance that the moral element in legislation is a discourse of justification, while adjudication involves discourses of application; legislation can involve an applicatory moment, while adjudication can involve elements of justification; see Günther, *Sinn*, p. 317, for example. To be sure, Habermas appears to make this correlation in LM, p. 277; FG, pp. 212f. Such a correlation is criticized by Peters, *Rationalität*, pp. 297–309.

political issues concerning a society's shared goals and self-under-standing, as well as bargaining processes requiring fair compromises. One could criticize a decision in view of certain technical facts as an ineffective solution to a conflict. On the other hand, a zoning decision about whether to allow a business into a given area can have a significant impact on the quality of life for the area residents. This means that ethical arguments involving what the residents want, what they consider desirable as a way of life, become relevant. A further example is found in the question of whether to allow researchers to patent human genomes in the United States. Inasmuch as such a decision will affect a nation's competitiveness in international markets, the nation's economic good is at stake. Finally, bargaining issues arise when particular (as opposed to generalizable or shared) interests clash, so that some compromise is necessary to reach a decision. In that case, one party might object that the other enjoyed a power advantage that undermined the fairness of the compromise.

In short, an analysis of the rationally motivating force of a legal validity claim involves a number of aspects that a formal-pragmatic analysis would have to pull apart. Moral discourse achieves empirical reality not by itself but only as intertwined with an entire range of discourse types. The foregoing suggests that one can pull these different discourses apart by thematizing the variety of potential criticisms to which a given legal decision is susceptible.[21]

(3) The third link further extends the second. In attempting to justify a claim to correctness, legal proceedings employ discursive procedures that display structural similarities with the rules of moral discourse. As we have seen, Habermas considers Alexy's treatment of such similarities problematic inasmuch as it tends to assimilate law to morality. On Habermas's view, one does better to analyze such similarities at the level of (D), in terms of the idealized requirements of impartial justification in general. In that case, one can see legal procedures as aiming at the production of impartially justified decisions within the framework of existing law. Even with this qualification, however, an examination of such

---

21. One might also include truth and sincerity as potentially relevant validity dimensions. Thus one can criticize a decision for failing to uncover the facts of the case (criticism of the truth claim underlying the decision). There is also some evidence that participants' assessment of the fairness of an authority's decision depends on their perception of the authority's sincerity (in the sense of "effort to be fair"); see Tom R. Tyler, *Why People Obey the Law* (New Haven: Yale University Press, 1990), pp. 135–146. For Habermas's attempt to interrelate the various modes of validity in a "process model" of political will-formation, see FG, pp. 195–207, 217–226.

similarities could be a fruitful test of the intuitions explicated in (U)—
i.e., it would show that certain intuitions about impartial justification
can have an institutional effect. In any case, I will treat this particular
link as one holding between legal procedures and *impartialist* idealizations that at most display certain similarities to impartial moral justification.

One of the most striking of these similarities is the legal principle that
like cases be treated alike. This directly corresponds to Hare's notion of
semantic universalizability, which I discussed in Part One. Alexy connects this with a form of legal argument employed to resolve cases where
a general law clearly applies. In such cases a decision to treat a particular
person in a certain way is justified by the fact that some feature of that
person falls under a general law. For example, if an existing law maintains that "soldiers on official business must tell the truth" and M is a
soldier on official business, then a court order constraining M to tell the
truth can be legally justified.[22]

Unfortunately, Alexy restricts his treatment of this point to the forms
for producing particular legal arguments.[23] This is too narrow, as a look
at the three levels of argumentative speech will show. Habermas distinguishes these levels as follows: (1) The "process" level has to do with
argumentation as a form of communication that depends on idealizing
suppositions about the freedom and equality of the participants (this is
the level at which (U) operates). (2) The "procedural" level, which corresponds to Aristotle's dialectic, has to do with argument as subject to
rules of interaction that organize a debate as a cooperative search for the
better argument. (3) The logical level, finally, pertains to the production
of individual valid arguments.[24] On this analysis, Alexy's treatment remains largely at the dialectical and logical levels. Hare's universalizability principle, for example, can be seen as a logical rule for moving from
a general law to a particular judgment. The rule that allows for a transition to empirical argumentation represents a dialectical move, i.e., a
rule governing the interplay of logically valid arguments. To be sure, these
levels have a "legitimating force," as Habermas points out.[25] What falls

22. Alexy, *Legal Argumentation*, pp. 289–290, 222.
23. *Legal Argumentation*, pp. 290f, lists the presence of empirical argumentation, canons of interpretation, structures of dogmatic legal science, the doctrine of precedent, and
"special legal argument forms" (e.g., *argumentum e contrario*) as corresponding to aspects
of general practical argumentation.
24. See TCA 1:25–26.
25. Although Habermas does not explicitly draw a connection between these various
legal forms and the levels of argumentative speech, his own description justifies our doing
so: "What has legitimating force are the procedures that distribute burdens of proof, define

from view, however, is precisely the "process" level at which impartialist idealizations call for symmetrical and distortion-free conditions of communication. Thus Habermas goes on to argue that "we can find the rational core . . . of legal procedures only by analyzing how the idea of impartiality in the justified choice and application of binding rules can establish a constructive connection between the existing body of law, legislation, and adjudication."[26]

To complete Alexy's analysis, then, we must look beyond the legal procedures that secure a cooperative production of arguments and ask how these procedures screen out bias and other distortions in communication. Of course, well-designed procedures for producing sound arguments are an important element in impartial justification, so that the process level depends on the logical and dialectical levels. But to get at the process level we must go beyond these. One possible way of doing this can be illustrated in the case of court procedures.

To see how rules of court procedure secure an impartial *process* of justification, we could examine how they provide opportunities for the disputants to voice their point of view as clearly and forcefully as possible, on the one hand, and compensate for the very partiality such voicing normally involves, on the other. We could then locate impartialist idealizations in the very *structure* of court proceedings, at least to some extent. The overall structure puts partiality to work for the production of the best available argument for each side while separating such partiality from the decision mechanism proper, which it hands over to a relatively detached judge or jury. This illustrates Habermas's point that legal structures "define, protect, and structure the spaces" within which discourse and the logic of argumentation can operate; to this extent, such structures represent more than limits on idealized discursive intuitions.[27] At least in some cases, one must view them as artful devices for reproducing the intended effect of these idealizations in less than ideal circumstances. If two opponents in a dispute cannot realistically expect that

---

the requirements of justification, and set the path of argumentative vindication." LM, p. 242. His language here suggests the dialectical level, where the primary goal is argument as a "cooperative division of labor," TCA 1:25.

26. LM, p. 242.

27. FG, p. 219. Habermas's analysis of court procedures, however, largely locates the discursive elements *outside* the procedure proper, in the judge's own separate evaluation of the evidence and legal assessment; see FG, pp. 287–291. I argue here that the procedure itself also embodies some of the intuitions we think should govern rational discourse. For social-psychological evidence for the view I am presenting here, see John Thibaut and Laurens Walker, *Procedural Justice: A Psychological Analysis* (Hillsdale, N.J.: Lawrence Erlbaum, 1975).

they will take each other's perspectives, then they can at least suppose
that the jury can do so after having heard the best arguments each side
can muster. Here we have two elements of rational discourse—arguments made from the standpoint of each affected individual and mutual
perspective taking—artfully approximated by a division of labor (between disputants and jury) that isolates the distorting effects of bias, i.e.,
compensates for the inability of the participants to take one another's
perspective. On the one hand, disputants present their own cases (generally with the help of lawyers); on the other hand, the judge or jury
weighs the relative force of each side's arguments, thereby compensating
for the inability of the disputants to take one another's perspective.

(4) The fourth link between legal and moral discourse is the need for
forms of moral discourse *within* legal discourse. Alexy notes a number
of points where this can occur: the justification of normative premises in
a legal argument, the justification of a choice between argument forms
that lead to different results, and the justification for introducing distinctions or overruling precedents are only three.[28] Here I want to high-
light one dimension of this that Habermas has emphasized. Insofar as
legal proceedings and above all legislative proceedings are public events,
they remain open or "pervious" to broader, less constrained processes of
discourse in the public sphere—i.e., the ongoing discourse that occurs
face-to-face; in journals, newspapers, and magazines; and on the radio
and television.[29] Because this public discourse is not as institutionally
confined as processes of adjudication and legislation, the arguments and
results issuing from these latter institutions can be submitted to a direct
moral criticism in the forums of public discourse, assuming that such discourse has not been subverted by other forces.[30] Conversely, a robust
public sphere can supply judges, legislators, and government administrators with potential justifications at the points noted above. Rather
than pursue an analysis of the public sphere directly, limitations of space

28. Alexy, *Legal Argumentation*, pp. 284–286, 291–292.
29. See Jürgen Habermas, *The Structural Transformation of the Public Sphere: An Inquiry into a Category of Bourgeois Society*, trans. Thomas Burger (Cambridge: MIT Press,
1989), for Habermas's attempt at a thorough analysis of the emergence of the bourgeois
public sphere and the subsequent effects of mass media and capital concentration. This
study, which appeared in German in 1962, is in need of certain revisions, as Habermas
admits in "Further Reflections on the Public Sphere," in *Habermas and the Public Sphere*,
ed. Craig Calhoun (Cambridge: MIT Press, 1992), pp. 421–461; more recently, see FG,
chap. 8.
30. LM, pp. 248–249, 278–279; also Jürgen Habermas, "Volkssouveränität als Verfahren: Ein normativer Begriff der Öffentlichkeit," in *Die Moderne—Ein unvollendetes
Projekt: Philosophisch-politische Aufsätze* (Leipzig: Reclam, 1990), esp. pp. 204ff; re-
printed in FG, Appendix II.

force me to approach it in the context of the aporias suggested by the foregoing account of law and morality.

III. DECENTERING RATIONAL CONSENSUS: FURTHER QUESTIONS

The foregoing account of law and morality, with their relations to a public sphere of ongoing critical debate, must remain suggestive at most. My aim was simply to indicate how the strong idealizations developed in Part One have effect in real discourses. In this section I want to supplement the foregoing by indicating directions of further research. These are revealed by various follow-up problems or aporias encountered in the attempt to link discourse ethics as a regulative moral idea with real discourses. The first problem concerns whether discourse ethics does not boil down to a theory of democratic legitimacy rather than morality; to defuse this objection, it is necessary to connect discourse ethics with the broader moral structures of the lifeworld. The second problem calls our attention to the gap between (U) and real discourses. In particular, one must ask whether (U) can adequately account for the peculiar moral demands connected with real limits on the degree of participation and the possibility of intractable disagreement. Each of these difficulties indicates how it is necessary to carry through the break with subject-centered reason—a break thus far only adumbrated—and revamp the notions of insight and solidarity accordingly. I cannot here argue these points with the requisite detail; that would, in any case, require a separate study (or studies) beyond the scope of the present project. In each case I can only tentatively suggest a further direction of analysis.

1. TOWARD A GENERALIZED DISCOURSE-ETHICAL ANALYSIS

Albrecht Wellmer has objected that (U) does not sufficiently differentiate "between problems concerning the *legitimacy* of norms and the problem of morally right action"; on the contrary, Wellmer argues, Habermas's formulation of discourse ethics falls behind the Kantian distinction between law and morality.[31] To be sure, Wellmer's critique predates Ha-

31. Wellmer, "Ethics and Dialogue," p. 117; also pp. 193–195. One should note that this work originally appeared in German in 1986, and thus does not benefit from Habermas's 1988 "Law and Morality," let alone from *Faktizität und Geltung* (1992); in these works it is Kant who stands charged with too closely linking law and morality; e.g., LM, pp. 269–271.

bermas's more recent work on law, and the stress Habermas now lays on the complexity of legal validity certainly addresses this critique from the side of law. But Habermas's complementary point—that the moral principle (U) pertains primarily to informal everyday interaction—remains comparatively undeveloped. As long as this is the case, everyday practices of reason giving in normatively charged situations will appear rudimentary in comparison to (U), leading to doubts about whether discourse ethics spells out a moral theory or, rather, merely the moral dimension of legitimate democratic institutions. In view of this it is not surprising that some commentators prefer to restrict discourse ethics to just such institutions.

One could respond to Wellmer by questioning his tendency to overemphasize the concrete applicatory aspect of morality to the detriment of its orientation to general norms, which for Wellmer apparently boil down to mere rules of thumb.[32] However, to spell out the relevance of (U) for ordinary life (and counter Wellmer's objection), one must ultimately establish a clearer link between everyday reason giving and discourse proper. Given the attenuated character of the individual's everyday practice of argument, which rarely if ever involves detached reflection with all the affected parties, in what sense can it be plausibly construed as an instance of a (U)-governed discourse? Here I continue to assume that to arrive at (U) one must extrapolate a good distance from the very limited exchanges of reasons used as evidence in Part One.

To address this difficulty, one must, I think, supplement and generalize the foregoing analysis of legal-political discourse. The necessary supplementary step is already evident in the very reason giving that one might consider too simple for a (U)-governed discourse. Consider a fairly typical schema of everyday norm "justification" that would fit many of the examples I have used throughout this study:

Person A challenges B's action as immoral.

B asks for A's grounds, and A points to a norm N.

B asks A why N is valid, and A points to certain values N incorporates, or values that the consequences of following N would preserve.

As I have continued to point out, consensus in these cases usually depends on agreeing that the norm at stake incorporates a basic moral value or values. Granted, the relationship between the norm and such

32. See Günther, *Sinn*, pp. 65–81.

values may involve a number of twists and turns, since the decisive value could be directly incorporated in the norm or it could emerge only through the wider impacts of the norm's observance. The important point is that generalized moral values do much of the work in the effort to reach agreement, insofar as the agreement is reconstructible in terms of moral discourse. Naturally such values can themselves become problematic; then one would expect local disagreements to reflect deeper social rifts. But in a great many cases the participants do not problematize the value as such, i.e., they do not ask whether one should or should not consider it a moral value at all; rather, they argue about the interpretation of the value, or the extent of its relevance, or whether it supports the norm in question.

The upshot is that such everyday disputes can be seen either as "foreshortened" discourses set against an unproblematic background of moral values, or—especially in more difficult cases where the values themselves are in some sense problematic—as local expressions of broader processes of discourse carried on at different levels in a society. To see everyday disputes as discourses in the fuller sense one must take in a larger picture that distinguishes between more specific, thematized conflict issues and the background values that are themselves often expressible in the form of very abstract moral norms. The latter values/ norms then either allow a quick and harmonious conclusion to the local dispute or—assuming the parties do not come to blows or simply strike an uneasy truce—are more finely interpreted, creatively altered, or sensitively applied in the local dispute. To conceive the "discourse" over such values one need only step back and view the entire process of scattered disputes, local innovations, public debates and even philosophical reflection on the issues in which such values are at stake. In this way one can conceive of a moral tradition, i.e., an ongoing process of social debate that brings a tradition of moral values to bear on historically specific problems and thereby interprets and perhaps even changes those values.

From the participant perspective, these background values appear as moral certitudes to which one can confidently appeal in order to settle a conflict on a less general level. They embody one's confidence that certain modes of interaction enjoy a general and unquestioned approbation. This confidence can, of course, be disappointed.[33] In that case an element

33. Habermas speaks of such confidence as a "type of anthropologically basic trust [*Urvertrauen*]" in a tradition. In Germany such trust was deeply disappointed when traditional continuities led to National Socialism, with the result that "a *conscious* life is no longer possible without mistrust" for such unquestioned continuities; Jürgen Habermas,

in a society's tradition(s) has become thematized vis-à-vis a problematic norm. Those involved in such conflicts must renegotiate both the underlying value and the specific norm. One should not expect this to be a tidy process. In real discourse, moral argumentation will generally not stand alone, but will be interwoven with other forms of argumentation and reasoning—ethical-existential discourse, strategic and instrumental reasoning, personal narratives, and so forth. Moreover, not just arguments are involved, but real experiments in lifestyle and mutual cooperation. This makes it difficult to separate discourse from the clash of actual life practices. A discourse ethics of everyday life would require the theorist to reconstruct "discourse" and individual "insight" by situating these in ongoing life practices.

Having supplemented the earlier discourse-ethical analysis of law by situating it in a study of the lifeworld background, we can also reasonably generalize the application of discourse ethics beyond the legal sphere. For if discourse ethics is more than a theory of legal-political legitimacy, then one should expect to find analogous normative intuitions guiding decision-making procedures (and the criticism of such procedures) in any number of institutions. In fact, there is a growing body of empirical evidence indicating that notions of procedural justice operate across a variety of institutional spheres, though it remains to be seen how closely such notions match discourse-ethical reconstructions like (U).[34] Again, one should not expect moral intuitions always to be the sole or even primary factor in the validity of such decision making. Hence, to carry out this generalizing move, for each institution one would have to analyze an interpenetrating set of discourse types, taking an approach not unlike that illustrated above in the analysis of law. Such analyses take a theory of moral judgment beyond the ken of moral theorists, for domain-specific considerations enter into the assessment of even the moral quality of a particular decision.

Such an analysis would both situate and decenter the real practice of discourse. It would situate it in a multidimensional field composed of shared background values informing lifeworld cooperation, formal institutional decision-making procedures, and scattered processes of ar-

---

"Ethics, Politics and History: An Interview with Jürgen Habermas." Conducted by Jean-Marc Ferry, *Philosophy and Social Criticism* 14 (1988): 434–435.

34. See Lind and Tyler, *The Social Psychology of Procedural Justice*, esp. chap. 6; the pervasiveness of discourse ethics should already be at least plausible in view of Jean Piaget's *The Moral Judgment of the Child*, trans. Marjorie Gabain (New York: Free Press, 1965), which traced out, in various contexts, the preadolescent development of the intuitions Apel and Habermas would later incorporate in discourse ethics.

gument, be they local face-to-face encounters or broader discussions carried on in the public media of mass communication. It would also decenter it, for "the moral discourse" about a given norm would be the sum of a complex network of overlapping processes. Whether (U) adequately reconstructs the rationality of such a decentered process I shall address below. Here I want to note that insofar as substantive moral values on the one hand, and idealizing moral intuitions of fair procedure on the other inform the decision-making procedures across a variety of institutions and spheres of action, one can mitigate the impression that discourse ethics pertains less to morality than to legitimacy. To think otherwise risks endorsing a recalcitrant individualism.[35]

2. THE VESTIGES OF SUBJECT-CENTERED REASON IN (U)

One cannot carry out the broader discourse-ethical analysis projected above without facing a number of difficulties. Again, these bear on the move from the idealized to the real procedure, only in this case the question is not whether discourse ethics falls too readily into legal-political categories but whether it falls too far, so to speak. For if real discourses can at best only approximate the idealizations, one may ask whether morality stands on too high a pedestal. Why should a proceduralization defined *externally* to morality be necessary for procedural morality itself? Here I refer to institutionalized procedures in a very broad sense, as taking in any social decision-making procedure that enables a group to reach clear, definite, and timely resolutions of morally relevant problems of cooperation.

This engenders some instructive problems. Two are especially important for our purposes. The first has to do with the justification of specific procedural shortcuts. If to make a real practical judgment it is necessary that one descend from the idealized heavens of complete universal reversibility and take the realistic (and even reasonable) shortcuts of institutionalized procedures, then how does one justify the *morality* of such shortcuts? According to (U) this is impossible, for real procedures would have to be subjected in turn to an equally idealized discourse of all those affected. But if one cannot justify the morality of real procedures, then one cannot show that real judgments are procedurally correct. That is, one cannot *morally* justify the specific limitations imposed by the real

35. Cf. Robert Bellah, Richard Madsen, William Sullivan, Ann Swindler and Steven Tipton, *The Good Society* (New York: Knopf, 1991).

procedure on the moral idealizations: from the moral standpoint any limitation—cutting off debate at a certain point, setting up criteria for participation, and so on—must remain problematic inasmuch as such limitations depend on extra-moral considerations. One cannot fully dispel
this objection by recurring to the fallibilism of moral judgment, since the
results of a real discourse will be fallible in any case, i.e., even if the real
procedure were clearly the best at producing probable moral judgments.
The question I am raising is this: why stop the debate here rather than
there? Why admit x number of representatives rather than y? Why a two-
thirds majority and not a four-fifths majority? In short, how does one
identify in moral terms which of several possible procedures is clearly the
better when every real procedure departs from moral standards at some
point?[36]

The second problem has to do with compliance. If reaching concrete
decisions in specific institutional contexts necessitates procedural shortcuts that leave some parties unconvinced of the rightness of the decision,
then why should those parties comply, morally speaking? According to
(U), they would always be justified in criticizing the decision as unjust:
after all, *they* were not convinced, their arguments not adequately re-
butted. But clearly one should not comply with an unjust decision. To
respond to this, one would seemingly have to explain how the specific
institutional limitations on (U) in a given domain enjoy a certain moral
force. Or one would have to show that individuals generally attribute a
moral force to procedural limitations on (U)—a paradoxical endeavor,
given that the unlimited demands of (U) first define moral force. Like the
first difficulty, the second too points to certain advantages in bringing (U)
closer to earth.

Alexy seems to be aware of such problems, but is willing to live with
them; for Habermas, they simply issue from the unavoidable "tension
between facticity and validity."[37] Enduring such tension is not necessarily
so difficult; in fact, it has certain advantages, as we shall see. One need
only simultaneously emphasize both the reasonableness and fallibilistic
character of empirical procedures, moves we indeed made in section II
of this chapter.[38] (U) is, after all, a regulative idea spelling out what a

36. In EzD, pp. 161–162, Habermas speaks of "sufficiently" satisfying pragmatic presuppositions contained in (U); institutional procedures such as parliamentary deliberations
should guarantee "the probability of a sufficient satisfaction of the demanding presuppositions of communication." My question concerns how one knows, or justifies the guarantee, that this sufficiency actually obtains.
37. See Alexy, "Theory of Practical Discourse," pp. 180–183; Habermas, FG, chap.1.
38. See, for example, Alexy, *Legal Argumentation*, pp. 207–208, 292–295.

complete rational conviction would have to look like; one should not expect its empirical representation.

I do not insist that such difficulties are insuperable within the bounds of a viable discourse ethics. They do, however, betray vestiges of a subject-centered notion of reason, and this makes their investigation worthwhile. To get at these it helps to recall the derived formulation of (U):

> A consensus on a norm is rational (and the norm valid) if and only if
>
> (a) each of those affected can convince the others, in terms they hold appropriate for the perception of both their own and others' interests, that the constraints and impacts of the norm's general observance are acceptable for all; and
>
> (b) each can be convinced by all, in terms she or he considers appropriate, that the constraints and impacts of the norm's general observance are acceptable for all.

I have already discussed the reversibility paradox this contains. I suggested earlier the following resolution of the paradox: If my rational conviction that a norm is valid depends on yours and vice versa, then the site where such conviction develops must be a public or common one existing "between" individual speakers and hearers. Language presents a natural candidate for such common space, as thinkers such as Humboldt and Mead realized. Mead, for example, found such a space in the identical aural stimulation provided by the spoken word. Because speech offers the same sensory input to both speaker and hearer, a common meaning is possible on its basis.[39] In order to understand (U) in these terms one must simply elaborate such linguistic commonality as a process of symbolic exchange. That is, (U) requires each member of a deliberative group to enter the common linguistic space of every other member. As each face-to-face encounter is reiterated across the entire group, a common meaning shared by the group is gradually built up, the sum result of the individual pairings. Of course, we saw in Part One that this must be qualified: beyond what is necessary to agree to the norm at issue, this meaning need not be a *single* semantic framework. The specific arguments that each person finds convincing can differ from perspective to perspective, so long as each person has confirmed this convincingness for each of the affected viewpoints.

39. See Mead, *Mind, Self, and Society*; also TCA 2:3–42.

Strictly speaking, however, the above formulation of (U) only takes us to the threshold of this common space. For it still assumes that each individual is the ultimate site of rational conviction or insight, the common space of exchange notwithstanding; its advance over individualism consists in linking such conviction to a complete perspective taking in which each person has convinced every other and vice versa. It is precisely the attempt to formulate such perspective taking on the basis of a subject-centered notion of insight that constitutes the paradoxical appearance of this formulation of (U). Hence the derivation of (U) takes the subject-centered approach to the point where it must be abandoned or destroy itself.

The root difficulty lies in conceiving reflective insight as something had by each *individual* and then, on that basis, attempting to link it with the conviction of *all other individuals*. One can, to be sure, point to experiences in which one's own tentative conclusion becomes conviction only when it finds the other's support. But once this interdependence expands to include all those affected by a moral norm, it is hardly possible to satisfy the demands for mutual perspective taking in the one-to-one manner envisioned in (U). At the very least there are insuperable "logistical" difficulties, which raise precisely those questions of material feasibility that make the turn to procedural shortcuts a necessity, as shown in section II.

At the same time, taking the individual subject as the site for rational conviction offers definite advantages. It clearly links consensus with each individual's insight into the better argument, at least as a counterfactual supposition. As a regulative idea it at least offers a clear *target* for real discourses. And if the normative rationality of an empirical procedure is not measured by the attempt to approximate the complete cognitive perspective taking of (U), then on what basis can we measure its rationality? However difficult this question may appear, to back off at this point risks overlooking important elements in the rationality of real dispute settlements and institutional proceduralization—a rationality that is not angelic but all too human. And as human, its intersubjective character is not fully captured by the still rather angelic rationality of (U). My thesis, then, is that we can only fully carry out the paradigm shift away from the philosophy of the subject by taking in not just the counterfactual but also more of the *factual*—i.e., empirically limited—rationality guiding real moral discourses.

The presence of a "factual" rationality betrays itself most quickly in two basic theoretical aporias that underlie the difficulties mentioned above (having to do with the justification of shortcuts and compliance). On the one hand, *participation is incomplete* in real discourses; on the other, *agreement is incomplete*. These two problems are not unrelated, to be sure, but for analytic reasons it helps to separate them. I will treat each in turn.

Incomplete participation. Once we consider justification discourses in cases other than the face-to-face encounters involving only a small group, the problem of full participation becomes acute. In fact, even local disputes, if viewed as attempts at a partial justification of general norms, must tacitly refer to *all* those possibly affected by the norm in question. This means that each of the affected persons must be able to convince and be convinced by each other affected person, each from his or her own perspective. But certainly everyone cannot speak to everyone in a dispute of any scope. A single author, of course, might be able to make her perspective and arguments known to an entire society, but she could not learn of all her readers' reactions. This means she cannot be *fully* convinced even of the correctness of her own views on the disputed issue, since that conviction partly depends on others' reactions.

This problem is compounded if an issue involves a weighing of empirical consequences from the standpoint of different disciplines. For example, decisions affecting environmental quality, or the health standards of a population, usually involve a number of expert viewpoints and disciplines. If these various experts cannot fully assess the opinions of their colleagues from neighboring disciplines, one can hardly expect "all those affected" to do so.[40] Thus the problem of participation includes not only limits on perspective taking but limits on any person's ability to participate fully in all branches of the relevant argumentation. Unlike Descartes with his deductions, no one individual commands the entire "chain" of arguments and counterarguments on the way to reaching a valid conclusion.

In at least two ways, then, a discourse escapes the individual's full participation: no individual has a full familiarity with all the relevant considerations, and no individual has argued the matter out with all other affected individuals. One person may have discussed the issue with a

---

40. On this point see Charles Arthur Willard, "The Problem of the Public Sphere: Three Diagnoses," in *Argumentation Theory and the Rhetoric of Assent*, ed. David Cratis Williams and Michael David Hazen (Tuscaloosa: University of Alabama Press, 1990), pp. 135–153.

small circle of acquaintances, another may have closely followed public debates; yet another has a deep appreciation of the environmental impact of a decision but not of its impact on the business community.

If this description is accurate—and is becoming more and more accurate in today's society—then the cooperative element in reaching a rational consensus goes even deeper than (U) would suggest. On the above scenario, it is not just that your input broadens the range of views and arguments I can consider in forming my opinion; rather, at a certain level I simply *cannot take in your input at all*, as an individual. For example, your expert analysis of the likely consequences simply exceeds my powers of assessment, while my perspective is never well represented in the particular circles with which you are familiar. For rational consensus to be at all possible in such cases, the "common space" in which reflective insight occurs cannot be conceived in any way as that of a collective subject. Reflective insight cannot rest even on the "summation" of individual insights or acts of mutual convincing: this is where (U), as presently formulated, still betrays its allegiance to the monadic subject. Even if the individual's conviction is indissolubly linked to that of other individuals, and even if this conviction must be confirmed across the various languages and conceptual frameworks appropriate to each other individual's need interpretation, (U) still apparently posits a counterfactual end state in which each *individual* would be sure of his or her conviction as well as that of everyone else.

To get beyond the residues of a collective subject, Habermas has made the following suggestion:

> The "self" of this self-organizing society then disappears in those subjectless forms of communication that are supposed to regulate the flow of discursively shaped opinion-formation and will-formation in such a way that their fallible results can claim to be reasonable. Such an intersubjectively dispersed, anonymous popular sovereignty withdraws into democratic procedures and the demanding communicative presuppositions of their implementation. They find their non-locatable location in the interactions between legally institutionalized will-formation and culturally mobilized public spheres.[41]

Now the foregoing analysis suggests that to work out the "subjectless" notion of reason projected in the above quotation, a still more radical step is necessary, one that breaks with the subject-centered overtones in the "demanding communicative presuppositions" found in (U) itself. But it is far from clear how to do this without losing sight of the individual

41. NR, p. 196.

in some huge procedural machine cranking out presumably correct results independently of human subjects.

Here I can only tentatively suggest a promising route. If real processes of discourse are decentered in the manner described above, such that individual conviction becomes impossible; if rational consensus is cooperative even to the degree of requiring a decentered, "cooperative insight," then it would seem that something like trust must inhabit the heart of rational conviction. To link up with our earlier descriptions, participants must at some point trust the opinions of experts on likely consequences of a norm—a position that experts themselves occupy vis-à-vis other experts and even with respect to nonexperts' perspectives.[42] We have also seen how the substantive, tradition-mediated background values can be the object of a fragile trust. Similarly, participants must eventually trust the public processes of debate and decision-making procedures. Finally, they must have some confidence in one another's sincerity, the good will of concerned citizens involved in circles of debate beyond their own, the representatives' capacity to consider thoughtfully a variety of viewpoints, even the media through which arguments and viewpoints are disseminated.[43] On this view, the individual's confidence in the validity of a decision is based not so much on his or her overview of the relevant arguments as on the procedures for processing various arguments and how faithfully their administrators carry them out.[44]

Such trust, of course, need not be blind or naive, and any examination of the trustworthiness of these processes and those involved in them would have to draw upon a cognitive notion of rational consensus something like that presented in (U). But a notion of trust able to shorten the

42. Trusting experts is rational, according to Stephen P. Stich and Richard E. Nisbett, "Expertise, Justification, and the Psychology of Inductive Reasoning," in *The Authority of Experts: Studies in History and Theory*, ed. Thomas L. Haskell (Bloomington: Indiana University Press, 1984), pp. 226–241. And it need not be blind: as Willard, "Problem of the Public Sphere," points out, experts often contradict each other even within a discipline, which allows the nonexpert to test the strength of one expert's views against other experts.

43. The effect of electronic media of mass communications on discourse still remains to be worked out from the ground up in critical social theory; until this is done, it is difficult to shake the suspicion that discourse ethics pertains more to eighteenth-century salon societies than to our own, despite Habermas's early attempt to indicate how a critical public sphere is possible under twentieth-century conditions; *Structural Transformation*, esp. pp. 222–250; see also the critical assessment in John B. Thompson, *Ideology and Modern Culture: Critical Social Theory in the Era of Mass Communication* (Stanford: Stanford University Press, 1990), pp. 109–121.

44. The "rationally motivated trust" Habermas introduces as a "relief mechanism" for risky processes of reaching agreement has other *individuals* for its object: such trust has its source either in another's personal prestige or in his or her "disposition over knowledge"; TCA 2:181, also 181–185. My own analysis would extend such trust to institutional procedures.

gaps noted above would also have to bring specifically moral criteria of its own to such an assessment, criteria that do not appear in (U). This calls for the development of criteria of rational trust that are not rationalistic, i.e., criteria of cooperation in consensus formation that are defined not simply in terms of their approximation to (U) but rather as having a moral weight of their own. Because philosophers have neglected the concept of trust for so long, such a project remains in its infancy.[45]

The analysis of trust in this context would no doubt involve several levels. The most cognitive would perhaps be displayed by a trust in decision-making procedures and systems, inasmuch as these procedures could be analyzed as reasonable attempts to approximate (U). But if one is not to reduce trust to a mere approximating derivative of (U), then it must in some sense *itself explain* the very need for procedural shortcuts. Otherwise these approximating shortcuts can only appear as incompletions: as something that makes the real procedure somehow less moral in relation to (U). But if human moral rationality is cooperative from the start, then shortcuts enjoy a specific morality of their own insofar as they actualize the cooperative side of will-formation. In other words, it is rational to trust other participants in discourse, and one should not presume that this rationality can be explained in terms of (U)—as would be the case, for example, if a "rational trust" were defined by conditions making it *probable* that (U) was sufficiently satisfied on some point. If the conditions leading individuals to trust one another seem to bypass the idealizations found in (U), then this may only show that (U) has not fully thematized the cooperative, intersubjective side of rational consensus.

Incomplete agreement. The outcome of more significant disputes is commonly not an agreement even remotely approximating (U). Precisely this makes empirical proceduralization necessary, as we saw in the discussion of law and politics. In that discussion, however, we took the parties as presuming that their arguments would converge if only given sufficient time. But is such an assumption necessary—or even reasonable? Here again, I can only briefly suggest some of the difficulties in this idea and how one might deal with them.

The basic problem stems from Habermas's desire to conceive universal

45. Annette Baier attempted to kindle an attention to trust in her "Trust and Antitrust," *Ethics* 96 (1986): 231–260; see also Lars Hertzberg, "On the Attitude of Trust," *Inquiry* 31 (1988): 307–322; *Trust: The Making and Breaking of Cooperative Relations*, ed. Diego Gambetta (New York: Basil Blackwell, 1988); and Anthony Giddens, *The Consequences of Modernity* (Stanford: Stanford University Press, 1990), esp. pp. 21–36, for more recent attempts to deal with this topic.

consensus—the uncoerced agreement of all those affected by a norm—without recourse to notions of deductive or intuitive compellingness or certainty. As Habermas himself notes, the cogency of moral argumentation rests on the fact that an inference is *possible* and thus requires only a *"sufficient* motivation for considering [a norm] plausible."[46] But this would seem to make room for the existence of multiple possible conclusions, none of which would have to be necessary.[47] And this would in turn allow for intractable disputes on practical matters.

In recent decades theorists of argumentation—drawing to some extent on the rhetorical tradition—have been engaged in a reinvigorated attempt to work out a rational but nondeductive basis of assent. A broadly acceptable solution, however, does not seem to be in sight.[48] (U) is one approach to the problem, for it provides something analogous to the principle of empirical induction by which one can move from a host of individual data to a general conclusion. By styling moral argumentation along the lines of inductive inferences, Habermas loosens the link between "premises" and the norm inferred therefrom. But then how plausible is it to attach normative validity to *universal* consensus? Even if a handful of basic moral values could plausibly enjoy such consensus under the right conditions, most real disputes concern finer specifications and interpretations of such values, additional mediations that are contestable at each step. Add to this the need to assess likely future consequences, and we have what would appear a sure recipe for irresolvable differences. For if such assessments divide experts, even at the empirical level, then an evaluation of their acceptability should prove even more controversial.[49] Precisely this

---

46. W, p. 164.

47. The notion of sufficiency remains vague in this context: does it imply that reasons A, B, and C *must* move one to accept conclusion D, or that they make it *possible* for one reasonably to accept D? As it is difficult to see how the first interpretation would differ from a deduction, I lean toward the second.

48. I have already made reference to Stephen Toulmin's *The Place of Reason in Ethics* and *The Uses of Argument*, classics to which Habermas is strongly indebted. Also significant in this endeavor are Wayne C. Booth, *Modern Dogma and the Rhetoric of Assent* (Chicago: University of Chicago Press, 1974), and C. Perelman and L. Olbrechts-Tyteca, *The New Rhetoric: A Treatise on Argumentation*, trans. John Wilkinson and Purcell Weaver (Notre Dame: University of Notre Dame Press, 1969; French edition, 1958); a good historical overview is available in Robert J. Cox and Charles Arthur Willard, "Introduction: The Field of Argumentation," in *Advances in Argumentation Theory and Research*, ed. Cox and Willard (Carbondale: Southern Illinois University Press, 1982), pp. xiii–xlvii; for a sense of the current discussion see *Argumentation Theory*, ed. Williams and Hazen.

49. As McCarthy has pointed out in "Practical Discourse," in *Ideals and Illusions*, pp. 189–192.

sort of evaluative complexity motivates the idea that "essentially contested concepts" underlie intractable disputes in politics, religion, and art. As Gallie defined the term, such concepts involve arguable value appraisals of objects (or "achievements") that are at once internally complex and "variously describable" as well as open to unpredictable modifications in changed circumstances.[50] The considerations entering into (U)-governed discourse—the values that must be specified for the conflict at hand, the estimation of consequences, the need to adjust one's arguments to various perspectives on a situation, the possibilities for different ways of linking values with possible norms—all this lends the notion of an essentially contested concept a certain relevance for moral discourse. And if moral discourses often turn on such concepts, then one must face the possibility that specifically moral issues are open to an ongoing *reasonable* disagreement.[51]

It will not do to relegate all such disputes to the realm of compromise, for they turn on how recognizably moral values are to be incorporated into a norm. This makes them cases of moral discourse, so that an agreement should be possible in principle. One might reply that an ongoing reasonable disagreement does not necessarily imply that neither side can be ultimately *mistaken*.[52] But what could a mistake mean in this context? That the arguments on one side did not rightly foresee the future, perhaps? Rather than take this dubious route, I would suggest we consider a path that undercuts the tacitly deductivistic assumption that there exists somewhere "one right answer" or a set of correct arguments.[53] Again, I can only indicate the general direction one might take.

The key to getting around the above problem, I believe, lies in the notion of "audience" developed by Perelman and Olbrechts-Tyteca. According to these authors, argumentation always addresses an audience

50. W. B. Gallie, "Essentially Contested Concepts," *Proceedings of the Aristotelian Society* 56 (1955–56): 167–198; here pp. 171–172; Gallie makes the same argument in his *Philosophy and the Historical Understanding* (New York: Schocken Books, 1964), chap. 8.

51. For further discussion of the notion of an essentially contested concept, see William E. Connolly, *The Terms of Political Discourse* (Lexington, Mass.: D.C. Heath, 1974); also, more recently, Andrew Mason, "On Explaining Political Disagreement: The Notion of an Essentially Contested Concept," *Inquiry* 33 (1990): 81–98; see also Rawls's account of reasonable disagreement in "Domain of the Political," pp. 236–239.

52. See Mason, "Explaining Political Disagreement," p. 87.

53. Cf. also Hans Blumenberg, "An Anthropological Approach to the Contemporary Significance of Rhetoric," in *After Philosophy: End or Transformation?*, ed. Kenneth Baynes, James Bohman, and Thomas McCarthy (Cambridge: MIT Press, 1987), pp. 429–458, for an argument along similar lines. Habermas himself still holds a "one right answer postulate" as concerns sufficiently precise moral questions; EzD, pp. 165–166.

whose adherence it seeks.[54] Now the deductivistic models of argument favored by Enlightenment rationalism address an ideal "universal audience," since any rational being should be able to assent to them.[55] Whence the difficulty for Habermas's notion of universal consensus: how does one define such universality without implicit recourse to a universal audience and thence to deductive notions of self-evidence?[56] Habermas's language of "convincing," as opposed to "persuading," likewise implies an "argumentation that presumes to gain the adherence of every rational being."[57] By contrast, everyday instances of argument have less ambitious goals: "In ordinary dialogue the participants are simply trying to persuade their audience so as to bring about some immediate or future action; most of our arguments in daily life develop at this practical level."[58] As "persuasive," such everyday argumentation "only claims validity for a particular audience," which suggests that such argumentation can take in all the prethematic particularities, narratives, and unspoken shared experiences of the participants.[59]

If we link the notion of a particular audience with the decentering of (U) sketched above in the treatment of incomplete participation, a possible solution is at hand: the universality in (U) need not be insured by any instance of real discourse but only as the *result* of a decentered social process involving a series of ongoing discourses before a variety of more or less particular audiences. On this view, a norm that can be successfully argued before enough particular audiences enjoys the rebuttable presumption of validity or rightness—i.e., one may suppose that adoption of the norm is justified for the time being. By dispersing consensus throughout various particular audiences one can perhaps obtain a notion of universal agreement that does not rely on the deductive argumentation required to convince a universal audience. Crucial in such a process, of course, are the institutions and procedures that link the outcomes of local discourses in a definite decision binding on all.

54. Perelman and Olbrechts-Tyteca, *New Rhetoric*, p. 19; for a condensed presentation of their views, see Chaim Perelman, *The Realm of Rhetoric*, trans. William Kluback (Notre Dame: University of Notre Dame Press, 1982).

55. Perelman and Olbrechts-Tyteca, *New Rhetoric*, pp. 31–35.

56. In fact, Habermas considers Perelman's image of a universal (or "ideal") audience "too concretistic" and suggests the model of a wholly porous public sphere instead; EzD, p. 159.

57. Perelman and Olbrechts-Tyteca, *New Rhetoric*, p. 28; also pp. 26–31.

58. Perelman and Olbrechts-Tyteca, *New Rhetoric*, p. 39.

59. Perelman and Olbrechts-Tyteca, *New Rhetoric*, p. 28; the French terms here are *persuader* and *convaincre*; see the French edition of Perelman and Olbrechts-Tyteca, *La Nouvelle Rhétorique: Traité de l'Argumentation*, 2 vols. (Paris: Presses Universitaires de France, 1958), 1:34–40.

To understand why the outcome of such a dispersed and imperfect process is binding, one could recur to a notion of trust like that hinted at earlier. If one looks simply to (U), reasons for noncompliance can always be manufactured, for the individual rational conviction projected by (U) will almost never accompany a concrete decision about a social norm. A decentered conviction, however, defined partly by (U) and partly by trust in the cooperative process of will-formation, might reasonably attach to the outcome of ongoing particular discourses bound together by healthy public media and institutional procedures. At the same time, (U) continues to be relevant insofar as it supplies a counterweight to keep such dispersed consensuses from degenerating into group relativism or a crude majoritarianism.[60] No real consensus can ever exult itself as definitively *right*, however extensive the de facto agreement. This means that dissent always has its *justified* place in such processes, and that decisions must ever remain open to reconsideration.

Now how does this solution deal with the problem of ongoing reasonable disagreement? On the above scenario, individuals involved in discourses are from the very start *not* oriented by the search for knockdown deductions that would eliminate all opposition. Anyone experienced in real political discussions, for example, *already knows* that such arguments are not to be had except in exceptional cases. One might even see opposed reasonable arguments as the *typical* case without surrendering the quest for validly binding decisions. But this quest must be redefined as the attempt to bring different (initially opposed) particular audiences, each disposed to its own conclusion supported by plausible arguments, mutually to shift their allegiances enough to converge on *other* plausible arguments striking a middle path between the various parties.[61] Note here that these other arguments do not necessarily *defeat* the arguments they replace; the shift from one set of arguments to another is founded on the pragmatics of reaching agreement and not, in the first instance, on semantic-syntactic weak points in initial arguments. In fact, (U) itself implies this attention to what we might call the "pragmatic weakness" of opposed arguments: according to (U), the awareness of opposed arguments should weaken the strength with which each group holds its position. As long as others do not find my arguments accept-

60. See Earl Croasmun, "Realism and the Rhetoric of Assent," in *Argumentation Theory*, ed. Williams and Hazen, pp. 33–49, for a scathing critique of such views.

61. Here I assume that a particular audience, even if defined independently of the conflict issue, will usually tend to coalesce around similar outlooks on the issue. Admittedly, the notion of particular audience would have to be more precisely defined to carry out this analysis.

able, a degree of uncertainty attaches to those arguments, assuming the issue is a moral rather than an ethical one.[62] This uncertainty should in turn motivate attempts to find a middle ground upon which a norm can be justified to all those affected.

The above approach might at first appear at cross-purposes with earlier formulations of the illocutionary force of normative validity claims. At the beginning of this chapter, for example, I noted that "the force of the validity claim posits the acceptability of that claim by any rational person able to grasp the situation," and so on. Must this now be jettisoned? Two considerations indicate that such a reaction would be rash. First, (U) itself ties validity to a series of exchanges, each of which argues a norm's validity relative to a different hearer's own need interpretation. Thus even if (U) still ultimately locates the site of rational conviction in the individual, it does not tie such conviction to a single set of reasons addressed to a universal audience. Rather, (U) allows for multiple reasons *universally tested*, which is a slightly different notion. The second consideration actually underlies the first: one can distinguish between the force of a claim and the arguments that back it up. If we drop the assumption that argumentation must proceed by self-evident intuitions and deductions, then it is possible to conceive of universally valid claims that nonetheless must be defended in terms tailored to particular audiences. This means that at the level of argumentation, speakers in real discourses must grant their particular audience a privileged position vis-à-vis all other rational persons. In this context, the point of striving to approximate (U) is to insure as much as one can that the reasons persuading one audience constitute good reasons, an outcome presumed to result from the indefinite reiteration of such local argumentation processes until a general consensus has developed. The middle ground that such reiteration yields is not necessarily defined by a single knock-down justification, but rather is a field in which different but not mutually exclusive arguments and justifications can coexist, thereby bringing a variety of particular audiences into a stable cooperation.

This leaves the question of compliance. If a decision must be made before a middle ground of argumentation has been reached, then why should the dissenting parties comply? To the extent that individual conviction no longer constitutes rational consensus, to the extent that the

62. In this context a sign that the issue at stake is ethical, or has a strongly ethical component, would be found in the fact that each side continues to be unmoved by the others' doubts and counterarguments, despite all their efforts at mutual understanding; see EzD, pp. 165–166.

consensus grounding presumptive validity lies rather in a socially dispersed and complex process, and to the extent that this process satisfies criteria of rational trust (however these are defined), the individual has less reason to take his or her dissent as grounds for noncompliance. To be sure, dissenting individuals also have grounds for expecting decisions to be periodically reconsidered so long as their arguments are able to win a sufficient number of adherents. Nor can one ever rule out the possibility that the majority could suffer from a self-deception so profound that a minority's civil disobedience is the only *moral* course available. What is striking in a modern democracy, however, is the degree of compliance that does exist despite deep, ongoing differences. I doubt that one can explain this on the basis of legal sanctions alone. Could it be that for many individuals the value of maintaining a cooperative relationship with the group outweighs their reservations about this or that law or social norm? The answer to this question is too obvious even to dwell on. A more interesting question, perhaps, is whether the ethics of care can contribute to the analysis of compliance by persons with moral reservations. It may well be that to explain such cooperation one must supplement the principled perspective defined by (U) with an explicitly relational one developed from a "care" perspective. In terms of moral theory, such an explanation would have to develop criteria for "drawing the line," i.e., for determining the point at which compliance slides from a justifiable care in morally ambiguous situations to an immoral collaboration with evil.

IV. INSIGHT AND SOLIDARITY: A WRAP-UP

We can conclude with a backward glance. I have been concerned to show that the discourse ethics elaborated by Jürgen Habermas, while primarily inspired by Kant, has the resources to address some of the central objections leveled against neo-Kantian moral theory. Discourse ethics can thus contribute to efforts to get beyond the dichotomies currently afflicting recent debates in moral and political theory. Although discourse ethics can, I think, address utilitarian objections, I have been more concerned with the charge that Kant's focus on an abstract, universal and impartial "right" projects an individualistic morality that overlooks the moral significance of goods constituted by one's particular community, tradition, and special interpersonal relationships.

To be sure, as a deontological moral theory discourse ethics accords priority to justice; it thus anchors morality in an irrevocable respect for the integrity of the person's rational autonomy. But this autonomy is based neither in the noumenal reason posited by Kant nor in the possessive individualism dominating British empiricism and its heirs. Thus the communitarian intuition that individuals depend on real communities for their very identities need be no more alien to discourse ethics than the utilitarian intuition that consequences have moral significance. The primary intuition behind the discourse-ethical approach to these intuitions, however, lies still deeper, in a move beyond the individualism inhabiting Cartesian rationalism. Discourse ethics locates an interpersonal, "communitarian" moment at the very heart of moral insight. This move has systematic implications for current debates, and it is in these that we find the central contribution of discourse ethics.

In Part One I attempted to ground this move in a formal-pragmatic analysis of practical argumentation. That analysis arrived at the puzzling conclusion that the individual's practical insight is inseparably bound up with the insight of every other individual affected by the issue at hand. Contrary to Descartes, one arrives at rational conviction not in isolation but only in a public space, however much a certain solitude might be necessary as one moment in this process. We thus find justice linked—at its very basis in rational autonomy—with a real dependence on others' rational autonomy. For inasmuch as my conviction about moral obligation cannot come at the expense of yours, in disregard for your inviolable right to say no, it must submit itself to the testing of the deliberating community of all those affected. Precisely the effort to convince others of the justice of a normative expectation demands that I attend empathetically to its effects on others' welfare. Both the community whose cooperative structures are at stake in moral deliberation as well as the concrete others involved in such cooperation enter into the very constitution of justice under the aegis of a rational solidarity.

Subsequent parts of the investigation attempted to develop the implications of this intersubjective notion of insight and solidarity in specific contexts of debate. In Part Two I turned to a central issue in the communitarian-liberal debate, the relation between justice and the good life. That debate calls into question the neo-Kantian prioritization of justice over the good life, suggesting that such a prioritization merely elevates one particular good over others. My treatment of this debate focused above all on three questions: How do particular goods enter into moral discourse? In what sense does justice have priority over the pursuit of such goods? and Does discourse ethics not presuppose that its practitioners subscribe to a certain vision of the good life? In reply, I argued that individual and group notions of the good life *must* enter into moral discourse insofar as the attempts to actualize such notions of happiness affect others and depend on their cooperation. This already gives priority to justice, for it limits the individual's pursuit of particular goods by others' ability to acknowledge that such goods make a legitimate claim on everyone's cooperation. Finally, I argued that discourse ethics does indeed presuppose the good of rational cooperation, but that in today's world such a good admits less and less of stable alternatives for persons who consider themselves rational.

These replies both rely upon and develop the ideas set forth in Part One. Crucial here is the kind of coordination problem at stake in justice issues: reaching agreement on how to get past a conflict and arrive at a basis for rational cooperation. Part One implies that the objective constraints on what will count as a rational solution to this kind of problem are *intersubjective*, i.e., the nature of the problem is such that an insight into the legitimate solution can *only* be constituted intersubjectively. Therefore, the rational pursuit of one's own interest or happiness must be conditioned by a consensus on cooperative structures within which such pursuit can accord with others' pursuit of their interests. To be sure, this assumes a rationality governed by the good of cooperation based on mutual understanding. But this "good" is not simply one option among others, once problems of social coordination arise in which actors who consider themselves rational adhere to different interests and conceptions of the good life. For in such situations my personal justification for my normative expectations *must* deal with others' views on the issue: their own expectations and counterclaims, objections and proposals. That is, I disregard these views only at the risk of my *own* self-ascription of rationality. Within the very structures of language use there exists a cognitive exigency to redeem one's views in discourse with others. Whether and to what extent this exigency gets actualized depends on whether the surrounding historical and cultural environment allows for countervailing pressures. But the presence of this exigency is just as "objective" as the canons governing modern scientific method, and the option to actualize it no less arbitrary and dispensable than an "option" to govern scientific inquiry by the canons of empirical method.

By the same token, the intersubjectivity of moral insight calls forth a solidarity that goes at least part way in meeting communitarian concerns. Moral discourse not only attends to the concrete goods at stake in justice issues, it issues in a "common good," albeit not one displaying the concreteness communitarians desire. Rather, moral discourse involves a

movement from the particular notions of the good life, around which
concrete lifeworld solidarities take shape, to a consensus on *specific
moral* solidarities that govern cooperation between persons who do not
share the same thick conception of happiness. This movement does not
necessarily undo or level out traditional solidarities but rather lays down
between them a network of norms based on generalizable values and interests. Such values allow for modes of cooperation and mutual recognition that constitute a solidarity between different groups and individuals. This moral solidarity takes on social reality in the basic rights one
grants to persons who do not share a given lifestyle, a particular religious
tradition, a "correct" political orientation, or a particular corporate allegiance. It is also displayed in the cooperative behavior one gives and
expects from others, for example, in one's expectation of and willingness
to pay for benefits that further individual welfare irrespective of lifestyle,
etc. At the basis of moral solidarity, finally, there lies a *rational human
solidarity*, the counterweight pulling practical reason out of its ego- and
ethnocentric centripetal spiral, orienting it rather toward the cognitive
force of the other's presence and claim. Though more immediate interests
and local solidarities can easily suppress this universalistic solidarity, it
continues to exert its pull over the long haul, aided and abetted by the
external historical and economic forces that bring peoples together and
make cooperation increasingly desirable.

Part Three attempts to extend the above analysis into an area that has
traditionally resisted deontological approaches to morality: concrete
particularity. In response to concerns expressed by the ethics of care, I
tried to show that the universalistic dimension of discourse-ethical solidarity need not level out differences between individuals. Not only does
its notion of ethical discourse *make room for* the intrinsic value of particular relationships, its recognition of the need for application discourses *builds* the moment of particularity *into* the very heart of impartialist morality. Specifically, I argued that impartial application must take
account of particular circumstances in such a way that it need not issue
in simply another, albeit more detailed, general norm. Again, the analysis
links practical insight and solidarity. In this case, however, the participants strive for an insight into a host of situational particulars, both cir-
cumstantial and personal. At issue is not the justification of a general
norm but rather the question of which concrete action is warranted in
the light of prima facie norms and situational particulars. Given the limited scope of those involved in an application question and the possible
situational complications, these warrants need not amount to new norms

that would generalize beyond the situation in any useful way. This suggests that the kind of insight governing application depends on a *concrete moral solidarity* with those involved in the situation, i.e., participants must appreciate precisely the exceptional and unique dimensions of the individual welfares at stake in an application.

Do such idealizations as govern discourse-ethical justification and application have any real life counterparts? In this last chapter I have tried to indicate that they do insofar as they inform real decision-making procedures such as those found in law and politics. I have indicated that a discourse-ethical analysis of real procedures would have to work at a number of levels, taking into account not only institutionalized procedures but also the shared background of moral values and less formal processes of public discussion and communication. This suggests yet a further development in the concept of solidarity: insofar as real institutional procedures represent attempts to approximate the rational intersubjective will-formation idealized in (D)—thus insofar as they carry a supposition of valid insight in specific contexts or realms of decision making and action—one could call the willingness to engage in such procedures a *concrete rational solidarity*. The point of focus here would be the actual cooperative procedures used by the various institutions of a given society for reaching decisions in the respective spheres of cooperation. One might think of the procedures as giving the structures of rational human solidarity a certain empirical realization.

In sum, discourse ethics offers something both nuanced and substantive in response to demands to redress Kant's undue emphasis of the abstract moral 'ought' over community and friends. To be sure, it neither pines for an idyllic past nor assumes that "community" can be formed at the level of the pluralistic nation-state; even less does it imagine that we could dispense with moral impartiality and restrict our attention to the more immediate requirements of particular relationships and concrete situations. Rather, it directs our attention to the *multiple* kinds of solidarity at work today: from those very particular and concrete solidarities that bind together friends, families, and communities of work and recreation; through the most basic solidarity by which we acknowledge and respond to the questions and needs of any human being; to the specific moral solidarities that issue from mutual solidaristic responsiveness to shape forms of cooperation that transcend local traditions while remaining sensitive to local differences. A discourse-ethical critique of society would have to address each of these levels: the stock and variety of cultural traditions, the shared moral values and intuitions about human rights, and the willingness to listen and discuss. It would, moreover, have to examine the actual decision-making procedures by which specific conflicts are resolved: how well such procedures draw on the foregoing solidarities, whether the participants find them satisfying or unsatisfying, whether they can allow for individual differences.

This analysis, of course, has hardly even begun at a philosophical level. Moreover, it harbors theoretical difficulties of its own; as I indicated, these difficulties crucially bear on the conception of insight guiding the present study. At issue is how adequately (U)—or more broadly, discursive idealizations in general—captures the rationality of *real* proceduralization in all its gritty details and shortcuts that fall short of full cognitive reversibility. There is actually a certain irony in this. If the practical reason and "insight" inhabiting real procedures involve an element of trust, for example, then the intersubjective concept of insight found in (U) would appear not intersubjective *enough*. After opening the door to the intersubjectivity and cooperative character of practical insight, (U) itself hesitates to cross the threshold to a fully cooperative concept of rational collective will-formation. For (U) still seems to conceive the insight grounding rational consensus as something located in the individual's head, even if only after an exchange with other individuals. But if insight is essentially constituted in a cooperative social network that requires trust on the part of each individual; if, strictly speaking, insight resides in no single individual, then (U) at best provides an incomplete thematization of rational consensus. To be sure, (U) can explain the fallibilism and ongoing criticizability of real decisions. But the positive force such decisions can enjoy involves more than the absence of glaring departures from a regulative idea of unlimited consensus. To fully capture the sense of a truly cooperative moral legitimacy, therefore, we must go beyond the current formulation of discourse-ethical universalization. What we need, presumably, is something like a genuinely social concept of practical judgment.

Bibliography

Ackerman, Bruce. "Neutralities." See Douglass et al., *Liberalism and the Good*, pp. 29–43.

———. *Social Justice in the Liberal State*. New Haven: Yale University Press, 1980.

———. "What Is Neutral about Neutrality?" *Ethics* 93 (1983): 372–390.

———. "Why Dialogue?" *Journal of Philosophy* 86 (1989): 5–22.

Alexy, Robert. *Theorie der Grundrecht*. Frankfurt: Suhrkamp, 1986.

———. *Theorie der juristischen Argumentation: Die Theorie des rationalen Diskurses als Theorie der juristischen Begründung*. Frankfurt: Suhrkamp, 1978.

———. "Eine Theorie des praktischen Diskurses." *Normenbegründung, Normendurchsetzung*. Ed. Willi Oelmüller. Materialien zur Normendiskussion 2. Paderborn: Schöningh, 1973. Pp. 22–58.

———. *A Theory of Legal Argumentation: The Theory of Rational Discourse as Theory of Legal Justification*. Trans. Ruth Adler and Neil MacCormick. Oxford: Clarendon, 1989.

———. "A Theory of Practical Discourse." See Benhabib and Dallmayr, *The Communicative Ethics Controversy*, pp. 151–190.

Apel, Karl-Otto. "The *a priori* of the Communication Community and the Foundations of Ethics." See Apel, *Towards a Transformation of Philosophy*, pp. 225–300.

———. *Charles S. Peirce: From Pragmatism to Pragmaticism*. Trans. John Michael Krois. Amherst: University of Massachusetts Press, 1981.

———. "Normatively Grounding 'Critical Theory' through Recourse to the Lifeworld? A Transcendental-Pragmatic Attempt to Think with Habermas against Habermas." See Honneth, McCarthy, et al., *Philosophical Interventions*, pp. 15–65.

————. "Das Problem der Begründung einer Verantwortungsethik im Zeitalter der Wissenschaft." *Wissenschaft und Ethik*. Ed. Edmund Braun. New York: Lang, 1986. Pp. 11–52.

————. "The Problem of a Macroethic of Responsibility to the Future in the Crisis of Technological Civilization: An Attempt to Come to Terms with Hans Jonas's 'Principle of Responsibility.'" Trans. Wilson Brown. *Man and World* 20 (1987): 3–40.

————. "Scientism or Transcendental Hermeneutics?" See Apel, *Towards a Transformation of Philosophy*, pp. 93–135.

————. *Towards a Transformation of Philosophy*. Trans. Glyn Adey and David Frisby. London: Routledge, 1980.

Aquinas, Thomas. *Summa Theologiae*. 3 vols. Ottawa: Institute of Medieval Studies, 1941.

Baier, Annette. "Trust and Antitrust." *Ethics* 96 (1986): 231–260.

Baier, Kurt. *The Moral Point of View*. Ithaca: Cornell University Press, 1958.

Baynes, Kenneth. "The Liberal/Communitarian Controversy and Communicative Ethics." *Philosophy and Social Criticism* 14 (1988): 293–313.

————. *The Normative Grounds of Social Criticism: Kant, Rawls, and Habermas*. Albany: SUNY Press, 1992.

Bellah, Robert N., et al. *The Good Society*. New York: Knopf, 1991.

————. *Habits of the Heart: Individualism and Commitment in American Life*. Berkeley: University of California Press, 1985.

Benhabib, Seyla. "Autonomy, Modernity, and Community: Communitarianism and Critical Social Theory in Dialogue." See Honneth, McCarthy, et al., *Zwischenbetrachtungen*, pp. 373–394.

————. *Critique, Norm and Utopia: A Study of the Foundations of Critical Theory*. New York: Columbia University Press, 1986.

————. "The Generalized and the Concrete Other: The Kohlberg-Gilligan Controversy and Feminist Theory." See Benhabib and Cornell, *Feminism as Critique*, pp. 77–95.

————. "In the Shadow of Aristotle and Hegel: Communicative Ethics and Current Controversies in Practical Philosophy." *Philosophical Forum* 21 (1989–90): 1–31.

————. "Liberal Dialogue versus a Critical Theory of Discursive Legitimation." See Rosenblum, *Liberalism*, pp. 143–156.

Benhabib, Seyla, and Drucilla Cornell, eds. *Feminism as Critique: On the Politics of Gender*. Minneapolis: University of Minnesota Press, 1987.

Benhabib, Seyla, and Fred Dallmayr, eds. *The Communicative Ethics Controversy*. Cambridge: MIT Press, 1990.

Bennett, Jonathan. "The Conscience of Huckleberry Finn." *Philosophy* 49 (1974): 123–134.

Berver, Kitty, Don Kurtz, and Eliot Orton. "Off the Track, But in the Fold." *Academe* 78, no. 6 (November-December 1992): 27–29.

Blum, Lawrence A. *Friendship, Altruism and Morality*. London: Routledge, 1980.

————. "Gilligan and Kohlberg: Implications for Moral Theory." *Ethics* 98 (1988): 472–491.

————. "Iris Murdoch and the Domain of the Moral." *Philosophical Studies* 50 (1986): 343–367.

————. "Moral Perception and Situational Particularity." *Ethics* 101 (1991): 701–725.

————. "Particularity and Responsiveness." *The Emergence of Morality in Young Children*. Ed. Jerome Kagan and Sharon Lamb. Chicago: University of Chicago Press, 1987. Pp. 306–337.

Blumenberg, Hans. "An Anthropological Approach to the Contemporary Significance of Rhetoric." *After Philosophy: End or Transformation?* Ed. Kenneth Baynes, James Bohman, and Thomas McCarthy. Cambridge: MIT Press, 1987. Pp. 429–458.

Bohman, James. "'System' and 'Lifeworld': Habermas and the Problem of Holism." *Philosophy and Social Criticism* 15 (1989): 381–401.

Booth, Wayne C. *Modern Dogma and the Rhetoric of Assent*. Chicago: University of Chicago Press, 1974.

Braaten, Jane. *Habermas's Critical Theory of Society*. Albany: SUNY Press, 1991.

Buchanan, Allen E. "Assessing the Communitarian Critique of Liberalism." *Ethics* 99 (1989): 852–882.

Callahan, Sidney. *In Good Conscience: Reason and Emotion in Moral Decision Making*. San Francisco: Harper, 1991.

Cohen, Jean. "Discourse Ethics and Civil Society." *Philosophy and Social Criticism* 14 (1988): 315–337.

Cole, Eve Browning, and Susan Coultrap-McQuin, eds. *Explorations in Feminist Ethics: Theory and Practice*. Bloomington: Indiana University Press, 1992.

Connolly, William E. *The Terms of Political Discourse*. Lexington, Mass.: Heath, 1974.

Cox, Robert J., and Charles Arthur Willard. "Introduction: The Field of Argumentation." *Advances in Argumentation Theory and Research*. Ed. Robert J. Cox and Charles Arthur Willard. Carbondale: Southern Illinois University Press, 1982. Pp. xiii–xlvii.

Croasmun, Earl. "Realism and the Rhetoric of Assent." See Williams and Hazen, *Argumentation Theory*, pp. 33–49.

Darwall, Stephen. *Impartial Reason*. Ithaca, N.Y.: Cornell University Press, 1983.

Doppelt, Gerald. "Beyond Liberalism and Communitarianism: Toward a Critical Theory of Social Justice." *Philosophy and Social Criticism* 14 (1988): 271–292.

————. "Is Rawls's Kantian Liberalism Coherent and Defensible?" *Ethics* 99 (1989): 815–851.

Douglass, R. Bruce, Gerald M. Mara, and Henry S. Richardson, eds. *Liberalism and the Good*. New York: Routledge, 1990.

Dworkin, Ronald. *A Matter of Principle*. Cambridge: Harvard University Press, 1985.

————. *Taking Rights Seriously*. Cambridge: Harvard University Press, 1977.

Edelstein, Wolfgang, and Jürgen Habermas, eds. *Soziale Interaktion und soziales*

Verstehen: Beiträge zur Entwicklung der Interaktionskompetenz. Frankfurt: Suhrkamp, 1984.

Eder, Klaus. "Critique of Habermas's Contribution to the Sociology of Law." *Law and Society Review* 22 (1988): 931–944.

——. *Geschichte als Lernprozess? Zur Pathogenese politischer Modernität in Deutschland.* Frankfurt: Suhrkamp, 1985.

Eisenberg, Nancy. *Altruistic Emotion, Cognition, and Behavior.* Hillsdale, N. J.: Lawrence Erlbaum, 1986.

Eisenberg, Nancy, and Janet Strayer, eds. *Empathy and Its Development.* Cambridge: Cambridge University Press, 1987.

Flanagan, Owen, and Jonathan Adler. "Impartiality and Particularity." *Social Research* 50 (1983): 576–596.

Flanagan, Owen, and Kathryn Jackson. "Justice, Care and Gender: The Kohlberg-Gilligan Debate Revisited." *Ethics* 97 (1987): 622–637. Rpt. in Sunstein, pp. 37–52.

Frank, Manfred. "Gibt es rational unentscheidbare Konflikte im Verständigungs-handeln?" *Das Sagbare und das Unsagbare: Studien zur deutsch-französischen Hermeneutik und Texttheorie.* Expanded ed. Frankfurt: Suhrkamp, 1990. Pp. 590–607.

Frankena, William K. *Ethics.* 2d ed. Englewood Cliffs, N. J.: Prentice-Hall, 1973.

Fraser, Nancy. "Talking about Needs: Interpretive Contests as Political Conflicts in Welfare-State Societies." *Ethics* 99 (1989): 291–313.

——. "Toward a Discourse Ethic of Solidarity." *Praxis International* 5 (1986): 425–429.

Frug, Jerry. "Argument as Character." *Stanford Law Review* 40 (1988): 869–927.

Gadamer, Hans-Georg. *Truth and Method.* 2d, rev. ed. Trans. Joel Weinsheimer and Donald G. Marshall. New York: Crossroad, 1990.

Gallie, W. B. "Essentially Contested Concepts." *Proceedings of the Aristotelian Society* 56 (1955–56): 167–198.

——. *Philosophy and the Historical Understanding.* New York: Schocken, 1964.

Gambetta, Diego, ed. *Trust: The Making and Breaking of Cooperative Relations.* New York: Blackwell, 1988.

Gardbaum, Stephen. "Law, Politics, and the Claims of Community." *Michigan Law Review* 90 (1992): 658–760.

Garfinkel, Harold. "A Conception of, and Experiments with, 'Trust' as a Condition of Stable Concerted Actions." *Motivation and Social Interaction.* Ed. O. J. Harvey. New York: Ronald, 1963. Pp. 187–238.

Giddens, Anthony. *The Consequences of Modernity.* Stanford: Stanford University Press, 1990.

Gilligan, Carol. *In a Different Voice: Psychological Theory and Women's Development.* Cambridge: Harvard University Press, 1982.

——. "Moral Orientation and Moral Development." See Kittay and Meyers, *Women and Moral Theory*, pp. 19–33.

————. "Remapping the Moral Domain: New Images of the Self in Relationship." *Reconstructing Individualism: Autonomy, Individuality and the Self in Western Thought.* Ed. Thomas C. Heller et al. Stanford: Stanford University Press, 1986. Pp. 237–252.

Gould, Carol C. "Philosophical Dichotomies and Feminist Thought: Towards a Critical Feminism." *Feministische Philosophie.* Ed. Herta Nagl-Docekal. Vienna: Oldenbourg, 1990. Pp. 184–190.

Grimshaw, Jean. *Philosophy and Feminist Thinking.* Minneapolis: University of Minnesota Press, 1986.

Gripp, Helga. *Jürgen Habermas: Und es gibt sie doch—Zur kommunikationstheoretischen Begründung von Vernunft bei Jürgen Habermas.* Paderborn: Schöningh, 1984.

Grundmann, Reiner, and Christos Mantziaris. "Fundamentalist Intolerance or Civil Disobedience? Strange Loops in Liberal Theory." *Political Theory* 19 (1991): 572–605.

Günther, Klaus. "Impartial Application of Moral and Legal Norms: A Contribution to Discourse Ethics." *Philosophy and Social Criticism* 14 (1988): 425–432.

————. "Ein normativer Begriff der Kohärenz für eine Theorie der juristischen Argumentation." *Rechtstheorie* 20 (1989): 163–190.

————. *Der Sinn für Angemessenheit: Anwendungsdiskurse in Moral und Recht.* Frankfurt: Suhrkamp, 1988.

————. "Universalistische Normbegründung und Normanwendung in Recht und Moral." *Generalisierung und Individuierung im Rechtsdenken.* Ed. M. Herberger et al. *Archiv für Rechts- und Sozialphilosophie.* Beiheft 45 (Stuttgart: Steiner, 1992), pp. 36–76.

Gutman, Amy. "Communitarian Critics of Liberalism." *Philosophy and Public Affairs* 14 (1985): 308–322.

Gutman, Amy, and Dennis Thompson. "Moral Conflict and Political Consensus." *Ethics* 101 (1990): 64–88. Also in Douglass et al., pp. 125–147.

Haan, Norma. "Two Moralities in Action Contexts: Relationships to Thought, Ego Regulation and Development." *Journal of Personality and Social Psychology* 36 (1978): 286–305.

Habermas, Jürgen. *Autonomy and Solidarity: Interviews.* Ed. Peter Dews. London: Verso-New Left Books, 1986.

————. *Communication and the Evolution of Society.* Trans. Thomas McCarthy. Boston: Beacon, 1979.

————. "The Concept of Practical Reason Revisited." Northwestern University. Evanston, Ill., 10 October 1988.

————. "Discourse Ethics: Notes on a Program of Philosophical Justification." See Habermas, *Moral Consciousness,* pp. 43–115.

————. "Diskursethik—Notizen zu einem Begründungsprogramm." See Habermas, *Moralbewußtsein,* pp. 53–125.

————. "Erläuterungen zum Begriff des kommunikativen Handelns." See Habermas, *Vorstudien,* pp. 571–606.

————. *Erläuterungen zur Diskursethik.* Frankfurt: Suhrkamp, 1991.

———. "Erläuterungen zur Diskursethik." See Habermas, *Erläuterungen*, pp. 119–225.

———. "Ethics, Politics and History: An Interview with Jürgen Habermas." Conducted by Jean-Marc Ferry. *Philosophy and Social Criticism* 14 (1988): 433–439.

———. *Faktizität und Geltung: Beiträge zur Diskurstheorie des Rechts und des demokratischen Rechtsstaats*. Frankfurt: Suhrkamp, 1992.

———. "Further Reflections on the Public Sphere." Trans. Thomas Burger. *Habermas and the Public Sphere*. Ed. Craig Calhoun. Cambridge: MIT Press, 1992. Pp. 421–461.

———. "Gerechtigkeit und Solidarität: Eine Stellungnahme zur Diskussion über 'Stufe 6'." *Zur Bestimmung der Moral: Philosophische und sozialwissenschaftliche Beiträge zur Moralforschung*. Ed. Wolfgang Edelstein and Gertrud Nunner-Winkler. Frankfurt: Suhrkamp, 1986. Pp. 291–317.

———. "Historical Materialism and the Development of Normative Structures." See Habermas, *Communication*, pp. 95–129.

———. "Intention, Konvention und sprachliche Interaktion." See Habermas, *Vorstudien*, pp. 307–331.

———. "Justice and Solidarity: On the Discussion Concerning Stage 6." Trans. Shierry Weber Nicholsen. See Wren, *Moral Domain*, pp. 224–251.

———. *Kultur und Kritik*. 2d ed. Frankfurt: Suhrkamp, 1977.

———. "Labor and Interaction: Remarks on Hegel's Jena *Philosophy of Mind*." *Theory and Practice*. Trans. John Viertel. Boston: Beacon, 1973. Pp. 142–169.

———. "Law and Morality." Trans. Kenneth Baynes. *The Tanner Lectures on Human Values*. Vol. 8. Ed. Sterling M. McMurrin. Salt Lake City: University of Utah Press, 1988. Pp. 217–279.

———. "Lawrence Kohlberg und der Neoaristotelismus." See Habermas, *Erläuterungen*, pp. 77–99.

———. *Legitimation Crisis*. Trans. Thomas McCarthy. Boston: Beacon, 1975.

———. *Moralbewußtsein und kommunikatives Handeln*. 1st ed. Frankfurt: Suhrkamp, 1983.

———. *Moral Consciousness and Communicative Action*. Trans. Christian Lenhardt and Shierry Weber Nicholsen. Cambridge: MIT Press, 1990.

———. "Moral Consciousness and Communicative Action." See Habermas, *Moral Consciousness*, pp. 116–194.

———. "Moralität und Sittlichkeit: Treffen Hegels Einwände gegen Kant auch auf die Diskursethik zu?" See Kuhlmann, *Moralität*, pp. 16–37. Rpt. in Habermas, *Erläuterungen*, pp. 9–30.

———. "Morality and Ethical Life: Does Hegel's Critique of Kant Apply to Discourse Ethics?" See Habermas, *Moral Consciousness*, pp. 195–215.

———. *Die nachholende Revolution*. Kleine Politische Schriften 7. Frankfurt: Suhrkamp, 1990.

———. *Nachmetaphysisches Denken: Philosophische Aufsätze*. 2d ed. Frankfurt: Suhrkamp, 1988.

———. *On the Logic of the Social Sciences*. Trans. Shierry Weber Nicholsen and Jerry A. Stark. Cambridge: MIT Press, 1988.

————. *The Philosophical Discourse of Modernity: Twelve Lectures.* Trans. Frederick Lawrence. Cambridge: MIT Press, 1987.

————. "Philosophy as Stand-In and Interpreter." See Habermas, *Moral Consciousness*, pp. 1–20.

————. *Postmetaphysical Thinking: Philosophical Essays.* Trans. William Mark Hohengarten. Cambridge: MIT Press, 1992.

————. "A Postscript to *Knowledge and Human Interests*." *Philosophy and the Social Sciences* 3 (1973): 157–189.

————. "Questions and Counter-Questions." *Praxis International* 4 (1984): 229–249. Rpt. in *Habermas and Modernity*. Ed. Richard J. Bernstein. Cambridge: MIT Press, 1985. Pp. 192–216.

————. "Reconstruction and Interpretation in the Social Sciences." See Habermas, *Moral Consciousness*, pp. 21–42.

————. "A Reply." See Honneth and Joas, *Communicative Action*, pp. 214–264.

————. "A Reply to My Critics." Trans. Thomas McCarthy. See Thompson and Held, *Habermas*, pp. 219–283.

————. *Staatsbürgerschaft und nationale Identität: Überlegungen zur europäischen Zukunft.* St. Gallen: Erker, n.d.

————. *The Structural Transformation of the Public Sphere: An Inquiry into a Category of Bourgeois Society.* Trans. Thomas Burger. Cambridge: MIT Press, 1989.

————. *Strukturwandel der Öffentlichkeit: Untersuchungen zu einer Kategorie der bürgerlichen Gesellschaft.* 1962. Preface J. Habermas. Frankfurt: Suhrkamp, 1990.

————. *Texte und Kontexte.* Frankfurt: Suhrkamp, 1991.

————. *Theorie des kommunikativen Handelns.* 3d ed. Frankfurt: Suhrkamp, 1988.

————. *Theory of Communicative Action.* 2 vols. Trans. Thomas McCarthy. Boston: Beacon, 1984, 1987.

————. "Towards a Communication-Concept of Rational Collective Will-Formation: A Thought Experiment." *Ratio Juris* 2 (1989): 144–154.

————. "Über Moralität und Sittlichkeit—Was macht eine Lebensform rational?" *Rationalität: Philosophische Beiträge.* Ed. Herbert Schnädelbach. Frankfurt: Suhrkamp, 1984. Pp. 218–235. Rpt. in Habermas, *Erläuterungen*, pp. 31–48.

————. "Volkssouveränität als Verfahren: Ein normativer Begriff der Öffentlichkeit." *Die Moderne—Ein unvollendetes Projekt: Philosophisch-politische Aufsätze.* Leipzig: Reclam, 1990. Pp. 180–212.

————. "Vom pragmatischen, ethischen und moralischen Gebrauch der praktischen Vernunft." See Habermas, *Erläuterungen*, pp. 100–118.

————. "Vorlesungen zu einer sprachtheoretischen Grundlegung der Soziologie." See Habermas, *Vorstudien*, pp. 11–126.

————. *Vorstudien und Ergänzungen zur Theorie des kommunikativen Handelns.* 2d ed. Frankfurt: Suhrkamp, 1986.

————. "Wahrheitstheorien." See Habermas, *Vorstudien*, pp. 127–183.

————. "What Is Universal Pragmatics?" See Habermas, *Communication*, pp. 1–68.

————. "Wie ist Legitimität durch Legalität möglich?" *Kritische Justiz* 20 (1987): 1–16.

Hampshire, Stuart. *Morality and Conflict.* Cambridge: Harvard University Press, 1983.

Hare, R. M. *Freedom and Reason.* Oxford: Clarendon, 1963.

————. *Moral Thinking: Its Levels, Method, and Point.* Oxford: Clarendon, 1981.

Hegel, G. W. F. *Phenomenology of Spirit.* Trans. A. V. Miller. Oxford: Oxford University Press, 1977.

Held, Virginia. "Feminism and Moral Theory." See Kittay and Meyers, *Women and Moral Theory,* pp. 111–128.

Heller, Agnes. *Beyond Justice.* Oxford: Blackwell, 1987.

————. "Habermas and Marxism." See Thompson and Held, *Habermas,* pp. 21–41.

Heritage, John. *Garfinkel and Ethnomethodology.* Cambridge: Polity, 1984.

Herman, Barbara. "Integrity and Impartiality." *Monist* 66 (1983): 233–250.

————. "The Practice of Moral Judgment." *Journal of Philosophy* 82 (1985): 414–436.

Hertzberg, Lars. "On the Attitude of Trust." *Inquiry* 31 (1988): 307–322.

Hoffman, Martin L. "Empathy, Its Limitations, and Its Role in a Comprehensive Moral Theory." See Kurtines and Gewirtz, *Moral Development,* pp. 283–302.

————. "The Contribution of Empathy to Justice and Moral Theory." See Eisenberg and Strayer, *Empathy and Its Development,* pp. 47–80.

Hollenbach, David. "Critical Discussion of *Whose Justice? Which Rationality?,* by Alasdair MacIntyre." Thirteenth Annual Meeting of the Society of Christian Ethics. South Bend, Indiana, 15 January 1989.

Honneth, Axel. *Kritik der Macht: Reflexionsstufen einer kritischen Gesellschaftstheorie.* Frankfurt: Suhrkamp, 1985.

Honneth, Axel, and Hans Joas, eds. *Communicative Action: Essays on Jürgen Habermas's "The Theory of Communicative Action."* Trans. Jeremy Gains and Doris L. Jones. Cambridge: Polity, 1991.

————. *Kommunikatives Handeln: Beiträge zu Jürgen Habermas' "Theorie des kommunikativen Handelns."* Frankfurt: Suhrkamp, 1986.

Honneth, Axel, Thomas McCarthy, et al., eds. *Philosophical Interventions in the Unfinished Project of Enlightenment.* Trans. William Rehg. Cambridge: MIT Press, 1992.

————. *Zwischenbetrachtungen im Prozeß der Aufklärung: Jürgen Habermas zum 60. Geburtstag.* 2d ed. Frankfurt: Suhrkamp, 1989.

Hooper, J. Leon. *The Ethics of Discourse: The Social Philosophy of John Courtney Murray.* Washington, D.C.: Georgetown University Press, 1986.

Humboldt, Wilhelm von. *Schriften zur Sprachphilosophie.* Vol. 3 of *Werke in Fünf Bänden.* Ed. Andreas Flitner and Klaus Giel. Stuttgart: Cotta'sche; Darmstadt: Wissenschaftliche, 1963.

Ingram, David. *Habermas and the Dialectic of Reason.* New Haven: Yale University Press, 1987.

Kant, Immanuel. *Critique of Practical Reason.* Trans. Lewis White Beck. Indianapolis: Bobbs, 1956.

———. "On the Proverb: That May Be True in Theory, But It Is of No Practical Use." *Perpetual Peace and Other Essays*. Trans. Ted Humphrey. Indianapolis: Hackett, 1983. Pp. 61–92.

Keller, Monika. "Rechtfertigungen: Zur Entwicklung praktischer Erklärungen." See Edelstein and Habermas, *Soziale Interaktion*, pp. 253–299.

Kelly, Michael, ed. *Hermeneutics and Critical Theory in Ethics and Politics*. Cambridge: MIT Press, 1990.

Kennedy, Duncan. "Freedom and Constraint in Adjudication: A Critical Phenomenology." *Journal of Legal Education* 36 (1986): 518–562.

Kittay, Eva Feder, and Diana T. Meyers, eds. *Women and Moral Theory*. Savage, Md.: Rowman and Littlefield, 1987.

Kohlberg, Lawrence. "From *Is* to *Ought*: How to Commit the Naturalistic Fallacy and Get Away with It in the Study of Moral Development." Kohlberg, *Philosophy of Moral Development: Moral Stages and the Idea of Justice*. Vol. 1 of *Essays on Moral Development*. 2 vols. San Francisco: Harper, 1981. Pp. 101–189.

———. "A Reply to Owen Flanagan and Some Comments on the Puka-Goodpaster Exchange." *Ethics* 92 (1982): 513–528.

Kohlberg, Lawrence, et al. "The Return of Stage 6: Its Principle and Moral Point of View." See Wren, *Moral Domain*, pp. 151–181.

Kuhlmann, Wolfgang, ed. *Moralität und Sittlichkeit: Das Problem Hegels und die Diskursethik*. Frankfurt: Suhrkamp, 1986.

———. *Reflexive Letztbegründung: Untersuchungen zur Transzendentalpragmatik*. Freiburg: Alber, 1985.

Kurtines, William M., and Jacob L. Gewirtz, eds. *Moral Development through Social Interaction*. New York: John Wiley, 1987.

Kymlicka, Will. *Liberalism, Community and Culture*. Oxford: Clarendon, 1989.

LaMoyne, James. "Troops in Gulf Talk of War, and of Vietnam and Respect." *New York Times*, 30 September 1990, natl. ed.: A1.

Larmore, Charles. *Patterns of Moral Complexity*. Cambridge: Cambridge University Press, 1987.

———. Rev. of *Whose Justice? Which Rationality?*, by Alasdair MacIntyre. *Journal of Philosophy* 86 (1989): 437–442.

Leist, Anton. "Diesseits der 'Transzendental-pragmatik': Gibt es sprachpragmatische Argumente für Moral?" *Zeitschrift für philosophische Forschung* 43 (1989): 301–317.

Levin, David Michael. *The Listening Self: Personal Growth, Social Change and the Closure of Metaphysics*. New York: Routledge, 1989.

———. *The Opening of Vision: Nihilism and the Postmodern Situation*. New York: Routledge, 1988.

Lind, E. Allan, and Tom R. Tyler. *The Social Psychology of Procedural Justice*. New York: Plenum, 1988.

Littlejohn, Stephen W. *Theories of Human Communication*. 3d ed. Belmont, Calif.: Wadsworth, 1989.

Locke, John. *An Essay Concerning the True Original, Extent, and End of Civil Government*. *The English Philosophers from Bacon to Mill*. Ed. Edwin A. Burtt. New York: Modern Library, 1967. Pp. 403–503.

Lonergan, Bernard J. F. *Insight: A Study of Human Understanding*. 1957. 3d ed. New York: Philosophical Library, 1970.

MacIntyre, Alasdair. *After Virtue: A Study in Moral Theory*. 1981. 2d ed. Notre Dame: University of Notre Dame Press, 1984.

———. *Whose Justice? Which Rationality?* Notre Dame: University of Notre Dame Press, 1988.

Mackie, J. L. *Ethics: Inventing Right and Wrong*. New York: Penguin, 1977.

Maihofer, Andrea. "Ansätze zur Kritik des moralischen Universalismus: Zur moraltheoretischen Diskussion um Gilligans Thesen zu einer 'weiblichen' Moralauffassung." *Feministische Studien* 6, no. 1 (1988): 32–52.

Mason, Andrew. "On Explaining Political Disagreement: The Notion of an Essentially Contested Concept." *Inquiry* 33 (1990): 81–98.

McCarthy, Thomas. "Complexity and Democracy: The Seducements of Systems Theory." McCarthy, *Ideals*, pp. 152–180.

———. *The Critical Theory of Jürgen Habermas*. Cambridge: MIT Press, 1978.

———. *Ideals and Illusions: On Reconstruction and Deconstruction in Contemporary Critical Theory*. Cambridge: MIT Press, 1991.

———. "Philosophy and Social Practice: Avoiding the Ethnocentric Predicament." See Honneth, McCarthy, et al., *Philosophical Interventions*, pp. 241–260.

———. "Practical Discourse: On the Relation of Morality to Politics." See McCarthy, *Ideals*, pp. 181–199.

———. "A Theory of Communicative Competence." *Philosophy of the Social Sciences* 3 (1973): 135–156.

Mead, George Herbert. *Mind, Self, and Society from the Standpoint of a Social Behaviorist*. Ed. with an Introduction by Charles W. Morris. Chicago: University of Chicago Press, 1934; Charles W. Morris, 1962.

———. *Selected Writings*. Ed. with an Introduction by Andrew J. Reck. Indianapolis: Bobbs-Library of Liberal Arts, 1964.

Meehan, Mary Johanna. "Justice and the Good Life: An Analysis and Defense of a Communicative Theory of Ethics." Dissertation Boston University, 1989.

Miller, Max. *Kollektive Lernprozesse: Studien zur Grundlegung einer soziologischen Lerntheorie*. Frankfurt: Suhrkamp, 1986.

Nagel, Thomas. *The View from Nowhere*. New York: Oxford University Press, 1986.

Noddings, Nel. *Caring: A Feminine Approach to Ethics and Moral Education*. Berkeley: University of California Press, 1984.

Nunner-Winkler, Gertrud. "Moral Relativism and Strict Universalism." See Wren, *Moral Domain*, pp. 109–126.

Nussbaum, Martha. *The Fragility of Goodness: Luck and Ethics in Greek Tragedy and Philosophy*. Cambridge: Cambridge University Press, 1986.

———. "It Has Nothing to Do with the Law." Lecture 3 of "The Literary Imagination in Public Life." Northwestern University School of Law. Chicago, 10 April 1991.

Okin, Susan Moller. "Reason and Feeling in Thinking about Justice." *Ethics* 99 (1989): 229–249.

O'Neill, Onora. *Constructions of Reason: Explorations of Kant's Practical Philosophy.* Cambridge: Cambridge University Press, 1989.
———. "Ethical Reasoning and Ideological Pluralism." *Ethics* 98 (1988): 705–722.
Ophir, Adi. "The Ideal Speech Situation: Neo-Kantian Ethics in Habermas and Apel." *Kant's Practical Philosophy.* Ed. Y. Yovel. New York: Kluwer, 1989. Pp. 213–234.
Perelman, Chaim. *The Realm of Rhetoric.* Trans. William Kluback. Notre Dame: University of Notre Dame Press, 1982.
Perelman, C., and L. Olbrechts-Tyteca. *The New Rhetoric: A Treatise on Argumentation.* Trans. John Wilkinson and Purcell Weaver. Notre Dame: University of Notre Dame Press, 1969.
———. *La Nouvelle Rhétorique: Traité de l'Argumentation.* 2 vols. Paris: Presses Universitaires de France, 1958.
Peters, Bernard. *Rationalität, Recht und Gesellschaft.* Frankfurt: Suhrkamp, 1991.
Piaget, Jean. *The Moral Judgment of the Child.* Glencoe, Ill.: Free Press, 1965.
Power, Clark, Ann Higgins, and Lawrence Kohlberg. "The Habit of the Common Life: Building Character through Democratic Community Schools." *Moral Development and Character Education: A Dialogue.* Ed. Larry P. Nucci. Berkeley: McCutchan, 1989. Pp. 125–143.
Rasmussen, David. *Reading Habermas.* Cambridge, Mass.: Basil Blackwell, 1990.
———, ed. *Universalism vs. Communitarianism: Contemporary Debates in Ethics.* Cambridge: MIT Press, 1990.
Rawls, John. "The Domain of the Political and Overlapping Consensus." *New York University Law Review* 64 (1989): 233–255.
———. "The Idea of an Overlapping Consensus." *Oxford Journal of Legal Studies* 7 (1987): 1–25.
———. "Justice as Fairness: Political not Metaphysical." *Philosophy and Public Affairs* 14 (1985): 223–251.
———. "Kantian Constructivism in Moral Theory." *Journal of Philosophy* 67 (1980): 515–572.
———. "The Priority of Right and Ideas of the Good." *Philosophy and Public Affairs* 17 (1988): 251–276.
———. *A Theory of Justice.* Belknap-Harvard University Press, 1971.
Rehg, William. "Discourse and the Moral Point of View: Deriving a Dialogical Principle of Universalization." *Inquiry* 34 (1991): 27–48.
———. "Discourse Ethics and the Communitarian Critique of Neo-Kantianism." *Philosophical Forum* 22 (1990): 120–138.
Richardson, Henry S. "The Problem of Liberalism and the Good." See Douglass et al., *Liberalism*, pp. 1–28.
———. "Specifying Norms as a Way to Resolve Concrete Ethical Problems." *Philosophy and Public Affairs* 19 (1990): 279–310.
Ricken, Friedo. *Allgemeine Ethik.* Stuttgart: Kohlhammer, 1983.
Rödel, Ulrich, Günter Frankenberg, and Helmut Dubiel. *Die demokratische Frage.* Frankfurt: Suhrkamp, 1989.

Roderick, Rick. *Habermas and the Foundations of Critical Theory*. New York: St. Martin's, 1986.

Rorty, Amélie Oksenberg, ed. *Explaining Emotions*. Berkeley: University of California Press, 1980.

Rosenblum, Nancy L. Introduction. See Rosenblum, *Liberalism*, pp. 1–17.

———, ed. *Liberalism and the Moral Life*. Cambridge: Harvard University Press, 1989.

Sandel, Michael. *Liberalism and the Limits of Justice*. Cambridge: Cambridge University Press, 1982.

———. "The Procedural Republic and the Unencumbered Self." *Political Theory* 12 (1984): 81–96.

Scanlon, Thomas. "Contractualism and Utilitarianism." *Utilitarianism and Beyond*. Ed. Amartya Sen and Bernard Williams. Cambridge: Cambridge University Press, 1982. Pp. 103–128.

Scheit, Herbert. *Wahrheit, Diskurs, Demokratie: Studien zur "Konsensustheorie der Wahrheit."* Freiburg: Alber, 1987.

Scott, Marvin B., and Stanford M. Lyman. "Accounts." *American Sociological Review* 33 (1968): 46–62.

Seel, Martin. "Die zwei Bedeutungen 'kommunikativer' Rationalität: Bemerkungen zu Habermas' Kritik der pluralen Vernunft." See Honneth and Joas, *Kommunikatives Handeln*, pp. 53–72.

Sher, George. "Other Voices, Other Rooms? Women's Psychology and Moral Theory." See Kittay and Meyers, *Women and Moral Theory*, pp. 178–189.

Solomon, Robert C. "On Emotions as Judgments." *American Philosophical Quarterly* 25 (1988): 183–191.

Spohn, William C. "Passions and Principles." *Theological Studies* 52 (1991): 69–87.

Stern, Paul. "On the Relation between Rational Autonomy and Ethical Community: Hegel's Critique of Kantian Morality." *Praxis International* 9 (1989): 234–248.

Stich, Stephen P., and Richard E. Nisbett. "Expertise, Justification, and the Psychology of Inductive Reasoning." *The Authority of Experts: Studies in History and Theory*. Ed. Thomas L. Haskell. Bloomington: Indiana University Press, 1984. Pp. 226–241.

Stout, Jeffrey. *Ethics After Babel: The Language of Morals and Their Discontents*. Boston: Beacon, 1988.

Strawson, P. F. "Freedom and Resentment." *Freedom and Resentment and Other Essays*. London: Methuen, 1974. Pp. 1–25.

Strayer, Janet. "Affective and Cognitive Perspectives on Empathy." See Eisenberg and Strayer, *Empathy and Its Development*, pp. 218–244.

Strydom, Piet. "Collective Learning: Habermas's Concessions and Their Theoretical Implications." *Philosophy and Social Criticism* 13 (1987): 265–281.

Sunstein, Cass, ed. *Feminism and Political Theory*. Chicago: University of Chicago Press, 1990.

Taylor, Charles. "Comments and Replies." *Inquiry* 34 (1991): 237–254.

————. "Cross-Purposes: The Liberal-Communitarian Debate." See Rosenblum, *Liberalism*, pp. 159–182.

————. "The Diversity of Goods." See Taylor, *Papers* 2: 230–247.

————. *Ethics of Authenticity*. Cambridge: Harvard University Press, 1992.

————. "Inwardness and the Culture of Modernity." See Honneth, McCarthy et al., *Philosophical Interventions*, pp. 88–110.

————. "Justice after Virtue." *Kritische Methode und Zukunft der Anthropologie*. Ed. Michael Benedikt and Rudolf Burger. *Philosophica* 6. Vienna: Wilhelm Braumüller University Press, 1985. Pp. 23–48.

————. "Language and Society." See Honneth and Joas, *Communicative Action*, pp. 23–35.

————. "Die Motive einer Verfahrensethik." Kuhlmann, *Moralität*, pp. 101–135.

————. "The Nature and Scope of Distributive Justice." See Taylor, *Papers* 2: 289–317.

————. *Philosophical Papers*. 2 vols. Vol. 1: *Human Agency and Language*. Vol. 2: *Philosophy and the Human Sciences*. Cambridge: Cambridge University Press, 1985.

————. *Sources of the Self: The Making of the Modern Identity*. Cambridge: Harvard University Press, 1989.

————. "Sprache und Gesellschaft." See Honneth and Joas, *Kommunikatives Handeln*, pp. 35–52.

————. "What Is Human Agency?" See Taylor, *Papers* 1: 15–44.

Taylor, Charles, Alasdair MacIntyre, and Frederick Olafson. "Author Meets Critics: *Sources of the Self*." Central Division Meeting of the American Philosophical Association. Chicago, Illinois. 27 April 1991.

Thibaut, John, and Laurens Walker. *Procedural Justice: A Psychological Analysis*. Hillsdale, N.J.: Lawrence Erlbaum, 1975.

Thompson, John B. *Ideology and Modern Culture: Critical Social Theory in the Era of Mass Communication*. Stanford: Stanford University Press, 1990.

Thompson, John B., and David Held, eds. *Habermas: Critical Debates*. Cambridge: MIT Press, 1982.

Toulmin, Stephen Edelston. *An Examination of the Place of Reason in Ethics*. 1950. Cambridge: Cambridge University Press, 1970.

————. *The Uses of Argument*. 1958. Cambridge: Cambridge University Press, 1964.

Tyler, Tom R. "Justice, Self-Interest, and the Legitimacy of Legal and Political Authority." *Beyond Self-Interest*. Ed. Jane Mansbridge. Chicago: University of Chicago Press, 1990. Pp. 171–179.

————. *Why People Obey the Law*. New Haven: Yale University Press, 1990.

Wallace, James D. *Moral Relevance and Moral Conflict*. Ithaca: Cornell University Press, 1988.

Walzer, Michael. "A Critique of Philosophical Conversation." *Philosophical Forum* 21 (1989–90): 182–196.

————. *Spheres of Justice: A Defense of Pluralism and Equality*. New York: Basic, 1983.

Wellmer, Albrecht. "Ethics and Dialogue: Elements of Moral Judgement in Kant and Discourse Ethics." *The Persistence of Modernity: Essays on Aesthetics, Ethics, and Postmodernism*. Trans. David Midgley. Cambridge: MIT Press, 1991. Pp. 113–231.

———. *Ethik und Dialog: Elemente des moralischen Urteils bei Kant und in der Diskursethik*. Frankfurt: Suhrkamp, 1986.

———. "Terrorism and the Critique of Society." *Observations on "The Spiritual Situation of the Age."* Ed. Jürgen Habermas. Trans. Andrew Buchwalter. Cambridge: MIT Press, 1985. Pp. 283–307.

White, Stephen K. *The Recent Work of Jürgen Habermas: Reason, Justice and Modernity*. Cambridge: Cambridge University Press, 1989.

Wiggins, David. "Universality, Impartiality, Truth." *Needs, Values, Truth: Essays in the Philosophy of Value*. Aristotelian Society Ser. 6. Oxford: Blackwell, 1987. Pp. 59–86.

Willard, Charles Arthur. "The Problem of the Public Sphere: Three Diagnoses." See Williams and Hazen, *Argumentation Theory*, pp. 135–153.

Williams, Bernard. *Ethics and the Limits of Philosophy*. Cambridge: Harvard University Press, 1985.

———. *Moral Luck*. New York: Cambridge University Press, 1981.

———. "Moral Luck." See Williams, *Moral Luck*, pp. 20–39.

———. "Persons, Character and Morality." See Williams, *Moral Luck*, pp. 1–19.

Williams, David Cratis, and Michael David Hazen, eds. *Argumentation Theory and the Rhetoric of Assent*. Tuscaloosa: University of Alabama Press, 1990.

Wingert, Lutz. "Gemeinsinn und Moral: Elemente einer intersubjektivistischen Konzeption der Moral." Dissertation. University of Frankfurt (am Main). 1990. Forthcoming, Suhrkamp, 1993.

Wolf, Susan. "Moral Saints." *Journal of Philosophy* 79 (1982): 419–439.

Wren, Thomas E., ed. In cooperation with Wolfgang Edelstein and Gertrud Nunner-Winkler. *The Moral Domain: Essays in the Ongoing Discussion between Philosophy and the Social Sciences*. Cambridge: MIT Press, 1990.

Young, Iris Marion. "Impartiality and the Civic Public: Some Implications of Feminist Critiques of Moral and Political Theory." See Benhabib and Cornell, *Feminism as Critique*, pp. 57–76.

———. *Justice and the Politics of Difference*. Princeton: Princeton University Press, 1990.

Index

Certainty, 85–86, 239. *See also* Cognitive
uncertainty
Ceteris paribus (qualification), 60, 70,
190, 197
Christian Platonists, 116
Cognitive uncertainty, 156, 166–167,
210, 242–243. *See also* Fallibility
Cognitivism, 21–22, 27, 31, 38, 123,
172; and intersubjectivity, 151, 163–
169, 234, 246; moral cognitivism,
155–157
Common good, 4, 5, 80–81, 91–92, 95,
97–101, 102–110, 246; thin common
good, 106–108, 112, 114, 118, 136,
170
Communication, universal structures of,
145, 151–154
Communication-theory method, 23, 26–
27, 34, 35, 119–120, 172
Communicative action, 78, 119, 141–
143, 160–161; theory of, 67, 142,
146–148, 154, 158, 162
Communitarianism, xiv, 11, 16, 22, 82,
113 138, 181–183, 245–246; critique
of liberalism, 3–9, 80; and notion of
good, 91, 94, 102, 147
Community, 4, 8, 15–16, 45–46, 137,
155, 244–245, 248; ideal communication community, 63, 212
Competence, 62–69, 86–87, 139, 154–
157, 178, 193–194, 209; competent
speakers 26–27, 63–68, 154, 212
Compliance, 61, 70, 190, 203; with real
decisions, 232–235, 242–244. *See
also* Action constraints
Compromise, 39, 75, 98, 104, 136, 149,
156, 173, 210, 219, 223
Concrete totality, 102, 150–151, 155,
157
Confidence, 74, 229–230, 237. *See also*
Validity claims: and confidence
Conflict, 9, 46, 51, 57ff, 70, 99–100,
137, 163–166, 174–175; in application discourse, 184, 188, 191–195,
197, 209–210, 229–230; of interests,
32, 53–55, 58–59, 64–67, 76, 83,
97, 103; social conflict, 2, 6, 9, 148–
149, 177
Conflict resolution, 1, 5–6, 8, 10, 15, 17,
68–69, 73, 80, 96, 118–122, 136,
185. *See also* Consensus, rational
Consensus, 6–7, 31–35, 46, 64, 69, 103–
106, 156, 207–208, 210, 220–221,
233–234, 246–247; background consensus, 32, 45–46, 131, 147, 229,
237, 248; local consensus, 207; moral
consensus, 1, 6, 54–55, 69, 81, 91–

92, 110, 119; overlapping consensus,
38–40, 126–130; rational consensus,
8, 37–39, 41–45, 56–57, 62–63, 74,
77, 82–83, 91, 97–98, 107–108, 111,
122, 176, 207–208, 211, 227ff, 236–
238, 243–244, 249; social consensus,
2, 79–80, 123, 130, 133–134; universal consensus, 238–241
Consequences, 15, 24, 32, 49, 54, 68,
110–111, 114, 181–182, 185, 189,
208, 245; evaluation of, 72, 106, 194,
236, 239–240; and perspective taking, 38–40; role in moral discourse,
41–45, 56–61, 79–82, 197. *See also*
Action constraints; Impacts; Side-
effects
Consequentialism, 22, 45, 47, 56, 66, 79,
82
Constitutive good, 116–117, 131–133,
159; and discourse ethics, 17, 118–
123, 134–149, 152, 161–163, 169,
141, 174, 176
Content Premise (CP), 58–61, 66, 69
Contested concepts, 240
Conviction. *See* Rational conviction
Cooperation, 5, 33–35, 46, 68, 81, 83,
135–136, 151, 173–177, 188, 230–
231, 236–238, 243, 246, 248; and
conflict resolution, 57–58, 64, 66–70,
120; rational cooperation, 17, 138–
139, 141–149, 151–154, 159–161,
163, 167–171, 174, 246; social cooperation, 1–2, 6, 8–10, 13, 32, 34, 97–
105, 110–112, 127, 130–132, 134,
138, 148, 170
Critical theory, xiv, 21

Decisionism, 21, 133
Decision making, 17, 21, 31, 34, 78, 80–
81, 108, 117, 162–163, 196, 237–
238, 248, 249; hypothetical scenario,
197–207; institutional, 216–217,
220–223, 230–232, 237–238, 248
Democratic system, 32, 80–81, 124–
134, 227, 228, 236. *See also* Liberal-
democratic tradition
Deontological ethics, 5, 22, 31, 47, 82,
95, 107, 244, 247
Descartes, René, 235, 245; Cartesian individualism, 15, 245
Desires. *See* Needs and wants
Dialectics, 224–225
Discourse, 33, 57–60, 103, 108, 149,
161, 170, 192, 217, 228; and everyday interaction, 24–26, 60, 143, 207,
213, 229–230; as incomplete or ongoing, 65, 235–242; as objective ba-

sis, 33, 38, 246; in the public sphere, 215, 226–227, 231, 236, 245; real discourse, 17, 35, 78–79, 182–183, 195–196, 213, 230, 243; "super" discourse, 189–190. See also Application discourses; Discourse principle (D); Ethical discourse; Justification discourses; Moral discourse; Practical discourse; Rules of rational discourse (RP)

Discourse ethics, xiii–xv, 11, 14–17, 21–22, 37, 78–83, 91–92, 103–105, 107, 112–115, 159, 233, 244–248; and constitutive good, 134, 141, 149, 160–163, 174, 176–178; and ethics of care, 185–188, 196–200, 205–208; and institutions, 217–220, 227–231; and the lifeworld, 23–26, 30–36, 61, 103–107, 181–183, 211–214; and solidarity, 167–172; and theory of communicative action, 2, 6, 26–27, 160; and theory of good, 115–123; and theory of justice, 123–134

Discourse principle (D), 30–35, 38, 65–67, 119, 138, 219, 221, 223, 248

Doppelt, Gerald, 127–128, 132

Duty. See Moral obligation

Egalitarianism, 128

Emotions and feelings, 13–14, 16, 49–52, 80, 185–187, 207, 213. See also Appetitive structures; Empathy

Emotivism, 21, 27

Empathy, 13–14, 17, 77, 120, 203, 205, 207; and solidarity, 82, 108–111, 245

Enlightenment ideals, 35, 41, 63, 68, 127, 241

Epikaia, 202

Equality, 1, 124–127, 130, 134, 224

Essentially contested concepts, 240

Ethical discourse, 54–55, 75, 82, 95–98, 104, 121, 147–148, 219, 230

Ethical domain, 118, 120, 122, 126, 133, 135, 173, 188, 203–209, 210. See also Moral-ethical relation

Ethics of care, 5, 9–13, 22, 182, 184–188, 196–200, 205–209, 244

Eudaemonism. See Teleological ethics

Evaluation and testing, 28, 38, 45, 53, 59, 71–72, 74, 77, 82, 101–103, 106, 153, 161, 167–168, 189–90, 195–196, 216, 219, 239–240, 243, 246; evaluative frameworks, 117–118; evaluative questions, 54, 75, 96–97; evaluative terms, 49, 51, 54, 122, 164; strong evaluation, 115–116

Examples: abortion, 194; capitalism,

173; capital punishment, 106; child development, 53; comatose persons, 78; corporate theft, 46–47; country houses, 49; courage, 116; critique of capitalism, 48; crossword puzzles, 85; curfew, 24; deception, 51; economics, 161; euthanasia, 192; excuses, 190; expert opinions, 235–237; harm, 106, 202–205; homemakers, 61; honesty, 53; human genomes, 223; loans, 41, 47; lying, 25, 50, 52–53, 163, 190, 192, 193, 196; market economics, 32; merit, 201–204; money, 32; murder, 114; nation, 174; Nazism, 59; office workers, 106–107; peasants, 106–107; promises, 61, 213; property, 127; religion, 53; religious freedom, 105, 170; religious intolerance, 163; religious preference, 81; relocation of employee, 70–72, 74–75; talent, 128; taxes, 81, 99; tenure appointment, 197ff, 200, 205, 208; theft, 43, 47, 114; thieves, 168; tort law, 222; truthfulness, 224; undeserved recognition, 50–52; welfare legislation, 104–105; workers, 173; zoning, 223

Fairness, 1, 7, 32–34, 57, 130, 198, 217, 223

Fallibility, 28, 45, 195–196, 215–216, 232, 236, 249

Feelings. See Emotions and feelings

Feminist critiques, 9, 16, 107, 173, 184–186

Flanagan, Owen, 200

Formalism. See Moral formalism

Formalism thesis, 145–146, 153–154, 159

Formal pragmatics, 23ff, 26–29, 31–33, 37

Frameworks, 1, 8, 12, 35, 42–44, 76, 81, 115–118, 120–122, 217, 233, 236. See also Language; Moral perspective; Tradition; Worldview

Frankfurt School, 21

Freedom. See Rights and freedoms

Free-rider problem, 94, 100n16, 141, 143, 175

Friendship, 11–13, 17, 137, 187, 205, 208–210

Functionalism, 48

Gadamer, Hans-Georg, 168, 172

Gallie, W. B., 240

Genealogical approach, 121, 134, 145, 148

Designer:	U.C. Press Staff
Compositor:	Wilsted & Taylor
Text:	10/13 Sabon
Display:	Sabon
Printer:	Thomson-Shore, Inc.
Binder:	Thomson-Shore, Inc.